Politics, power and old age

RETHINKING AGEING SERIES

Series editor: Brian Gearing
School of Health and Social Welfare
The Open University

The rapid growth in ageing populations in Britain and other countries has greatly increased academic and professional interest in gerontology. Since the mid-1970s there has been a marked increase in published research studies which have stimulated new ideas and approaches to understanding old age. However, such knowledge has not been widely disseminated. There continues to be concern about the education and training in gerontology of professional workers and whether research findings about ageing reach professionals and the general public.

The *Rethinking Ageing* series aims to fill this need for accessible, up-to-date studies of important issues in gerontology. Each book is intended to review and enhance understanding of a major topic in ageing, and to have particular relevance for those involved in age care, whether as researchers, service providers or carers. All the books in this series address two fundamental questions. What is known about this topic? And what are the policy, service and practice implications of this knowledge? At the same time, authors are encouraged to *rethink* their subject area by developing their own ideas, drawing on case material and their research and experience. Most of the books are multi-disciplinary and all are written in clear, non-technical language which appeals to a broad range of students, academics and professionals with a common interest in ageing and age care. The very positive response from readers and reviewers to the books published so far has encouraged us to extend the series with new titles while retaining this approach.

Current and forthcoming titles:
Simon Biggs *et al.*: **Elder abuse in perspective**
Ken Blakemore and Margaret Boneham: **Age, race and ethnicity**
Joanna Bornat (ed.): **Reminiscence reviewed**
Bill Bytheway: **Ageism**
Maureen Crane: **Understanding older homeless people**
Andrew Dunning: **Advocacy and older people**
Mike Hepworth: **Stories of Ageing**
Frances Heywood *et al.*: **Housing and home in later life**
Beverley Hughes: **Older people and community care**
Tom Kitwood: **Dementia reconsidered**
Eric Midwinter: **Pensioned off**
Sheila Peace *et al.*: **Re-evaluating residential care**
Moyra Sidell: **Health in old age**
Robert Slater: **The psychology of growing old**
John A. Vincent: **Politics, power and old age**
Alan Walker and Tony Maltby: **Ageing Europe**
Alan Walker and Gerhard Naegele (eds): **The politics of old age in Europe**

Politics, power and old age

JOHN A. VINCENT

OPEN UNIVERSITY PRESS
Buckingham · Philadelphia

Open University Press
Celtic Court
22 Ballmoor
Buckingham
MK18 1XW

email: enquiries@openup.co.uk
world wide web: http://www.openup.co.uk

and
325 Chestnut Street
Philadelphia, PA 19106, USA

First Published 1999

A catalogue record of this book is available from the British Library

ISBN 0335 201660 (hb)   0335 201652 (pb)

Library of Congress Cataloging-in-Publication Data

Vincent, John A., 1947–
    Politics, power and old age/John A. Vincent.
        p. cm. – (Rethinking ageing series)
    Includes bibliographical references and index.
    ISBN 0 335 20166 0 (hbk)   ISBN 0 335 20165 2 (pbk)
    1. Aged.   2. Ageing—Social aspects.   3. Power (Social sciences)
4. Intergenerational relations.   I. Title.   II. Series.
HQ1061.V54145   1999
305.26—dc21   99-20483
                                                           CIP

Typeset by Type Study, Scarborough
Printed in Great Britain by St Edmundsbury Press, Bury St Edmunds, Suffolk

Contents

List of tables

Series editor's preface

Since its inception in 1994 with Ken Blakemore and Margaret Boneham's *Age, Race and Ethnicity*, the Rethinking Ageing series has sought to fill a need for accessible, up-to-date studies of important issues in gerontology. Each book in the series seeks to review and enhance understanding of a major topic in ageing, and to have particular relevance for those involved in age care, whether they are researchers, service providers or carers. The series' authors are encouraged to address two fundamental questions: What is known about this topic? And, what are the policy and practice implications of this knowledge? At the same time, authors are encouraged to rethink their subject area by developing their ideas, drawing on case material and their own research and experience. Most of the books are multi-disciplinary and all are written in clear, non-technical language which appeals to a broad range of students, academics and professionals with a common interest in ageing and age care.

More than a dozen books have been published in the series so far, largely featuring topics which are already prominent in gerontology because of the widespread interest and concern that they evoke (e.g. ageism, elder abuse, dementia, etc.). Whilst the very positive response from readers and reviewers encourages us to maintain the style and accessibility of the series, we feel it is now time to extend its ambit to include topics of significance which have been neglected and whose importance in gerontology has not been widely appreciated. The first book to reflect this policy was Maureen Crane's *Understanding older homeless people*. We hope that by including titles on such 'emerging topics', as well as those of established interest, the series will continue to make a significant contribution to ageing studies.

Brian Gearing
School of Health and Social Welfare
The Open University

Acknowledgements

I should like to acknowledge with gratitude the help provided to me in writing this book. The responsibility for the opinions, and any errors or omissions, of course remain my own. Saira Vincent, Julie Morris, Brian Gearing, Nigel Pleasants and Pam Barnes helped with text editing and ideas.

Acknowledgement for making available data goes to the University of Keele Department of Politics for its archive of party political manifestos. For the *British Election Surveys*, the work of Professor Halsey and his colleagues at the University of Oxford is acknowledged and the detailed citation is included in the bibliography.

1

Introduction: politics, power and old age

In a survey of opinions conducted by Devon Age Concern to look at old age in the new millennium, a respondent aged over 80 wrote 'old people are not lesser beings'. What is it about being old in the UK at the end of the twentieth century which makes older people feel that their humanity is threatened? This book examines the social condition of older people through the study of power relations and the politics of old age. The book is not primarily about party politics but about political behaviour at its most general and ubiquitous and which can be identified when some people exercise power over others.

The book has ten chapters. The book follows a basic pattern of moving from micro-level day to day personal interaction, through pressure groups and institutional politics to national and global issues, ending up looking at macro-level issues of intergenerational solidarity, class politics and the construction of contemporary culture. Chapter 2 sets out the ideas and theories which form the background to the subject. It examines the way social science has dealt with old age, politics and power, pointing out the major alternative ways of thinking about these issues and suggesting the most fruitful lines of development which can be followed through the rest of the book. Chapter 3 is about the politics of interpersonal relationships, the micro-level politics which examines ways in which old age disempowers older people in day to day situations. It looks at issues about the ageing body, social relationships and the problem of identity in old age and, in particular, studies of Alzheimer's disease and the preservation of self-identity. Chapter 4 is about lifestyle politics and social movements and it concretely examines two lifestyle issues: first, gender and sexuality, and second, suicide, euthanasia and the 'right to die'. Chapter 5 examines professional politics and the medicalization of old age. Chapter 6 takes a look at party politics and the role of old age interests in the campaigning activities of current parliamentary politics. Chapter 7 examines the role of charities and pressure groups and looks at other ways in which older people's interests are expressed in western liberal democracies. Chapter 8 is about generational politics; in particular, this chapter tackles the 'new ageism' which identifies the current older generation as taking more than its fair share of the community's resources at the expense of succeeding cohorts. The cultural aspects of old age are examined in Chapter 9 which identifies consumerism as the key feature of the culture of the contemporary world and discusses how older people fit into such a cultural scheme and the extent to which this is disempowering. Chapter 10 brings together the various levels of analysis through the book and attempts to provide an overview which links the micro-level day to day interpersonal relationships to the macro-historical and global patterns of a changing society.

This volume is a timely contribution to the Rethinking Ageing series and social gerontology. The realization that we have an ageing population is now commonplace but the significance of this demographic change is not widely understood. This ignorance can be used in manipulative ways to present old people as a threat. There is a feeling that the changing age structure of the electorate in democracies will (or perhaps should) influence politics. Elderly people, themselves, are developing views of their position in society and developing institutions to reflect those ideas. They are becoming more articulate about themselves and their interests and have concerns about their powerlessness.

Material deprivation in old age

The current generation of older people is, measured in terms of material resources, over-represented at the bottom of society. Older people in the UK reflect the social inequalities of class, gender and race in the society in which they have lived. The added inequality of old age means that older women, older minorities and those who were manual workers are worse off than their peer equivalents in middle age (Palmore 1990; Vincent 1995). This is related, in particular, to the structure of the labour market. Income in later life tends to be dependent on pension rights acquired through employment supplemented by any savings and investments. Those who are materially best off in old age are those who received the largest material rewards in their working lives. Those who achieved poor rewards from their labour, and people who found difficulty entering the labour market at all, are those who have tended in their old age to be amongst the most materially deprived section of the British population. The fortunate few with accumulated wealth, and thus whose lifestyle is not dependent on a pension, do best of all.

In 1979 the average income of the poorest 20 per cent of pensioners was £55.90 per week, compared with £169.60 for the richest 20 per cent. Sixteen years later, the average income of the poorest 20 per cent had risen by £15.50 but the average income of the richest 20 per cent had risen by £103.40 (Department of Social Security (DSS) 1997). A quarter of all older people in Britain are either dependent on Income Support, or entitled to that benefit but not receiving it. For Europe, as defined by twelve members of the European Union (EU), Walker and Maltby (1997: 53) using data from the findings of the EU Observatory summarize the main trends in material standards as:

- rising living standards for older people, particularly those aged 50–74
- wide variations between countries
- poverty and low incomes amongst a significant minority of older people in most countries
- older women, particularly widows, have a higher incidence of poverty
- income inequalities are growing among pensioners.

Whilst there is evidence of rising average incomes for older people in the UK, there is also evidence of growing material inequality between some older people and the general population and a growing differentiation amongst older people themselves. There are concerns that this growing inequality will accelerate. Social inequalities are increasing in the younger age groups and because of the structure of welfare and pensions provision this may well lead to yet greater inequality in old age.

Material deprivation in old age is felt most strongly by particular groups. However, elderly people's subjective feelings about their standard of living are influenced by more than simply how much they can afford to spend. They have, for example, a variety of reference groups against which to compare their living standards. Contemporary elderly people's recollection of their personal history includes memories of the conditions in which older people lived in the early part of this century. They are likely to compare themselves positively to the past in material terms (but not necessarily moral or social ones). They are also aware of their former standard of living experienced before they retired – a process which for many has meant a lowering of living standards. Older people might also compare themselves, favourably or otherwise, with other retirees. They might also take a more general reference point such as the average living conditions of society as a whole. Thus, just as there is no clear single common experience of material deprivation amongst contemporary older people, so there is also no common interpretative framework by which older people come to feel a collective sense of their standard of living.

Other legacies of a stratified society follow people into old age (Allcock 1993). Health status and other indicators of social well-being follow gender, ethnic and class lines in old age. A survey sponsored by British Gas (Midwinter 1991) interviewed a sample of retired people aged 55 or over: 33 per cent had incomes of less than £88 per week, 41 per cent had an income between £88 and £144 per week, while 26 per cent of the sample had incomes of over £145 per week. The survey compared the richer and poorer sections of the sample and concluded: 'The survey demonstrates that, if money doesn't buy happiness, then, at least, a lack of it edges one toward misery' (Midwinter 1991: 31; see Table 1.1).

Elderly people are not a single group and should not be treated as such. Older people are as diverse as the rest of the population and simplistic stereotypes should be strongly resisted. For example, there are both rich and poor old people. The stereotypes of the impoverished pensioner, grateful for a kind word and a warm cup of cocoa, and of the high living old people, spending generous state subsidized pensions on seaside bungalows and four overseas holidays a year, are both misleading. They are very restricted images of older people and not applicable to the vast majority of the older population.

Table 1.1   Comparison of those on low incomes (under £88 per week) and high incomes (£145 or more) per week

Item	Total sample (%)	Low income (%)	High income (%)
Enjoying life more than previously	27	18	38
Good thing about growing old: none	29	36	20
Activities: taking exercise/going for a walk	70	66	80
Find need for extra care/attention	50	56	37
Did no planning for retirement	22	38	4
Often/occasionally lonely	32	45	18
Wish for more social contact	25	33	18
Have regular use of a car	50	32	74
In receipt of a private pension	22	18	42
Sometimes struggles to pay bills	31	53	8
Is concerned about paying bills	24	39	8
Often/occasionally cuts back on basics	28	44	12
Never cuts back on basics	72	56	89
No money left after basics have been paid for	11	19	3
Often/occasionally has problems with winter warmth	19	30	7
Home with central heating	81	79	90
Council tenancy	24	42	5
Owner occupation	60	37	87
Married	57	35	73
Preferred name: senior citizens	36	40	26
Preferred name: retired	36	26	45

Source: Table modified from Midwinter (1991: 31)

However, it will be one of the key arguments of the book that the social differences between older people are getting wider. The development, for some old people, of a 'Third Age', empowered by financial security and a sense of their own value and potential, is challenging thinking about older people. However, studies consistently show that older people are disproportionately represented amongst those who are the poorest and have the most limited quality of life. The meaning of old age is being challenged and disputed as never before. This book is intended as a contribution to that debate.

Literature and research

This book draws on a wide range of literature and research. It includes some original work reporting on my own analysis of survey and ethnographic data. Although my background is from social anthropology and I teach in a sociology department, the book also refers to political science, history, social policy, cultural studies, psychology, linguistics and social geography. The book is intended to be informative and challenging, not prescriptive. It is not about what should be done – either in social policy or in terms of care management. Rather, it is about *rethinking* old age. It should be of interest to practitioners who work with elderly people, not as a statement of best practice but as an aid to reflection on the way that power structures relationships between themselves and the older people with whom they work. The value of the book should be judged by the extent to which the ideas contained in it are found to be meaningful and insightful for people resisting the restrictions of ageism.

It is necessary in this introduction to establish some of the intellectual traditions and concerns that form the background and context to the debates about the ways in which old age is political. The literature that exists on some current political aspects of old age tends to be rather limited – not in the sense of quality – but of extent. Because old age is regarded as a highly undesirable condition in modern society, it is not a popular subject for study. This cultural devaluation of old age reflects on those people who work with, and study, old people. Old age has not formed part of mainstream political or sociological studies. Many standard textbooks in both subjects do not deal with old age, either as a conceptual issue or in terms of substantive description of the condition of older people in Britain, continental Europe or the USA. One widely read textbook by Giddens (1989: 84) is the exception, where a small subsection on age proves the rule. The third edition adds a further piece on old age, which is located with health issues (1997: 40, 132–5).

This book is largely written from the approach to the study of politics and society known as political economy. The approach seeks to link social structure and the way people think and act politically with people's material interests and the organization of economic life. The tradition of politics as political economy is well represented within social gerontology. Arising in the late 1970s and 1980s the political economy approach to ageing provided a critique of the exploitation of elderly people by various dominant groups including the medical industry and political and commercial elites. While social gerontology has tended to be under-theorized, the 'critical gerontology' approach has through the 1980s and 1990s provided a challenge to more conventional ways of thinking about issues of old age (Phillipson 1982; Phillipson and Walker 1986; Phillipson *et al.* 1986; Cole 1993; Street and Quadagno 1993; Estes *et al.* 1996; Phillipson 1998). Critical gerontology borrowed its name from the tradition of 'Critical Theory' as developed by the Frankfurt School including Max Horkheimer and Theodor Adorno. This critique was born out of deep disappointment with regard to the liberty and justice that scientific solutions to social problems had promised to achieve. It developed historically from German Marxist intellectuals responding to the rise of National Socialism. Not only is the project of controlling nature seen by Adorno and Horkheimer as a specific historical endeavour, but also human nature is seen in an historical and social perspective. According to them what is presented (implicitly or explicitly) as 'inevitable', 'normal' and 'healthy', in short as 'natural', is in reality 'second' nature. What is natural is not a fixed and stable starting point, but is the result of social structures and processes of domination that have their own momentum in creating and continuing to achieve an established order of reality (Connerton 1976; Baars 1991). This approach subjects any claim about normal or natural ageing to close critical scrutiny. At the core of critical gerontology literature lies a humanistic perspective and an overt espousal of liberal values. It values emancipation from the traditional constraints of ageing, and sees the function of social science as about the liberation of individuals. I intend that this book will be a development of the existing critical tradition in the political economy of old age.

Within the subdiscipline of political sociology the study of social movements, pressure groups and political parties is well developed (Barnes 1995). One kind of political science examines concretely the decision making and output of party political campaigns. Such an approach could be used to identify changing orientation towards, and sensitivity to, older voters on the part of power holders. In Chapter 6 I attempt to look at similar issues, and further in Chapter 7 I look at the role and effectiveness of pressure groups made up of older people or those seeking to represent their interests. A further political science skill is the study of public opinions and attitudes. Such surveys can be used for examination of public perceptions of the extent to which older people are seen as an interest group with power and influence and how legitimate that power and influence is regarded. There are a few studies on the influence of older people on elections. Studies in this field have previously been small scale and funded by charities (Midwinter and Tester 1987; Age Concern 1997). However, there are regular systematic surveys of opinions conducted by polling organizations which include data on different age groups. Further, in both the UK and the USA there are regular academic surveys at every national election, which provide data that are of use when trying to assess the impact of older people on the political process.

Since the 1980s previous modes of understanding politics have been challenged by a radically different way of approaching knowledge known as postmodernism. While not adhering to that approach to social science, it is necessary to pay attention to some of the problems which it has identified. Importantly, postmodernism challenges existing conventions for establishing authoritative knowledge. It does not accept the claim of science, or any other world-view, to be the single source of truth. A single authoritative voice cannot be sustained in the face of a lack of an all-embracing unified knowledge system and postmodernism requires us to listen to a variety of different people and their knowledge. The reality of globalization and (for want of a better word) multiculturalism in a pluralistic world cannot, and should not, be avoided, and will form a distinctive focus for this book. I believe it to be an important task of the book to try and encompass the multiplicity of ways of understanding politics and old age, but to do this in a manner which does not merely reduce the task to a language game, an intellectual strategy to which postmodern writing is prone. In debating politics and old age I shall endeavour to reveal more than the structures of discourse; my aim is also to understand the processes of power as they affect older people.

2

An overview of old age, politics and power

Age has been used in all societies as a way of differentiating people. In modern Britain it forms part of the power structure by which collective life is ordered. This book is about the ways in which power and age interact to structure social life and, in particular, how old age has come to carry political significance for people in contemporary Britain. Throughout this book the idea of 'politics' will be taken at its widest possible definition. It is an important function of social science to provide a critical perspective on society. We need to ask questions in new ways, query taken for granted positions and reveal new perspectives and new understandings. We start in this chapter with basic questions such as what are age, old age, politics and power? What are the major concepts and theories through which academics and others have sought to understand politics and old age?

Natural difference

Not only all people, but all organisms, age. Some people, therefore, see age as simply a 'natural' category. Is it then a sensible question to ask how ageing is *socially* constructed? When 'age' along with other criteria such as 'gender' and 'race' are labelled 'natural', we must be very cautious and unpick the meanings behind this apparently simple statement. 'Natural' has the meaning of 'obvious' or 'taken for granted' and consequently something which is seen as 'natural' takes the character of being unquestionably normal. Therefore if age is merely thought of as a natural phenomenon, an unquestioned assumption is all too easily made that certain behaviours are 'normal' for people of certain ages. 'Natural' has a further meaning that comes from the concept of 'the natural world'. Consequently, there develops a limited understanding of 'age' as merely the province of biological or other 'natural' sciences. This assumption leads to a strong temptation to think of age based categories as biological divisions rather than social ones, and to think of them as having an immutable normality. However, although there is an important interplay between the biological processes and social processes of ageing in humans, it is vital to appreciate that the meaning attributed to age and ageing is a social construction and varies fundamentally both between and within societies. People acquire grey hairs at various points in their maturation and incrementally with advancing years but how this is interpreted is not fixed by any 'natural' law. How this change in appearance is understood on a personal and a social level has nothing to do with the biochemistry of pigmentation or the distribution of genetic inheritance. Thus when we ask questions about politics and old age we do not assume there is a 'normal old age' but rather examine the impact of assumptions that such a normality exists. Further, we shall ask questions and pay careful attention to understanding the wide variety of meanings associated with old age, and examine the issues, opportunities and challenges which arise from this diversity.

Some analysts have conducted thought experiments to try and imagine societies in which age is not present (Mannheim 1927; Hazelrigg 1997). They suggest that without age society would be not only static but also boring. If all humans lived for ever, the sequences of generations and the consequent changes of personnel would not happen. Mannheim therefore argued that the implementation of new ideas and practices would be critically slowed and cultural life would become fossilized. An alternative thought experiment can be conducted which suggests a different kind of ageless society, one which would have features similar to certain insect societies. In this case one generation dies to be followed, in the new season, by a newly hatched generation which has had no direct interaction with the preceding one. All members of the society are therefore of the same age. This would be a society without socialization; without the capacity to learn from one generation to the next. Again, this picture of such a rigid and unprogressive society is a dystopian image. It further emphasizes that, although the biological characteristics of the human species give a very basic framework to the meaningful study of old age, it is the study of the variation in what it means to be older that is important to our understanding of the topic. The key information necessary to understand politics and old age is therefore a knowledge of the variety of social conditions which mean some older people are influential, powerful, rich and live meaningful lives, while others have no such advantages.

Age and difference

Anthropological studies suggest that age is one of the few genuinely universal social criteria. However, this fact in itself, although directing us to look towards issues of age, is not itself very informative. Understanding age as a method of social differentiation requires us to understand the wide variations in

- the degree to which age is used as a mechanism for social differentiation
- which age criteria are used
- the significance attached to these criteria.

All three of these factors are extremely varied. Societies range from those in which age is not particularly important to those in which it is the key structural principle, and from those in which old age is highly valued, to those in which it is of very low status. Further, what is thought to constitute old age varies not only cross-culturally but even within our own societies (Minois 1989; Schaie and Achenbaum 1993; Stoller and Gibson 1994).

In more egalitarian types of societies, neither age nor gender, as social categories, take on the rigid and determining quality that these criteria do in many other societies. The Mbuti, as described by Turnball (1984) and others, illustrate the highly flexible character of small scale societies who live by foraging. Many accounts (Lee and DeVore 1968; Dahlberg 1981) of foraging societies characterize them as living opportunistic lives in the natural environment, gathering and hunting a wide ranging diet. These people live together in small bands in which, although difference between men and women and old and young are acknowledged, all voices make some contribution to communal decision making. Accounts (Ingold and Woodburn 1988) of foraging societies also describe them as part of a complex social environment which contains other peoples and other ways of life which offers them opportunities to which they respond. Thus in some ways these apparently distant and exotic peoples' lives are not too different from the flexible lifestyles with which many people make a living within the complexities of the contemporary urban world. For example, both lifestyles have relatively simple and informal kinship structures. It is of interest that such nomadic societies seem to have better health and longevity than their settled neighbours. Some evolutionists have taken these band societies as a model for the social conditions for human evolution. From this point of view they have identified the significance of grandparents, particularly grandmothers, surviving beyond their own reproductive years, for the successful survival of their grandchildren.

In other societies where access to inherited property is crucial for economic well-being, age and sex criteria are frequently quite rigid and strongly sanctioned (Vincent 1995). The ideal of the patriarchal extended family, as found in parts of rural India or pre-revolutionary China for example, implies patriarchal power. But patriarchy is the domination not only by male members of the household over the female but also of the older (particularly the senior generation) over the younger. All household structures have potential for problems or conflicts. Thus the power and authority of the older over the younger and the duty and obedience owed by younger to older may create frustration in some circumstances. Waiting for the 'old man' to retire so that the younger generation can take control of the land and make their mark on the world is observed in literature (Shakespeare [1604] 1997; Hardy [1874] 1975; Synge [1907] 1995; Naipaul [1961] 1964) and ethnography (Arensberg and Kimbell 1940). From the opposite point of view, the older generation may feel a lack of filial piety on the part of children who have left to work in distant towns (cf. Asis *et al.* 1995). The frustrations of these rural family farmers have parallels in modern Britain, for example, in the emotions of elderly people and their families when making decisions about continued independent living in the face of increasing frailty. What is the right amount of duty owed, and what reasonable expectations can be anticipated from one generation to another? Society's norms can seldom be applied unambiguously to the complexities of individual circumstance.

'Age' can be both a verb (to age) and a noun (the age of consent). Ageing is a process that is continuous. Thus strictly age as an attribute requires an additional set of criteria to demarcate people into groups. People's ages are usually described in terms of calendar age – the numbers of years that have lapsed since birth. So to be described as aged '21' means that you have survived between 7665 days and 8030 days (give or take the odd leap year) since your birth. This is because we use the Gregorian calendar, which has become a worldwide standard. But there are other ways of measuring dates and times – the Jewish and the Islamic calendars are two such examples. In many societies the transitions from one 'age' to another are marked by ritual – ceremonies such as initiation rites – which publicly mark the change from one social role to another. The aspect of age that is significant to a society may be the accumulation of years, but in many societies without bureaucratic recording of age, people do not know their chronological age. People may measure the passing of the years by reference to personal, social and historical events – when they had their first child, when the pogrom took place, or when the great flood happened. In these ways people know who is older or younger.

Through a variety of means people may be differentiated into age strata. Society recognizes that a group of people, defined by chronological age or through collectively reaching a certain stage in their lives, should occupy certain social roles and be entitled to certain privileges or duties. Some age categories may be given a special significance. In modern society many legal rights are defined by age. For example, the age at which you can buy alcohol or tobacco, drive a car, have sex, leave home, marry, join the army, vote, serve as a juror or be expected to retire as a judge, are legally defined. Hence there is an association of 'old age' with those of 65 years and over; historically this has been the pensionable age for men in the UK. Similarly, in the UK centenarians are regarded as special and this status is acknowledged by the nation with a telegram from the Head of State.

Age and stratification

Given this wide variation in the way in which age is used as a social criteria it is important to be clear about the concepts with which we describe age-based features of society. 'Age classes' are groups of people of the same age who by virtue of this characteristic have similar social rights and duties. These are groups of people who, as a result of their common age, share a distinctive set of life chances. The roles and norms society allocates to age groups create both barriers and opportunities. This can be seen to give people of similar age common interests, mutual advantages or disadvantages, as compared to people of other chronological ages. A weak view of such age strata would be simply that they are people in the same chronological age band into which people come and go with the passing of time; a strong view would be that they are people who have common interests which conflict with those of other age classes (Riley 1979; Riley *et al.* 1983; Riley *et al.*

1988a). People in the modern world move in and out of age strata as they add years to their life. It is important to note that the boundaries of the age categories are not fixed by any objective criteria that are independent of society. The age categories thought up by demographers or legislators for their convenience (Kirk 1992) are just as much social constructions as any reported sense of common identity among teenagers, pensioners or the over-40s. Because of historical social change, the age at which individuals, born at different times, acquired these age-based rights and duties may have been different. Both the experience of growing older, and the common experience of those born at a particular time, can form part of age-based social structures (Riley 1988; Riley *et al.* 1988b).

The 'life cycle' is seen as the typical sequence of age categories in a society. It is most frequently looked at in terms of the sequence of generations, as a continually turning wheel. Thus, all members of society are thought to age by following typical sequences of roles, for example, child, adolescent, spouse, parent, grandparent, then ancestor. 'Lifecourses' are different although naturally they are structured by life cycles. 'Life cycle' is a static image of an unchanging society; 'lifecourse' is an image that reflects the flow of time and the sequencing of cohorts as well as generations. 'Lifecourses' happen to people in historical time and in particular places, and so reflect the fact that 'life cycles' change over time and place. 'Lifecourses' not only vary between different social groups, for example across genders, but significantly also vary historically (Hareven 1982; Kohli and Meyer 1986; Riley 1986; Ikels *et al.* 1992).

'Generation' refers to the fact of reproduction and that each family experiences a sequence of people passing through the life cycle (Eisenstadt 1956). Thus today's children will be tomorrow's parents and will subsequently take their turn as grandparents. The idea of 'age strata' is sometimes not clearly differentiated from that of 'generation' and 'cohort'. This confusion is easily made when the image of the nation or the society as a family is used, such that those over 60 can be referred to as the 'older generation'. Similarly, 'the 1960s generation' refers to people who were young during a particular period of history, i.e. a cohort. The idea of 'generation' can rather more usefully be used to refer to position within the family. Generation and age are not synonymous. For example, grandparenthood and retirement do not necessarily occur simultaneously and it appears that the age range during which both these events occur is widening (Bengston 1996). Further, chronological age is not always an accurate guide to kinship relationships; nephews and nieces may in some circumstances be older than their aunts or uncles.

Cohorts or age sets may also be socially recognized. These are a set of people who are given a common identity early in their lives and carry that common identity through the rest of their days. These groups may be named age sets, so, for example, all those initiated at a certain time together form a group which earns a reputation and feels a common sense of solidarity throughout their lives. This may take the form of class groups at school or college (the class of '47) who keep in touch and have reunions. In tribal societies, social structures made up of a set sequence of age grades will have successive age sets or cohorts passing through them. Just as age since birth is continuous, so

dates of birth are allocable into cohort categories only by the use of culturally constructed systems of classification.

Members of a cohort age at the same time and, consequently, have many
historical experiences in common. Rapid change in society means that people
with quite close dates of birth may well have distinctive sets of experience
(Cribier 1989). These common experiences may lead to a common sense of
identity and even common interests. So, for example, there is a set of people
in the UK who are now in their 80s and were born before the First World
War (1908–14), were getting married and having children at the height of the
economic collapse of the 1930s, had their family and occupational careers disrupted by the Second World War, and retired before earnings related pension
schemes had made a significant impact on retirement incomes. Similarly, it
has been argued that the cohort born in the post-war baby boom, who experienced the changes in social conventions of the 1960s, established a collective
sense of liberation at that time and consequently has a degree of common
identity. One social repercussion of this differing cohort experience is sometimes referred to as a 'generation gap'. However, these cohort differences are
not merely cultural; demographic change, and other changes in family structure, will mean that the experience of parenthood and other intergenerational social relations will change (Hareven 1994; Bengston 1996). The
lifecourse now, much more typically, will include the experience of being
grandparents in middle age and a great-grandparent in later life.

It is important not to let the metaphor of social structure lead us to think
of society in rigid terms. Unlike inanimate structures such as buildings or geo-
logical formations, patterns of social relationships are constantly renewed and
recreated. Stratification is a process of continued interaction, dispute and
struggle over the differentiation of people and their allocation to groups of
varying social power. Just as a change in the position of women requires
adjustment by men, or more power for employers implies less autonomy for
workers, age-based groups affect one another. For younger social groups to
gain power the older ones must lose it. Further, there is a complex, dynamic,
pattern by which the lifecourse of different cohorts affect one another. The
cohort who are currently 70–80 have had opportunities which were achieved
by the struggles, often through trade unions, of the preceding generation
who started the movement down the road to universal retirement pensions
(Macnicol 1998). The success of those struggles enabled them to retire in
greater security than their parents had enjoyed. Subsequently, they have been
affected by the increasing proclivity of their children to separate and divorce,
and thus they may be obstructed in meeting some of their previously held
expectations of grandparent–grandchild relationships. In other words the
experiences of this cohort have been in part determined by the actions of both
the cohorts that immediately preceded and succeeded it.

Age strata and cohorts are two separate bases on which social life is patterned. There are difficult methodological problems, when trying to study old
age and politics, in working out which phenomena are the result of becoming a certain age, and which result from being a member of a particular
cohort. The common life chances of people of a particular age may derive
either from their chronological age or from the common experiences of their

cohort or from having lived in a particular period in history. A common attitude expressed by people of a particular age may arise for a number of reasons. Cohorts whose formative years have given them common values and perceptions make take up particular attitudes. All those people whatever their age who experienced a particular historical event may, as a result, adopt a common attitude. The greater propensity of people with a particular attitude to die young will affect the age distribution of that attitude. Further, simply living long enough to have enough experience of life and to be closer to death than birth, may itself lead to a particular attitude. Thus for any specific moment in time those who are old may appear to share certain characteristics. However, these features may be to do with advancing years and age class processes, the result of cohort survival or other age set experiences, or to the specific historical events experienced by a generation.

Definitions of politics

This book is about both politics and old age. Just as we examined the social construction of age so we can also ask 'what is politics?' Politicians and party politics are not held in high esteem in the UK or the USA, although, almost by definition, politics is about what is important in society. However, politics is properly about much more than party politics (although it is clearly about that as well). Politics can be seen as being concerned with social stability – law and order, the rights and duties of people to each other, conflict resolution and social integration. It is also about social change. In essence politics is about power, both the power that people and groups exert over each other, and how society collectively wields power over people by imposing institutionalized constraints on the ways they think and act (Eriksen 1996).

Politics can be identified analytically in all societies, but not all societies that anthropologists have studied have political institutions that are distinct from other societal realms. In modern state societies, it may seem fairly easy to delineate what is politics and what is not. Political science, which was developed to study politics in such societies, deals with the formal political institutions, with legislative assemblies, local administrations, voting patterns and other aspects of society that are commonly recognized as political. However, although politics is about the activities of parliaments, legislatures, administrations, judiciaries, political parties and pressure groups, who readily describe their actions as political, it is also about newspapers, television and other media, economic institutions such as firms, professions and unions who have vital interests in political decisions and seek to influence them. Further, the ways in which we think, in which we assess what is right or wrong and define what is moral or expedient, relate to social and cultural processes. Most importantly these kinds of political processes are found in institutions such as schools, universities, churches and families, and their role in socialization. It is not useful to try to define politics by making a complete list of institutions and relationships which are political. Political anthropologists studying the full range of human societies have to look for the political that is embedded in complex and multifunctional institutions. They identify decision making mechanisms which do not conform to a narrow institutional definition of politics and they find political aspects of behaviour throughout society. They seek to understand the dominant ideas of a society and how these ideas come to be challenged. Most significantly they seek to identify the social patterns by which the material and cultural goods are distributed amongst the various sections of society. Thus the key questions to ask about the politics in any society are who gets what and why? Politics at its widest is a way of looking at all relationships. It should be viewed as a social process not an institution. Thus through this book we look at politics according to a very wide definition of the subject and seek to understand politics on both the small scale and the large. We ask questions about politics and old age in interpersonal contexts, in local and community contexts, in national contexts, in broad historical and cultural contexts.

Definitions of power

Given this broad definition of politics the central concern of this book becomes the exercise of power. What is power? What kind of power do older people have, if any? If they do not have power, why not? In other words, we are seeking some explanation of the distribution of power between people and groups in contemporary society. Power is a relationship. Power is not an object, a thing like a gun, a bag of gold, or an arrest warrant – it is a relationship between people. One of the oldest and yet still most influential definitions of power is that of Max Weber, who wrote that power 'is the ability to enforce one's own will on others' behaviour' ([1919] 1978); that is the ability to make someone do something they would otherwise not have done. Because power is a feature of social relationships it is observable only through identifying the ability of some people to have others act to their advantage. Power, then, is only ever a potential when future actions are to be considered because its true measure is established only by its consequences. Social actors can anticipate who is powerful, but they may get it wrong. Power may be identified with greater certainty through an examination of the consequences of past action. All social relationships involve a balance of power. Domination is a severely unequal balance of power in a relationship. The chief characteristic of the relationship of domination is a lack of reciprocity. This lack of reciprocity can frequently be identified in material terms. Who contributes what to the total social wealth generated through society? Who gets what out of the social division of labour?

Some writers argue that it is not possible to go beyond what social actors say and believe about power. Now, while it is true that power is a social relationship, power is more than merely ideas and beliefs. It is necessary to look at the resources both physical and cultural which are available to the protagonists in any conflictual situation. A materialist view stresses the importance of structural power embedded in the division of labour – the relationships which govern control of key resources. The most useful kind of definition of power for the purposes of this book will require a strong materialist component. To understand politics, power and old age we need to understand the position of older people in the overall political economy. While contemporary intellectual fashions emphasize social and cultural construction, power is more than merely intellectual or cultural domination. We need to do more than to reveal the social nature of how people come to define their reality; we also need to understand that the potential for power exists prior to that process. Power is embedded in a pre-existing structure of relationships and it is this power that enables some definitions of the situation to be more readily accepted than others. A materialist basis to the study of politics is necessary if we wish to understand how different sets of people come to have different interests. People with common interests can be described as an interest group or perhaps as a class. What interest groups are involved in the politics of old age? How do individuals know where their true interests lie? Do old people have common interests? If so, what are these interests and how are they expressed?

Within a bounded context interests can be defined in an objective manner. However, we also need to recognize that ideological blinkers may mean members of society are unable to articulate them. The idea of 'power' will be used in this book in a manner which incorporates the control of ideas as well as control of physical force and other resources impacting on people's material interests. 'Interest' is not a straightforward concept and can easily become used in a tautological manner. Interests may diverge between conflicting short and long term interests. There may be genuine ambiguity or lack of knowledge of what constitutes someone's best interests. People might not know what their interests are and it is possibly even more difficult for an outside observer to know what those interests are. Although we have to take account of the interpretation and negotiation of social meanings, behaviour, life chances and possibilities for action, are structured by such things as class or age. These structures have consequences even if the actors involved are not conscious, either of the existence of classes or age groups, or of themselves as being a member of a specific class or age group. For example, individuals living in a modern industrial society cannot escape the impact of unemployment rates and the consequences these have for their own wages and employment prospects and opportunities. The market for labour exists independently of people's consciousness of being a member of the working class or any understanding of their labour market interests. By analogy, you do not have to think of yourself as old for the consequences of a social definition of old age to fundamentally structure your individual identity. For example, your life chances as an elderly person in the job market are structured, and even if you as an individual may have been fortunate in how those life chances have fallen out, your life is still structured by what has happened to others. The meaning of your identity as someone with a full-time job at 70 is inevitably coloured by the fact that so many others do not have such jobs.

Common interests are real, even if we, as observers, and they, as the subjects, do not know what these interests are. They are real in the sense that they are real in their consequences. Old people may have common interests intrinsic to a particular social structure, they may have such interests forced upon them by the actions of others, or they may create them for themselves. They may have objective common interests derived from their exclusion from the labour market even if they are not, as individuals, aware of this. They may have common interests imposed on them by the development of professions and the resulting dependency relations, or they may, by collective action, create a common interest in subsidized travel or other specific public services.

Ideology and hegemony

Power also adheres to the realm of ideas. Weber ([1919] 1978) makes a distinction between power and authority. Power is the ability to make other people do things, authority includes the idea of legitimacy and consent. The probability of obedience is that much greater if one believes that the instruction is given by a legitimate authority with the right to give the order. Political scientists discuss these elements of power in terms of the concepts of 'culture', 'ideology' and 'hegemony'. Culture describes learned as opposed to instinctive and biologically determined behaviour. More usefully it is used to describe the whole intellectual apparatus which people share in order to make sense of, and control, the world around them. Thus culture describes the collective values and knowledge which enable people to live in their society and also the social processes by which such values and knowledge are produced and reproduced. Ideology also refers to values and knowledge but sees these things as tied to social classes and groups so that what counts as knowledge and virtue is related to people's position in society and its division of labour. Gramsci developed the concept of hegemony, which summarizes how the ideas – the ideology – of the dominant class become all pervading and are able to exclude the possibility of even thinking about alternatives (Gramsci 1971, 1978, 1985; Forgacs 1988; Gledhill 1994). If something cannot be thought, it cannot be done. Questions that seek to reveal and understand ideologies are important in this book. What are the dominant values which mediate involvement in politics in general and old people's involvement in particular? Does ageism have such a hegemonic hold over the ways we think that we cannot even see or imagine alternatives?

The concept of power should include not only the Weberian idea of the probability of obedience (Weber [1919] 1978) but also the ideological issues of constructing the agenda. Power is expressed through all processes by which collective interests become, not simply identified and pursued, but sometimes systematically suppressed. Power lies not only in winning the public debate but also in keeping issues out of public consciousness and off the agenda. Is this why elderly people in the UK have not been noticeably vocal or active in asserting their interests politically (Midwinter and Tester 1987)? Lukes (1974) suggests that a one-dimensional view of power focuses on political behaviour, on decision making and on observable and overt conflict. This one-dimensional view of power sees interests as policy preferences revealed by political participation. He also discusses a two-dimensional view of power which identifies both issues and potential issues, overt and covert conflict, but still identifies interests in a subjective way as grievances or preferred policies. Lukes' three-dimensional view of power is established through a critique of the limitations of the previous two approaches. It focuses on decision making and control over the political agenda, so that issues, potential issues and latent conflicts become legitimate areas of study. We need to pay careful attention that our language and conceptual apparatus do not silence less powerful groups.

> Because of lack of communication channels, lack of organisation or similar poverty in resources, they are prevented from promoting their interest in efficient ways. In Michel Foucault's terms, powerless groups are subjugated by the dominant discourses of society; the ways in which everyday language structures the world and confirms a set of values.
>
> (Eriksen 1995: 146)

Lifestyle politics

One aspect of a broad definition of politics is what Giddens (1991) has discussed in terms of 'life' or 'lifestyle' politics. Such politics concerns how one chooses to live everyday life, even down to details of domestic arrangements and personal appearance. As outlined above, it is usual in political theory to recognize a narrow and a broad conception of politics. The first refers to processes of decision making within the governmental sphere of the state; the second sees as political any modes of decision making which are concerned with settling debates or conflicts, where opposing interests or values clash. Life-politics is politics in both these senses. Although the conflicts and issues examined may appear to be intimate and personal, 'all issues of life politics involve questions of rights and obligation and the state thus far continues to be the main administrative locus within which these are settled in law' (Giddens 1991: 226).

This can be illustrated by examples from the fields of economics and health. Should people be able to choose to work or not (cf. Bauman 1998)? Should I get out of bed in the morning and go to work? Strong moral opprobrium is experienced by young men who feel no sense of obligation to work. States and governments construct legal frameworks which regulate access to unemployment and/or disablement benefit for those who do not work. But at what age is it reasonable to no longer desire or be expected to seek paid employment? Individuals who do not work have to negotiate their lifestyles not only within immediate interpersonal relations of family and community but with the macro-structures of state and economic institutions.

Should it be a matter of personal choice as to whether to smoke or not? The state sets an overall set of legal parameters with regard to this choice. In the UK people cannot legally buy cigarettes until they reach the age of 16. Many public and private institutions ban smoking in at least part of their premises and there is a legally upheld framework for this prohibition. The USA has gone much further down this road than the UK. However, even within families, there is negotiation and decisions are made about who can smoke where. Parents with children who want to smoke have to work through and decide as families at what point and under what conditions the young people can smoke. Residents and management in residential homes for elderly people have to negotiate similar rules. The extent to which the National Health Service (NHS) should treat conditions that are self-inflicted through smoking are part of the internal resource allocation politics of the NHS and this issue is starting to be aired in national political forums.

> The capability of adopting freely chosen lifestyles, a fundamental benefit generated by a post-traditional order, stands in tension, not only with barriers to emancipation, but with a variety of moral dilemmas.
>
> (Giddens 1991: 231)

Giddens makes the distinction between emancipatory politics and lifestyle politics. Emancipatory politics are post-enlightenment efforts at liberation, freedom from constraints of religion and tradition and superstition. The idea of emancipation also contains the demand for liberation from one group dominating another. Such demands have traditionally been made by nations, ethnic or linguistic groups, classes and more recently genders. Lifestyle politics is about personal choice and control over lifestyle and requires a degree of emancipation in terms of the absence of domination from both ideas and social groups. Thus, Giddens suggests that emancipation both from the fixities of tradition and from the condition of hierarchical domination are a necessary precondition for lifestyle politics. However, he makes the caveat that it would be too crude to say simply that life-politics focuses on what happens once individuals have achieved a certain level of autonomy of action. Other factors are involved, which include 'reflexivity' and 'globalization'. 'Reflexivity', put simply, is the continuing impact of the awareness of oneself and one's impact on others, on behaviour and it is suggested that in the modern world there are enhanced possibilities for such knowledge and adaptation. 'Globalization' is a term to summarize the social, economic and technical changes that make the world a smaller place. One of the cultural consequences of globalization is greater contact and familiarity with a wider range of value systems. Giddens puts these two ideas together in his formal definition of 'life politics' (Giddens 1991: 214).

An understanding of politics and old age cannot merely be based on the social construction of meaning. We not only have to understand the social construction of the categories of old age, but also have to appreciate the importance of power. Politics is about the social differences that are recognized in society but in addition we need a theory which specifies how differences come to be recognized and evaluated. Who in society has the power to have their definitions of categories accepted as positive or negative? Power is embedded in social categories and social evaluation of categories; such construction of inequality does not happen in the abstract but is the result of the exercise of power by some people over others. The lifestyle options of older people are not simply a matter of their choice, or even choice within a structure of constraint. In order to understand such lifestyle choices we must unpick layer upon layer of power structures in which older people are embedded. These power structures have both a hegemonic and a material dimension.

The role of theory in study of old age

It is important that 'the elderly' are not regarded as some alien 'other', not part of us and our society and thus rendered without a voice and incapable of expressing their real interests. There are questions to be asked about why active organizations of older people representing their own interests are not more in evidence. Where do older people articulate their claim to full citizenship and express a sense of collective self-worth? There is a danger of finding negative answers to these questions through failing to properly identify such collective actions and thus reinforcing stereotypes about age. However, it remains for me the most significant question. The touchstone for understanding politics and old age is appreciating the means by which older people can and do take action, struggle to express themselves and free themselves from the restrictions of ageism. There are clearly particular difficulties to be overcome in order for elderly people to organize and collectively express themselves. Many old people frequently deny that the negative stereotypes of old age apply to them, although they believe that they do apply to others. The conflicts are real but may well be hidden in the manner of Lukes' (1974) third notion of power, which suggests that there could be a kind of ideological blindness to the real interests of elderly people. There is the possibility that opposition to inequality based on age is expressed in ways which are not viewed as political or even as opposition.

The questions to ask about old age and politics must be about social processes not about categories. Understanding old age and politics requires an understanding of political processes – how differentiation and domination affect the lives of older people. These processes are interconnected – who is dominated depends upon who is differentiated and who is differentiated depends upon who dominates. These processes cannot be considered in some abstract ahistorical manner but as specifically situated in particular times and places. So the questions we need to ask about the politics of any given situation include: Who are the different kinds of people involved? What is the broader historical and social context? Who dominates and how is this achieved? What is the process whereby some people become dominant and others dominated? What part does age play in this? In the following chapters we ask these questions of a variety of different settings from the personal and the intimate to the large scale global and historical frame.

3

Personal politics

In what ways can politics be thought of as personal? Such a discussion requires us to look at issues of personal identity and issues about the body and who controls it. No one wishes to be old. The cultural devaluation of old age is so strong that the question of negotiating a valued individual identity as an older person becomes a problem and the ways in which this negotiation is conducted involves a struggle for many elderly people. We need to examine the manifestations of personal politics not only in day to day and domestic situations but also in medical and residential institutions.

Body politics

The literature on the sociology of the body (Turner 1984; Featherstone *et al.* 1991; Harding and Palfrey 1997: 133–6) has raised issues which can be usefully explored in the context of old age and the struggle of very old people with other people's reactions to their ageing bodies. This literature suggests that the body is something on which culture can be inscribed. This happens in characteristic ways in the west in the last part of the twentieth century, which are manifest, for example, in skin appearance, in musculature and in a wide variety of body modifications from piercing to dentistry. It can be argued that contemporary society requires maintenance of a certain kind of body image. Old people's bodies are widely regarded with repugnance because of their physical appearance. Older people's appearance is valued only insofar as individuals retain the characteristics of the young, which represent the standard against which their bodies are judged aesthetically. There are two principal lines of reasoning which can be used to explain this phenomenon. First, in modern mass society people interact only on a transient basis, and second, older people lose the kind of control and manipulation of the body required by modern culture. Each of these lines of argument will be elaborated in turn.

Modern urban life and mass culture contrast with traditional communities. Most people do not live in communities where people know each other's character and reputation. Our communities are too large and the division of labour so complex, that in the modern world we interact with strangers on a daily basis. This requires us to make instant judgements about those we interact with and to make decisions about people of whom our knowledge is limited to their outward appearance. The extent to which people encounter each other through transient social relationships and experience each other, not through interaction and dialogue, but as receivers and transmitters of mass images, appearance and display becomes crucial. Social knowledge of other people becomes limited to their appearance, we do not have the knowledge of the background, family, or reputation of most people we encounter. Reflexively, we come to regard who we are as being tied to what we look like.

This point of view reflects the ideas presented in the classic sociological essay of Simmel ([1902–3] 1950) 'The metropolis and mental life'. The starting point of Simmel's concerns is that the deepest problems of modern life derive from the claim of the individual to preserve the autonomy and individuality of their existence in the face of overwhelming social forces characteristic of modern urban living. He argues that there are a number of consequences which derive from the size, complexity and economic organization of the metropolis for the personalities of the people living there. These include a blasé attitude to others and a calculating instrumentality in relationships with other people. These traits of urban living create a potential loss of identity and thus a psychological need to stand out from the crowd. As a consequence people choose dress, appearance and behaviour to make an immediate visual impact. The thrill and sensation of recognition, in Warhol's terms one's 15 minutes of fame, is a product of modern urban life. Mass society produces mass culture, including rapidly changing fashions and styles. Bodies as well as clothes, cosmetics, hairstyles and other bodily adornment have become subject to fashion. Although people in many societies across the world tattoo, scar or modify their bodies in various ways in pursuit of aesthetic goals, modern medical and biological knowledge provides people with greater ability to consciously manipulate the body in order to enhance its appearance. Exercise, diet, surgery, piercing, plucking, dyeing, a whole plethora of procedures give people unprecedented choice over their size, shape and appearance. The current fashions concern themselves less about faces of a certain kind but about bodies, favouring particularly a young slim muscular body shape. Although women seem to suffer the social imperatives on the body most strongly, the body image ideal is androgynous – 'nice bum' could refer to men or women. The body has become a fashion accessory. Social processes which lead to the cultural dominance of spectacle and display, connect in the fetishism of body image with a sense of personal worth. The great spread of such depressive illnesses as bulimia and anorexia has been associated with adolescent girls, in particular, because it occurs at a time crucial to the establishment of an independent adult personality, which in western society has become tightly linked to body image (Featherstone 1982; Giddens 1991).

The second line of argument stems from Elias's (1982) work on the 'civilizing process'. In this work he described a process through which modern personalities have come to internalize self-control. Elias described the rise of manners alongside the rise of the modern state. Men during feudal times had to be able to fight successfully, leaders were required to lead in battle. Thus through the Middle Ages successful men had to have the necessary personal attributes, including the right personality. They had to have the 'balls' to defend themselves and to kill others. Thus violent uncontrolled anger and aggression, or at least lack of restraint, were reflected in the behaviour even (or especially) of the aristocracy. However, with the development of centralized political control and the monopoly of the legitimate use of violence by the state, both leaders and subjects had to develop internalized controls on their physical behaviour and emotions. The development of courtly society ensured that successful people needed personal restraint – calculated behaviour rather than outbursts of aggression. Strategic manipulation of people and networks at court, to gain grace and favour, were the route to power, wealth and influence. In the new courts, control of bodily functions accompanied self-controlled personalities – people came not to eat with their hands, urinate in the corner or exhibit other such unmannerly behaviour. Hence, as courtly society developed, manners elaborated as signs of distinction and status. Such codes of conduct and in particular internally controlled personalities, spread by emulation through the social structure. In the modern world manipulation of personality for economic ends is commonplace. Whole occupational categories, such as sales staff or airline cabin crew, are now required to conduct themselves in a way to make a specific corporately designed impression. Politicians' public appearances are marked by a statuesque performance, a highly controlled smile, a perfectly manipulated facial expression, any deviation from which sparks a frenzy of photographers' flash guns and glee in the cutting room as pictures presenting an alternative image of the glorious leader can be fed to the public. People judge others by their appearance: politicians know this, they have to be good television performers and present a highly controlled personal image to the electorate. In other words, control of appearance and personality is externalized and manipulated as a central concern of politics and power – at least in the major western democracies.

Failure to present an acceptable body image is a problem for both men and women in old age. Older people, in particular female older people, experience the tyranny of appearance. In extreme old age, loss of adult status and failure to properly control the body are closely linked. Reflexive control through such things as 'body sculpting', body piercing and flamboyant hairdressing has enabled younger people to develop their bodies as a means of display and fashion. Old people struggle to maintain an acceptable body image. Cosmetic surgery can be used to disguise the physical effect of age. The vast majority of older people do not, and cannot, afford to go as far as surgical manipulation. Men in later life tend to have greater access to other desirable images through displays of wealth and power, which are less frequently available to women. This last point should alert us to the need, not only to note how important body image is to status, but also to consider the relationship between culture and ideology, and ask how and why particular images come to be valued.

Older women suffer a double jeopardy: de Beauvoir's (1972) classic exposition of being old and female serves to illustrate how interconnected cultural constructions of undervalued social groups are (see Chapter 4 for a discussion of gender and old age). A woman who, in the face of advancing years, stops attempting to control her appearance in a way that is deemed attractive, is said to have 'given up the fight' or 'to have let herself go'. This is unlikely to be said about a man. But the epithet 'dirty old man' is gender specific and indicates that although the problems of body image and appearance differ between genders, they nevertheless affect both. The social pressures associated with body image are so strong that even those who seek a re-evaluation of the 'Third Age', by presenting positive images and role models of older people, tend to choose images of older people who have retained 'young' characteristics. Age Concern produced a controversial advertisement in January and February 1998 that was intended to challenge ageist stereotypes. It took the form of a mock bra advert of a beautiful well-developed mature woman under the slogan 'it's not her age you notice first'. The advertisement reinforced the accurate and important point that older women are physically attractive but the image was based on implicit assumptions about what shape, size and appearance were desirable in a body. Thus 'looking good' and 'looking healthy' imply looking young. Eventually for everyone, however, ageing bones and joints impair stylish deportment, thinning hair and changing skin tone make it difficult to look young. Why it is desirable to look young should not be taken for granted, but should be examined and challenged.

There is a clear link between modernity and the cult of youth. The modernizing regimes of the twentieth century, particularly those which have seen themselves as starting on the road to a utopian future, gave a special place to the young. They wished to create the 'new man' and the 'new woman' uncorrupted by the past but shaped by new institutions. The consumer capitalism of the late twentieth century thrives on rapid changes of fashion and design which quickly render obsolete last month's purchases. The young are thus a key market, as they are responsive to change and have a lifetime of consumption in front of them. They are also highly visible in ways older people are not (see Chapter 7 on consumption). Positive images of old age derive from elderly people with access to power; the patriarchs and matriarchs of extended families, where kinship and family labour give power, are seen as self-confident, handsome and respected. Where spiritual authority confirms power on older people, the older body form of those possessing power does not diminish their status. Such power may well be seen to shine through their eyes, or be self-evident in their serene demeanour. Although it seems almost unthinkable, given the hegemonic image of 'youthism', it is possible that old people are stereotyped as unattractive because they lack property and power, rather than disadvantaged because they are weak, slow, wrinkly and smelly.

As suggested above, when looking at Elias's (1982) civilizing process, it is not surprising that failure to control their bodies will lead older people to feel shame. These problems of body image and its control are particularly acute for older people with failing health. They see themselves as a burden on others and have to suffer indignities to their adult status. The core control functions taught at the earliest ages start to weaken – bodily fluids leak. Some older people find themselves organizing their social lives around access to a toilet. Others have problems maintaining body shape, as they shrink and bend with age. The Anchor Trust *Grey Matters* survey (Sykes and Leather 1997: 12) reported that: 'Losing physical health (45%), independence (31%) and mental health (18%) were the main concerns of older people about growing old.' These priorities are readily explicable when we look at research on the consequences for older people who cannot discipline their bodies to show the required characteristics of adult behaviour. Herskovits and Mitteness (1994) suggest that there are key cultural values which adults are meant to display. These values include mastery (ability to control their behaviour and their bodies), productivity (an ability to demonstrate that their behaviour is useful and purposefully directed), individual responsibility (to show they are responsible for their own actions) and cleanliness. Old age and age-related health problems are often stigmatizing, but there appear to be variations in the degree of stigma related to any single condition. A comparison of urinary incontinence, dementia and arthritis shows how the transgressions involved in incontinence and dementia, in particular, involve an 'overdetermined assault on adult status' (Herskovits and Mitteness 1994: 337). They argue that the strategies used by medical personnel to manage symptoms for these two conditions are as much directed to stigma reduction as they are to symptom alleviation. Arthritis, however, invites much less stigma. Herskovits and Mitteness (1994) are able to demonstrate that these issues over body image are important for the way older people get treated in medical and institutional settings.

The issues of personal politics in terms of elderly people's control of their bodies is problematic not only with respect to euthanasia, as discussed in Chapter 4, but also in the whole range of medical and social care. Older people too often suffer from the paternalistic attitudes of doctors, social workers and others 'who know better'. This issue can be explored by considering the literature on identity. We should not look on older people as simply passive recipients as to what happens to them. We can then look at strategies of identity preservation as a matter of small scale politics.

Identity: threats to, loss and preservation of identity in old age

Looking closely at the concept of identity can give us insights into other aspects of politics and old age. Writers exploring the idea that western society is in a condition of high-modernity or postmodernity have suggested that the whole idea of what constitutes personal identity has become a problem. People's 'identity' can no longer be taken for granted and identity particularly seems to be under threat for some older people. Those at the very end of life and in institutional care seem particularly vulnerable to 'loss of identity'. What is the nature of this concept 'identity' which seems so important yet problematic?

Identity, in a mathematical sense, means exact equivalence, and maths and logic have procedures and formal proofs through which to technically establish something called an identity. Social identity is the aggregate of similarities and differences recognized in the social world. Taking for granted 'common sense' notions of identity has considerable problems (Jenkins 1996: 14). Such unquestioned notions usually take one of two forms. They may stress that there are concrete things called 'individuals', which can be contrasted with 'society', which is a different set of things. Alternatively, they may take a completely methodologically individualist view, which assumes that only individuals are real and denies collective identities any reality ('there are only individuals and their families': Margaret Thatcher). These constructions of identity have an important place in the history of the highly individualistic cultures and societies of the west. In societies with a more collective tradition it is equally self-evident that people are a mere reflection of a greater whole. For example, Hindu philosophical traditions see the current earthly manifestation experienced as an individual person, as part of the unfolding of spiritual forces through time.

The idea of the interior self, the real 'me' talking from inside the head can be distinguished from the public persona or socially given identity. This image of identity is tied up with the distinction between mind and body and identified using concepts such as 'individuality', 'personality', 'consciousness' and 'the mind'. The individual self is distanced from the corporeal entity (body) in which it is housed. These assumptions lie behind much psychological writing. In particular, Freudian psychoanalysis has been one of the most powerful intellectual traditions of the twentieth century, and inherent to notions of the subconscious mind is that there are mental features derived from early socialization which shape the individual personality. The purpose of psychoanalysis is precisely to become more aware of this inner identity. Both academic and popular writers debate loss or change of identity in old age in growing volumes. Popular poetry on old age frequently draws images of the inner self distanced from the outer body by age:

> I'm an old woman now
> > and nature is cruel,
> 'Tis her jest to make
> > old age look like a fool.
> The body it crumbles,
> > grace and vigour depart,
> There now is a stone
> > Where once I had a heart:
> But inside this old carcass
> > a young girl still dwells
> (Carver and Liddiard 1978: ix)

The idea (which is frequently associated with Descartes) of an interior self, the real or inner person different from the external appearance, is the dominant common sense one. However, these common sense notions are, at the end of the twentieth century, becoming increasingly problematic and appear less 'commonsensical'.

Jenkins (1996) argues that individual and collective identities are both essentially social and are, for most practical purposes, inextricably entangled. Identities are neither chosen at will by individuals, nor rigidly determined by the social order; they are the consequence of a process by which internal and external events generate identities in particular contexts. So both the 'interior' and the 'exterior' processes of identity formation are social. They both

reflect patterns of power. Some approaches to the study of identity emphasize the sources of individuality – these approaches will tend to look at issues
of mind and body and how each of these may come to be considered to have
unique or individual characteristics. The question of social process then
becomes – how is the uniqueness of each person's various identities accom-
plished in social settings? How are these accomplishments problematic for
older individuals? Other approaches emphasize how social similarity is produced. These emphasize, on the one hand, historical and cultural features
which impinge on the possible range and variety of meaningful social identities. On the other hand, they draw attention to the production of institutionalized and administered identities associated with powerful groups such
as the state, commercial and administrative bodies. The same question about
the problematic nature of identity for older people can also be asked from
these various perspectives.

One of the most problematic situations for establishing personal identity is
in the area of mental and physical infirmity. If individual identity is a social
accomplishment based in interaction what disabilities inhibit its achievement? One may ask, when is a person so physically and mentally impaired
that they cease to be able to command an individual identity? One approach
to this issue might be through biology and neurophysiology, an investigation
into what dementia is in terms of the biochemistry or organic structure of the
brain. Identity from this perspective would seek to diagnose brain functions,
perhaps related to consciousness, perhaps to information processing, which
could be measured and would stand as a diagnostic tool for the identification
of the presence of an individual identity. A further approach might be to look
to the psychology of identity. Psychoanalysis of course involves a particular
view of identity. Personality change for those with Alzheimer's might thus be
associated with de-layering, or stripping away defences and/or inhibitions.
The sociologist is more likely to take a humanistic approach, stressing the self-
realizing actor in a social context. This is the approach which I shall follow in
the final section of this chapter.

Identity preservation in institutional care

This section is about the personal politics involved in caring for elderly people
in institutional and domestic settings. The struggle for control of personal time
and space is bound up with the issue of sustaining identity. Who we aspire to
be, what we are allowed to be and thus what we are able to become, is particularly a problem in 'total institutions' (Goffman 1961). Extreme cases can
be useful in providing insight into more mundane circumstances. Brian
Keenan's (1992) account of his three-year incarceration by kidnappers in
Lebanon provides a very useful commentary on the issue of sustaining an
intact identity and how important maintaining a coherent narrative to one's
life is in that process. Day by day, Keenan experiences constant imminent
danger of death, and the stress and search for meaning which are associated
with the nearness of death. In counterpoint most of his time is spent in
routine, mind numbing, boring confinement in which, by and large, his only
resources for distraction and meaningful activity are within himself. He

experiences many deprivations – from food and water to personal contact. His guards maintained a close personal and intimate supervision of his person. The book tells us much about Keenan's character but also a great deal about identity maintenance, which Keenan manages in the most adverse of circumstances. The parallels with residential care are striking. The close presence of death, the daily humiliations of personal hygiene and the dependence on the erratic attitudes of transient carers, all presented Keenan with a problem in sustaining his identity. They similarly create a problem for the inmates of residential facilities for frail older people.

As a participant observer in a residential home, I watched a middle-aged carer approach a resident in her late 60s who sat in a chair in the communal lounge. She smiled at her and the lady shifted her weight forward, smiling in anticipation. The care worker took her hand and went 'round and round the garden like a teddy bear, one step two steps ticklely under there' together with the actions. Both laughed and smiled at each other and this performance was repeated three times before the care worker said goodbye with a cheery voice and the lady settled back in her chair with a contented smile. As a male university-educated observer I not only could see the 'natural' caring talent of the untrained local woman who had brought up her own children and the pleasure she had given the resident but also was shocked by the infantilization involved in so blatantly treating a fully grown adult in such a manner.

If we examine the beginnings and development of communicative behaviour in childhood we can gain some insight into how the carer–old person communication can degenerate into infantile modes. A baby's first interactions are pre-verbal and involve mutual looking, smiling and burbling. Baby talk is to vocalize simple stock phrases, repeated, with simple rhythms that mimic speech. Subsequent toddler talk involves recognizable words, the development of a vocabulary and the beginnings of conversational exchange. Young children can quickly learn language games which involve displacement and construction of an imaginative world. There is a view that adult status is achieved through a biological and psychological process of maturation. To an interactionist the change to adult status would be validated only through the interactional consequences of skilled role performance by the growing adult. Learning to interact fully and to be accepted, first as a baby, then as a child and later as an adult, produces characteristic responses from the other parties. Is this reversed with the biological and psychological changes in old age, which are seldom seen as maturation, more usually depreciation? I am not arguing that the developmental sequence regresses, rather that the interactional structures based in impaired communication can increasingly generate features which look like a reversal of developmental trends. Failure on the part of older inmates to have their talk identified as appropriately verbally sophisticated would promote a tendency to 'baby talk' them. Infantilization of elderly people is associated with the care role. External supervision of biological functions from feeding and dressing to toileting, invokes in the carer, behaviour that one would give to a child. The role exchange involves an expectation of passivity in return for gentleness. An interactionist analysis would see a circular process by which infantilization might occur. Failure to communicate in a manner which is seen as fully adult leads to a response from a carer which assumes less than adult status; in return, being treated as less than adult elicits infantile responses from the cared for (Kemper and Lyons 1994).

Hockey and James (1993) *Growing Up and Growing Old* is an excellent account of the use of the metaphors of childhood to construct the identities of old people and in particular the processes of infantilization, based on research on old age by Hockey and on childhood by James. Hockey and James (1993) point out that elderly people do not simply accept the position of quasi infant in which they find themselves. They adopt various strategies of resistance to assert an element of a fully adult identity. Hockey draws on her fieldwork experience in old people's homes to illustrate the ways in which this can be done even by those in residential care and with multiple disabilities. The authors' examples resonate with my own fieldwork and observation of residential care. They suggest that 'very elderly people, positioned in a twilight marginal zone, may be those who, free from structural constraints, can offer a critique of dominant social forms' (Hockey and James 1993: 172) and in this they echo the analysis of the oppositional youth cultures studied, for example, by the Birmingham Cultural Studies Centre (Willis 1977; Hebdige 1979). Hockey and James demonstrate how residents found ways to subvert and exploit the second childhood imposed upon them and to adjust the balance of power. 'Elderly people being treated by adults as children, thus empower themselves in a child-like manner in their rejection of the process of infantilisation' (Hockey and James 1993: 175). For example, poking a tongue out when submitted to childlike control by staff, they interpret as using a 'child's' response to an infantilized position which offers symbolic resistance in a way which challenged the imposition of metaphors of childhood. More passive, but similarly effective, were those residents who were able to turn their 'child-like' dependency on care staff to their own advantage. They suggest that a slumped body and a deaf ear could be put to powerful effect when resisting the repeated demands of busy staff endeavouring to assemble the entire company in the dining room for their thrice daily meals in the care home.

> Another scarcely mobile woman invariably set off on her long journey to the toilets whenever the lunch bell was rung, thus disrupting the ordered flow of lunch-time routine. Endeavouring to circumvent her late arrival in the dining-room, a care aide asked her some 15 minutes before lunch if she needed the toilet. Managing not to hear the question until it had been shouted repeatedly, the resident held up her hand and replied: 'Please teacher. I don't. Not yet.' By dramatising the adult-to-child relationship set up by the care aide she reveals its inappropriateness. She thus, effectively, asserted her adult right to choose when *she* wanted to go to the toilet.
>
> (Hockey and James 1993: 173)

Hockey and James (1993) cite examples where assuming a childlike role enables the residents to be aggressive, make demands, even become abusive and violent in the manner of a naughty child. The staff are thus manipulated into meeting the concerns of residents by being unable to escape the 'parent' role. They are even able to demonstrate the conscious irony by which the participants can acknowledge this contested power relationship.

> Mabel Wilkenshaw, a female resident in her early eighties, drew on the metaphor of childhood when resisting the institutional system of doling out medicines, regardless of residents' wishes. Having managed to refuse her pills, Mabel smiled winningly and said 'I'm a naughty girl.' The officer-in-charge urges her, 'You take notice of me. They do you good!' But Mabel held her ground, replying 'If I'm going to die, then I'll die.'
>
> (Hockey and James 1993: 181)

Although playing the 'child' role, this resident totally undermines the category by reference to her own death. It has also been my experience of homes that staff find the issues of death much more difficult to deal with than the residents. Showing preparedness for death, actively asking for or inviting death challenges the whole role and relationship of care staff as quasi parents of their child-like wards.

Those close to death or unable to control their bodily functions also have power to pollute. Thus, even when apparently at their most vulnerable, people have some social resources with which to negotiate their position. The defilement associated with contact with death adheres to very old people. A special ambiguous and dangerous status between life and death has been referred to many times in the anthropological literature, sometimes labelled as a 'limbo' status or as a 'twilight' position and by others as 'marginal' or 'stranger' positions. Defilement associated with incontinence gives old people a certain dangerous element which can become power. The power of bodily wastes to mess up the established order may be similarly wielded by angry young children or even political prisoners, as in a 'dirty' protest. This idea parallels reports by Searle-Chatterjee (1979) on the untouchable castes in Benares. These people who, in Hindu terms, are the lowest of low because they clean the city of excrement, are able to walk boldly down a crowded street in an assertive manner and have the multitudes move aside before them for fear of contamination. They have unionized and effectively demanded higher wages from the city authorities because the threat to withdraw labour, which would leave the city contaminated and unpure is a powerful one (Searle-Chatterjee 1979: 282).

Identity issues for those with Alzheimer's and other dementias

Although these issues in the politics of identity may seem remote and esoteric, they have both profound philosophical and practical consequences. Recent work on Alzheimer's and identity questions both the notion of self and the place of the individual person in western thought and the very practical problems of caring for people with Alzheimer's disease who are described as having lost their 'identity'.

The social construction approach to Alzheimer's disease can give some insights into the problems it creates for older people and into the issue of identity in general (Harding and Palfrey 1997). Alzheimer's involves the progressive loss of brain function, including memory loss and communication failure. One of the painful features, for carers with a long-standing relationship to the sufferer, is the inability to continue a reciprocal social relationship based on shared memory. To what extent can mental impairment to memory and to communication prevent the achievement of a full identity? Or, from a slightly different perspective, what is the nature of identity which is destroyed, hidden or distorted by dementia? Does the perceived loss of personal identity in sufferers start with the observer's inability to detect appropriate signs of identity. Carers' attention is drawn to personality changes by the everyday reality of coping. One way in which carers (who are usually spouses) cope is to cling to memories of previous 'real' identity of their loved ones before they deteriorated and became 'like a ghost' of their former self.

Another approach to identity and Alzheimer's disease is to look at identity preservation measures and strategies used by dementia sufferers as their condition progresses. We can, for example, try and look behind the communication difficulties to assess levels of self-awareness and thus personal identity. These approaches may assist us in helping sufferers to find new ways to preserve and communicate old identities. Interaction techniques to disguise memory loss or incontinence have been documented and many of these analyses start with Goffman's (1968) *Stigma,* which is subtitled *Notes on the Management of a Spoiled Identity.* Research (Mercken 1997) on the interactions between children and elderly dementia sufferers suggests that the responses of older women to the presence of young children has a positive beneficial effect. One possible explanation of the increased purposeful and pleasurable activity noted relates to activating elements of maternal and caring roles. These are elements of role performance which are laid down early in socialization and deeply embedded in the personality and so survive as routines and attitudes despite the deprecations of the disease. Aspects of personal identity derived from maternal roles may be thought of as more permanent or resilient than other aspects of identity (for example, time and location) which more easily get lost.

The current conception of Alzheimer's disease emerged in the 1970s, achieved wide acceptance and popularization (Herskovits 1995; Harding and Palfrey 1997) and was given its own four-digit code when the ninth revision of the International Classification of Diseases was introduced in 1979 (*Population Trends* 92: 27). Herskovits (1995) argues that it achieved such acceptance because it effectively served important political-economic interests, whilst also solving pragmatic, clinical and psychological problems for practitioners and carers. He argues that bringing the concept of 'senility' within the disease framework was functional for dealing with philosophical and ethical problems encountered when dealing with some older people. However, the widespread acceptance and popularization of this approach has produced a troubling dilemma regarding the subjectivity of people diagnosed with Alzheimer's disease. A 'loss of self' is implicit in the current Alzheimer's construct, and it has been argued that, consequently, the subjective experience of being and becoming old has become increasingly distressing. Certainly fear of the loss of one's 'mind' is widespread and for some people it is felt to be more alarming than even loss of life. It has been further suggested that a response to this unintended assault on the self can be seen in the now burgeoning literature offering diverse representations of, and debates about, the 'self' in Alzheimer's. What appears to be at stake in this debate is our most fundamental knowledge of the human condition and what constitutes subjective experience. Herskovits (1995) amongst others (Gubrium and Holstein 1995; Sherman and Webb 1994) suggests that as a culture, as well as a community of gerontological thinkers and practitioners, we tell these stories about Alzheimer's, because our struggle with the nature of the self-in-Alzheimer's reflects our struggle to grapple with the nature of self and identity in modern society.

Sabat and Harré (1992) discuss dementia from a phenomenological point of view, that is systematic examination of the observed behaviour, including language, of those diagnosed with Alzheimer's disease (AD). A very similar approach has been developed independently by Kitwood, also drawing on ideas about personhood and coming to a similar conclusion about care (Kitwood and Bredin 1992). If identity is the social construction of the participants through interaction, what kind of identity is possible for those whose ability to interact is limited or lost? This places the issue in the context of communication rather than of cognitive function.

> from Wittgenstein we have learnt of the central importance of language in the creation of social reality, and from the latter [Vygotsky] the role of the acquisition of linguistic and manipulative skills on the organisation of thought and experience. Using the analytical techniques of the new approach we will show that (1) there is a self, a personal singularity, that remains intact despite the debilitating effects of the disorder, and (2) there are other aspects of the person themselves that are socially and publicly presented, that can be lost, but only indirectly as a result of the disease. In the second case, the loss of self is directly related to nothing more than the ways in which others view and treat the A.D. sufferer.
>
> (Sabat and Harré 1992: 444)

Sabat and Harré review empirical evidence and conduct conversational analysis on the linguistic exchanges through the progressive phases of the disease between a small set of Alzheimer's sufferers and others. They distinguish between the interior self-referencing self revealed by linguistic usage of personal pronouns, and the distinctive persona achieved through interaction. They conclude that the self of personal identity remains intact even in the face of quite severe deterioration in other cognitive and motor functions. These researchers suggest that if there is loss of self as a result of Alzheimer's, that loss is not in 'the management of the organising power of the indexical creation of self'. People seem to be able to maintain a coherent linguistic reference point for themselves through the course of the disease until the time when virtually no behaviour of any consequence occurs. They also claim that it is clear that the repertoire of selves, the personae that are socially and publicly presented and which require the cooperation of others in the social sphere in order to come into being, can indeed be manifested even in the later stages of the disease. However, in this sense of identity the threatened disappearance of self is not directly linked to the progress of the disease. Rather, it is related to the behaviour of those who are regularly involved in the social life of the sufferer. They suggest, difficult though it is to react positively to the fragile clues of identity presented, persistence and dedication in this respect will lead to positive reinforcement of identity. They comment on carers' interactional behaviour:

> If such behaviour is founded on story lines that position the sufferer as inadequate, confused, helpless, etc. then that person will be so positioned and will have his or her behaviour interpreted by others in such a way as to confirm the initial story line and position. The ultimate result of such a situation is the fencing off of the sufferer so that no adequate self can be constructed.
>
> (Sabat and Harré 1992: 459)

Sabat and Harré's ideas have been commented upon by, amongst others, Golander and Raz (1996). Their aim is not only to strengthen and support the insight which theories of social construction of identity can make, but also to suggest, from a position of greater experience of care provision for elderly people, how new identities for dementing people are constructed in the care setting. Their emphasis is on social reconstruction by others of the social personae of severely demented people. In particular they show how a prior reputation can become embedded in a narrative which provides a mechanism for interpretation of behaviour and thus a route to sustaining elements of social identity (cf. Gubrium and Holstein 1995). Such story lines have consequences for the construction of care plans. For example, irritability may be seen to conform with an account of previous character traits and not therefore seen by medical staff as a pathological symptom and not treated with medication. An alternative story line about personal characteristics may lead to an older person's complaints about the behaviour of other patients on the ward being seen as a symptom for which they need to be treated.

Kitwood has attempted to theorize the care of Alzheimer's sufferers from within an interactionist framework. Kitwood not only refers directly to the symbolic interactionist school of sociology but also draws on resources from psychoanalysis and counselling. Significantly in analysing the disease he includes the care team in the diagnostic frame. This stance enables him to break down the dichotomy between 'us' practitioners outside the disease and 'them' the patients who are the manifestation of the disease. His perspective enables him to develop specific recommendations for therapy (Kitwood 1993, 1997). Kitwood proposes offering counselling and therapy built around the assumption of a positive identity of the older person even to those with advanced symptoms and sees this as a cultural challenge to traditional dementia care (Kitwood 1997: 135–7). Robertson (1991) also identifies a politics of cultural struggle over the treatment of people diagnosed with Alzheimer's disease (PDWADs):

> little attention is paid to the ways in which AD may be socially produced and reproduced by the unequal power relations between PDWADs and family members, service providers, care settings, and the entire public

culture that has grown up around AD. The loss of autonomy and structured dependence, as well as the expectations on the part of others of inevitable increasing cognitive impairment place the PDWAD in a no-win position.

(Robertson 1991: 143)

However, it is important to point out that the power structures involved are not merely micro-level structures. They go beyond the specifics of particular wards or residential homes and are built into the macro-institutional structures such as professions, state welfare and financial structures and the cultural attributes embedded in intergenerational relationships. The personal politics of these identity issues are hardly on the agenda. They are articulated only at the micro-level. Nevertheless, they are political. The balance of power between people in families and in institutions relates closely to the ability to live meaningful lives. Active attempts to change lifestyles are manifest in the politics of social movements: these will be the subject of Chapter 4.

4

Lifestyles, politics and social movements

What control over their lifestyles can older people exert? Can they choose a lifestyle for themselves? What prevents them making such choices? Lifestyle politics is about the power of people to shape not only their work and leisure but also their sexuality and the style and manner of their death. The typical manifestation of lifestyle politics is the social movement. It has been suggested that the idea of lifestyle politics can be understood as a more general case of gender politics. In parallel to the feminist challenge to reassess ideas, practices and relationships based on gender so the implications on age and ageism can be re-examined on a personal level. Lifestyle politics is linked with a high-modern or postmodern condition and stresses the social fluidity and choice of lifestyles available to people at the end of the twentieth century (or at least available to some affluent people in the west). The idea of reflexivity summarizes the observation that people nowadays have much greater information and knowledge about different lifestyles and how to create them and thus have greater possibilities of exercising choice in modifying their own lives.

Weber ([1919] 1978) emphasized the importance of rationality and knowledge to the development of the modern world. Legal rational bureaucracies characterize modern society, not only in civil services, but also in armies, charitable institutions, universities and hospitals. The tools of mathematics and the sciences are applied to economic and political life. Examples can be seen in the social changes in business management where the executive's individual discretion is modified by systematic rational calculation through product testing and polling applied to forecasting sales, aptitude testing applied to personnel selection, or specially designed sampling of accounts to detect fraud. Highly educated experts and technicians understand and control small parts of these systems. Expertise has become highly specialized and fragmented. The success of this modern way of life in bringing a plethora of consumer and other benefits is no longer considered an unequivocal benefit. Different sections of society question the extent to which their life is controlled by such specialist technical and bureaucratic power. They seek to end their sense of anomie by finding what they see as a deeper and more meaningful personal life.

> Produced by the emancipatory impact of modern institutions, the life-political agenda exposes the limits of decision-making governed purely by internal criteria. For life politics brings back to prominence precisely those moral and existential questions repressed by the core institutions of modernity.
>
> (Giddens 1991: 223)

People may acknowledge the expertise of economists and managers and see the efficiency of open markets for rational profit maximizing behaviour. They may also ask 'why make a profit?' and query the materialism embedded in the modern technical control of the economy. They may seek answers outside of the experts' self-limiting frame of reference, in non-materialistic lifestyles, alternatives which give priority to 'living gently on the earth' or other values. Some people may, for example, seek to adopt lifestyles which do not involve work. Thus the adoption of lifestyles as diverse as those of New Age Travellers or those retiring to the Mediterranean (Williams *et al.* 1997; Warnes and Pearson 1998), can be seen as life-politics. Medical expertise is similarly linked to lifestyle politics. People may appreciate the science-based power of modern medicine to extend life, but ask the more fundamental questions about the meaning of life and ask 'Why is it better to live longer?' Key issues of personal morality, life and death, abortion and euthanasia are raised by questioning, not the efficacy of medicine, but its moral framework. We know the effects of smoking on health, yet some people still choose to smoke. How should this affect the moral standing of those people and their right to claim a share of health resources? These specific examples have a more general application, all lifestyle choices can be seen as political.

Postmodernism is seen by many intellectuals as a response to the failure of utopian visions derived from the belief that reason and/or science are progressive and can provide a better future. However, in rejecting grand schemes and utopian visions, these theorists throw out any referential framework for debating moral issues.

> Here we see the limitations of accounts of 'postmodernity' developed under the aegis of poststructuralism. According to such view, moral questions become completely denuded of meaning or relevance in current social circumstances. But while this perspective accurately reflects aspects of the internally referential systems of modernity, it cannot explain why moral issues return to the centre of the agenda of life politics.
>
> (Giddens 1991: 223–4)

From a postmodern perspective there are no firm reference points. There is no moral position better or worse than any other. So confronted with choices over life and death which science has given us, or choices over agricultural production between organic food or genetically modified crops, decisions have to be made and different people make different choices (or have them made for them). Postmodernism does not offer a method for dealing with these dilemmas, it merely celebrates the diversity of lifestyles which result.

Social movements are a typical way in which such lifestyle politics are manifest. Giddens suggests that in exploring the idea that the 'personal is political' both the student movement, but more particularly the women's movement in the 1960s, pioneered this kind of politics. These social movements were not simply or unambiguously about lifestyle politics. Members of the student movement, for example, tried to use personal gestures and 'lifestyle revolts' as a mode of throwing down a challenge to the 'establishment' or the 'system'. They wanted to show not only that daily life expresses aspects of state power, but also that by overturning ordinary daily patterns they could actually threaten the power of the state. Flower power is associated in many contemporary minds with a 1960s style visible in clothes, fashion and a particular style of interpersonal relations. However, it also involved putting flowers down the barrels of the rifles of soldiers or state troopers confronting the protesting students. The slogan 'make love not war' was only partially about sexual liberation and specifically about challenging the power of the US military industrial complex over the war in Vietnam. The experiences of this flower power generation as students in the 1960s has moulded their political opinions as a cohort ever since. Despite the ignominious end to the Vietnam War (from the American point of view), and education reforms in various places, student-led actions failed to significantly dent the power of capital and the established elites of the western nations. Flower power thus came to be more associated with escapism and alternative lifestyles which concentrated on 'inner space'. A social movement is not just a political campaign (like that to legalize cannabis) or a social organization (such as the Woodstock festival), although each of these may be a manifestation of such a movement. The key feature of a social movement is the spread of a set of values and attitudes which guide and pattern choice of lifestyle (cf. Barnes 1995).

In the following two sections I elaborate two of these life-politics issues in turn. The first of these issues relates to attitudes and beliefs about the relationships between men and women. Ageism and sexism coincide to make choices about sexuality in old age particularly problematic. Second, attitudes and beliefs about death are changing and lead to issues about euthanasia and the right to choose to die.

Social movement 1: gender and lifestyle politics – challenging double jeopardy

The first social movement we look at in detail is the women's movement. The majority of older people are women. Gender and old age affect one another in significant ways. Demographically, economically and culturally, old age is experienced differently by men and women. A necessary background to this discussion is a short introduction to the inequalities experienced by older women. The work of Arber and Ginn (1991, 1995) is particularly useful in this respect.

Gender inequality and age

There is the well known gender difference in life expectancy. Current British life expectancy at birth is approximately 74 years for men and 80 years for women. The life expectancy difference is somewhat less at age 60, when men can anticipate a further 18 years to age 78 while women can typically expect to have a further 22 years to age 82. This difference in life expectancy means that old age is most typically a female stage of life and is becoming increasingly feminine. In England and Wales 15.9 per cent of the population is over 65 with a sex ratio of 1.5 women to each man. For older age groups 7.1 per cent of the population is over 75 years with a sex ratio of 1.9 to 1 in favour of women, while for the over 85-year-olds who make up 1.8 per cent of the population there are 3 women for every man. Widowhood has become normal and feminized. Women will experience an average of 9 years' widowhood. Male widowers are much more likely to remarry.

Exit from employment is typically at age 61 for men and 57 for women (if they are in the labour market). This means that men typically have 17 years and women 25 years of life after leaving paid employment. Women are more likely to work part time. They tend not to have the benefit of occupational pensions to the same extent as men. With short or disrupted employment records, the resulting small occupational pensions tend only to bring women up to the income support level. As a result they do not really gain any benefit from paying the contributions. Only 24 per cent of all women aged 40–59 belong to an occupational pension scheme. When it comes to help with disability, older men are (pro rata) more likely to receive domicilliary support, while there is a higher proportion of women than men in residential care (about twice as many). In the 85 and over age group, 15 per cent of men and 27 per cent of women are in residential care (Arber and Gilbert 1989; Arber and Ginn 1991, 1995; Ginn and Arber 1996).

The women's movement provided a challenge to standard and conventional lifestyles. New values and attitudes became more widely held and were increasingly used as guides for behaviour. In particular there were challenges to household arrangements and subsequently to interpersonal and sexual relationships. A variety of new lifestyles were developed under the very broad banner of feminism. The women's movement in the first half of the twentieth century was concerned with legal, political and citizenship rights. The struggle for women to be equal citizens before the law, with rights to vote and own property were the extension of the values of liberal democracy to the second sex. After the Second World War the emphasis of the women's movement was equality at work and at home. Betty Friedan is an important figure who can be used to illustrate the lifestyle priorities of the women's movement of the time. Her book *The Feminine Mystique* (Friedan 1963) was highly influential in the second wave of feminism. She questioned the values and aspirations of the American suburban housewife which were dominant in the 1950s and 1960s. She and writers like her provoked an enormous response by pointing out how domesticity and male dominated images of femininity stifled women into meaningless and boring existence and shackled those who wished to engage in the world of work and career.

Friedan's deep disquiet about personal identity, she made clear, came about only because there were now more options available for women. It is only in the light of these alternatives that women have come to see that modern culture does not 'gratify their basic need to grow and fulfil their potentialities as human beings' (Friedan 1963: 68). Friedan's advocacy of both a work career and a family as a meaningful lifestyle option for women was a defining moment in lifestyle politics for women. These issues of personal politics expanded into the context of the family. Taken for granted assumptions about who makes what decisions in families were queried and women challenged patriarchal practices over family decision making. Equality in the right to work meant demands at home for equal sharing of domestic and child rearing duties.

What is the significance of this social movement for older women? De Beauvoir (1972) identified 'double jeopardy' as the combination of ageist and sexist stereotypes. Friedan moved on to consider the double jeopardy experienced by older women: how ageism combines with sexism to imprison older women within stereotypes which restrict and devalue them. Friedan's *The Fountain of Age* (1993) challenges ageism in general and within the women's movement in particular.

> When my friends threw a surprise party on my sixtieth birthday, I could have killed them all. Their toast seemed hostile, insisting as they did that I publicly acknowledge reaching sixty, pushing me out of life, as it seemed, out of the race. Professionally, politically, personally, sexually. Distancing me from their fifty-, forty-, thirty-year-old selves.
>
> (Friedan 1993: xiii)

There is a lifestyle politics of 'double jeopardy'; it is possible to query the implicit assumptions about age and gender which structure domestic arrangements. Jerrome (1993) suggests that:

> We know very little about the sexual politics of late-life marriages. Examining power relationships is a new feature which bring the study of elderly couples into line with feminist work on marriage in general. For many older women, a power imbalance has always existed in marriage. Power plays take different forms, often focusing on an apparently trivial but symbolic item or event. I recently encountered a woman whose husband demanded sole access to the television remote control unit, becoming angry if she attempted to use it. Their 2-year-old grandson handled it with impunity.
>
> (Jerrome 1993: 94)

The nature of double jeopardy is also revealed in research on widows. For example, Davidson (1998) discusses domestic and caring relationships through the language of the older widows she interviewed. The gendered nature of selfishness as articulated by these widows reflected the internalized expectations of normal gender relationships, and seemed to express both a desire to, but also some difficulty in, distancing themselves from normative lifestyles. Davidson suggests that selfishness to the widows meant doing what they wanted, when they wanted and not having to consider the needs of a partner. Several said the primary reason for not wishing to form a new partnership, particularly marriage, was because they had become so selfish.

> *Cynthia*: (I don't want to) Take the responsibility of washing for some-body and ironing for somebody. And I can do what I want to do. It is selfish, absolute selfishness.
> *Interviewer*: Is there anything wrong with being selfish?
> *Cynthia*: Well, I feel a bit guilty sometimes. You know, that I can do what I want to do and go out when I want to go out. I do feel a bit guilty.

They had been prepared, and for most of them, happy, to look after the man they had married when they were young and lived with for a number of decades, but they were not prepared to 'take on' another man. Beryl had had a 'gentleman friend' for ten years before increasing frailty precipitated a move into the home of one of his daughters. When asked if she had considered marrying him during their time together, Beryl said she had anticipated that he might have to be looked after at some stage and so she decided against it.

> . . . It is particularly interesting that when considering 'taking on' another man, the widows reflected the prevailing social norm of marrying a man older than they were.
>
> (Davidson 1998: 6–7)

Those who have looked at kinship and caring have demonstrated how families negotiate the obligations of care and support across the generations. There tends to be a consistent pattern of preferred carer, which is structured around intimacy, co-residence and gender. Much of this research has been done in the context of care for frail elderly people and Care in the Community initiatives (Wenger 1984; Qureshi and Simons 1987; Qureshi and Walker 1989; Qureshi 1996). Double jeopardy and lifestyle politics cannot be separated from issues of community care and power structures behind the policies and institutional arrangements for care of frail older people (Ungerson 1987).

Gender and sexuality in old age

Insofar as women's oppression was seen to be located in the family, domestic and reproductive arrangements, issues of sexuality became centrally significant to the women's movement. Women form the large majority of older people yet new lifestyles, including new approaches to sexuality, remain highly problem-atic for older women. The move from what is sometimes called the second to the third wave of feminism saw a shift in emphasis from politics which demanded equal civil and legal rights, along the lines of emancipatory move-ments from oppressed racial and ethnic minorities, to a personal liberation and a redefinition of interpersonal relationships in a non-gender-specific way. The logic of this shift came from the analysis that women's oppression lay at root in sexuality and procreation. This suggested that male control of female bodies was necessary to control procreation. The institution of the family and the associated morality of motherhood and conventional definitions of feminine sexuality, it was argued, performed the function of keeping women in their place as second class citizens. These views resonated in particular with young educated women struggling precisely with the vision offered by the second wave feminists of the possibilities of a career and raising a family.

This highly simplified account of the changing emphasis of the women's movement through the 1960s to the 1980s is recounted to draw attention to the significance of the change in the women's movement for older women. Feminists who emphasized the importance of new forms of sexuality and suggested that the route to female liberation lay in controlling and redefining their sexuality and abandoning or renegotiating the family, tended to be of a younger generation. Society and young people, however, tend to define old people as sexless. The double jeopardy is particularly fierce when it comes to sexuality. What meaning could the message of third wave feminism provide for older women who were excluded by society and themselves from a sexual identity?

> Research now indicated that people might have an active sex life into their seventies and eighties, and even into their nineties. Maggie Kuhn, feisty founder of the Gray Panthers (that powerful lobbying organization originally called the Consultation of Older and Younger Adults for Social Change), interrupted the polite jargon about women's problems at a Washington conference to ask with whom women were going to have sex until eighty or ninety, with so many men their age dead: ten widows for every widower, and that widower marrying a younger woman. Everyone laughed uneasily when Kuhn said that we shouldn't kid ourselves, that if we were going to have sex, it would have to be with younger men, someone else's husband, other women, or masturbation. No kidding, she said, and went on to describe how she had organized a commune and worked out a non-exclusive, part-time arrangement with a younger, married lover, rather than give up sex.
>
> (Friedan 1993: xxiv–xxv)

Such a radical approach is not the lived experience of the vast majority of older women.

> Sexuality in old age is a subject which is enveloped with secrecy and half-knowledge, and referred to in society in general with embarrassment and by joking allusions, that is if it is not dismissed altogether, the old so patently being 'past it'.
>
> (Pickard 1995: 268)

Ford and Sinclair (1987), in the course of their conversations with a sample of women aged over 60 in a local community, found the same inhibitions with regard to discussions of sexuality. They write:

> Long-established conventions that preclude the discussion of sexual matters remain quite strong amongst these old women, not only with regard to their own lives, but when commenting on other people and other activities.
>
> (Ford and Sinclair 1987: 269)

These older people have grown up with a different attitude to sex and the sexual mores of the early part of the century in which they grew up are carried with them into later life. Opinion surveys show a considerable age disparity in attitudes to family, sex and sexual orientation. Medical and other studies almost wholly rule out biological constraints on healthy older people being sexually active (Scott 1996). The principal constraints for older women are lifestyle choices. The combination of lack of partners, belief that sex should be confined to marriage and internalized ageist stereotypes are the major inhibitors. Male attitudes differ, but also reflect the gender stereotypes of their youth.

> Older men describe the women of their generation as rapacious and predatory for marriage partners, both in their youth and, interestingly, in old age, although the latter was contradicted by every old woman I spoke to as well as by my own observations of their interaction – or more usually lack of it – at day-centres.
>
> (Ford and Sinclair 1987: 270)

Ford and Sinclair (1987) suggest that the significance of this gendered difference in attitude to sex lies more in the fact that old men continue to see themselves as sexual beings. They quote one informant who expressed the opinion that if a man has no longer any thought of sex, then he is approaching death. These researchers concluded that for the old people they interviewed, to be a man is, by definition, to be a sexual being, whereas for the women, it is easier to define herself as a mother, or grandmother, or friend or neighbour. Some older women have taken an active role in challenging the double jeopardy which condemns them to a sexless existence and sought other lifestyle choices. The Hen Coop has been an example of heroic resistance or at least good fun (Bernard and Meade 1993; Hen Coop 1997). They are an exception which proves the general rule: they can represent the possibility of alternative lifestyles for older women which are in practice highly constrained.

Older women, pornography, body image and male fantasies

The women's movement has identified the realms of pornography and prostitution as key locations which reveal the nature of the link between sex and gender domination. It is suggested that public moralities about commercialized sex reflect gendered power and control. It might be naively thought that, following the double jeopardy argument, there would be no pornography that features older women. However, although there does not appear to be a great deal compared to the vast array of soft and hard core images of young women, and indeed of young men orientated to the homophile market, there are distinct genres of pornographic images of older women. An Internet search for information on 'older women' brings up a long list of pornographic sites of various kinds. The titles that are listed include such terms as 'in praise of older women', 'sexy seniors' or 'veteran vixens'. The women depicted in pornographic images appear to be in their 40s and 50s and very few appear to be over 60; these few are women whose handsome aristocratic appearance gives them a kind of token youth. The image is of a 'well preserved' woman or an 'as good as if they were young' appearance. The market niche at which this pornography is directed is similar to the so-called 'amateur' market. These images and stories are meant to depict the girl next door, or 'ordinary' women, on the basis that the men using pornography know, even in their fantasies, that they would have no sexual access to the stereotypical beautiful young models who are the standard fare of much soft core pornography. Thus pictures of 'readers' wives' or badly reproduced images of unglamorous 'amateur' women provide a route to a sexual fantasy less challenged by the brute facts of the viewer's inadequacies, financial or physical. Thus a number of outlets feature pictures and stories of 'aunty' or the older woman next door.

There appear to be two kinds of pornography depicting older women. The first of these, most frequently in the soft core porn field (i.e. pictures of naked women as opposed to depiction of sex acts) are presentations of glamorous sexy older women who will introduce an implied younger man into the joys of sex. This is the classic depiction of the role of the older woman courtesan (cf. Colette [1920, 1926] 1954) in initiating a young man into sexual activity, overcoming his fears and teaching the required techniques. In contrast to the soft porn, the second kind of presentation is distinctly misogynous and indeed mirrors the double jeopardy in also being ageist. This kind of pornography depicts older women as desperate sluts, who desire sex constantly but because they are old, and thus unattractive, need to make themselves available and engage in sexual practices which appeal to the audiences' fantasies. Because the combination of myths about women, and the taken for granted assumptions about age, make these fantasies apparently more accessible, they are functional in meeting the desires of the man/person using the pornography.

In parallel to the double jeopardy in pornography, there are reports that an age-segregated prostitution market exists. Barrett (1997) identified in his study, located in an anonymous European city, an age-structured sex market. He described a main area of the city he studied, where punters will pay a premium to have sex with younger women. However, in another area peripheral to the main location studied, the women were considerably older and in the age range of 50–55 years. His research experience suggested this to be an unusual age group. The neighbourhood was very run down and was in the process of major infrastructure and housing refurbishment. There were some similarities and differences between the activities of the younger (16–20-year-old) women being studied and older (50–55-year-old) female prostitutes working in the adjacent neighbourhood. Generally the older women would work between 11 a.m. and 8 p.m. and the younger women would work between 7 p.m. and midnight. Both groups of prostitutes had regular punters while the older women were less likely to have pimps.

> The younger women were in an area with a steady stream of car drivers looking for prostitutes. When a deal was agreed the woman would enter the car, be driven off, and would be returned by the car driver a little while after to resume. In contrast the older women tended to stand in doorways or sit on doorsteps; rarely did they walk about or sit on cars.
>
> (Barrett 1997: 7)

This section of the life-politics of gender and old age has demonstrated how the power structures of our society are worked out in the bodies and feelings of older people (Pointon 1997). The social movement which through the twentieth century has sought to redefine women's position in society and re-evaluate gender relationships has changed the nature of the double jeopardy. Examples of where older women are pushed to the margins, in situations as diverse as the feminist movement and urban prostitution, illustrate ways in which gender and age interconnect. There is clearly an age dimension to sexual politics.

To conclude the discussion of the social control of sexuality it is worth referring to Chapter 3 on identity politics and infantilization. The exclusion of both infants and the dependent elderly from full adulthood also denies them a sexual identity.

> Adults are deemed to be sexually attractive/active; children and 'the elderly' are not and . . . adults may work hard at denying or controlling any sign of sexuality in later life.
>
> (Hockey and James 1993: 37)

Similar modes of thought also constrain sexuality amongst disabled people. Combinations of old age and disability tend to make sex unthinkable. Dependent old people as well as children are vulnerable to abusive relationships including sexual ones. All gross power differentials, together with values and ideologies that dehumanize or treat people like objects, open the door to violation.

Social movement 2: the right to die

Euthanasia and control over the time and nature of one's death is the ultimate expression of personal politics. The power to control the manner of our death seems a key test of political emancipation and a clear example of lifestyle politics involving the intersection of personal choice, public morality and state regulation. Further, euthanasia as an issue, indeed a social movement, is becoming increasingly urgent as a combination of demography and medical practice create more and more situations in which the prolongation of life is possible but may not seem desirable. Who has the controlling power to dispose of life? To what extent do, and to what extent should, people have the ability to determine the circumstances of their own death? Many people are frightened of death but fear of dying is more widespread. The debate about euthanasia is, of course, far from exclusively about old people. But, as most people who are terminally ill are old, the two issues do become entwined. Should people have the right to choose to die? Should others help them to achieve their aims (assisted suicide)? Other closely related issues are involved in decisions to stop treatment or continue efforts to sustain life. Should people have the right to refuse life saving treatment? Should others be able to refuse treatment on behalf of those unable to make such a decision for themselves?

These kinds of issues are characteristic of the late twentieth century where control of biological functions and advances in medical technology break down previously taken for granted boundaries between life and death. Thus the politics about who controls and defines life and death becomes more uncertain and problematic. Those claiming authority on religious and moral values have to constantly revise/update their positions in response to new possibilities and dilemmas. The reaction to such moral dilemmas range from fundamentalism to complete *laissez-faire*/anarchy; various social movements espouse positions from the absolute statement that it is a sacred duty that all life must be preserved at all costs, to a view that all moral values are relative so that everyone should be free to do exactly what they want with their life.

The right to die, along with other values identified as human or civil rights, reflect the strong individualism of western societies. The 'Protestant ethic' tradition, which is strong in the USA and in northern European cultures, stresses self-reliance, individual responsibility and work as a vocation. Not all societies place such emphasis on the individual but rather see people as part of collectivities from whom they should not distinguish themselves nor should they place individual desires before those of the collectivity – be that the family, the clan or the nation.

Suicide amongst older people

In practice there are significant numbers of older people who make the ultimate lifestyle choice to end their own lives. Moody (1992, 1994) reports that for the USA suicide is amongst the top ten causes of death among the old. The suicide rate for the general population is 12 per 100,000 while the suicide rate for those over 65 is 17 per 100,000. In a survey of doctors in Oregon, USA, when that state was contemplating legislation on euthanasia, it was reported that some 21 per cent of physicians had received requests for assisted suicide, and 7 per cent complied (Lee *et al.* 1996). In Taiwan, elderly people have an unusually high ratio rate of suicide compared to other age groups. In 1996, the suicide rate among those aged 65 and over in Taiwan was around six times the rate for those in the 15–24 age bracket. Comparative figures for suicide are difficult to take at their face value, given the problems of the variation in the methods by which they are identified and processed into statistical data. Nevertheless, figures suggest that despite very different suicide rates in different countries, it appears that suicide is most frequent amongst elderly people (see Table 4.1).

Moody (1994) suggests that:

> For all age groups, men are much more likely to commit suicide than women and the difference between the sexes widens with advancing age. For example, according to 1980 data there were 66 completed suicides per 100, 000 white males above the age of 85 in comparison to a rate of only 5 for white females. In fact the highest rate of suicide in the United States occurs among older white men.
>
> (Moody 1994: 31)

Hu Yu-hui (Chang Chiung-fang 1998) found that in those Asian societies which emphasize 'three generations living under the same roof' and expect the family to be welfare-provider to the aged, elderly women are at higher risk of committing suicide than their counterparts in western countries. She suggests, because of the varying levels of accuracy between different country's suicide statistics, it is more reliable to compare suicide rates among different countries by looking at the relative rates for different groups. In Taiwan, the

Table 4.1   Suicide rates per 100,000 for selected countries *c.* 1988

Country	Men 15–24	Men 75 years and over	Women 15–24	Women 75 years and over
UK	12	24	3	8
Italy	5	49	2	12
France	15	113	4	29

Source: Kinsella and Taeuber (1993: 36)

rate of suicide among elderly women is 3.2 times higher than the rate for women in general, while the corresponding ratio is 4.2 in Singapore and 2.4 in Japan. In contrast, the ratio is only 1.2 in the USA and 1.5 in the UK, Sweden and Australia. These lower ratios she links to countries with a developed system of welfare provision for elderly people.

Elderly people have the highest rate of suicide among all age groups in Taiwan. Researchers note that the high rate of suicide among old people has to be viewed in connection with the problems of poverty, illness and low self-esteem. According to a government survey in 1989, 57 per cent of old people in Taiwan live in poverty. The lower down the social ladder old people are, the greater their economic dependence on their offspring. In the case of women who are old and illiterate, 78.6 per cent of living expenses are provided by their offspring. It is suggested that the lower status of the old in today's families can be inferred from the part of the home they are given to occupy. Traditionally, an old member of the family would have one of the principal rooms in the house. Today, however, old people are more likely to be crammed into the most out-of-the-way corner in the apartment. Chinese traditional values strongly emphasize the virtue in taking care of one's family elders, and in practice there is more reliance on relatives (Chang Chiung-fang 1998). Similar attitudes are reflected by the discussants in the Asian focus groups studied by John Knodel and his co-researchers (Asis *et al.* 1995). Privacy and independence are more strongly emphasized in the west, where old people are more likely to want to live alone and thereby seek to preserve their own sense of dignity.

Decisions about suicide by older people and older couples can be very calculated choices. Such decisions are sometimes made at home, in collaboration with close family (particularly spouses) and can be made not only in cases of extreme pain or physical degradation but also in anticipation of those circumstances. A local paper in the USA reported on a series of suicides by older people, stating that in one case where the husband's health was deteriorating he had first entered a nearby nursing home. Then a couple of weeks later, the wife obtained a day pass to bring him home. They died together in their car from carbon monoxide poisoning. The paper quotes the police reporting the deaths of the 81-year-old husband and 80-year-old wife:

'It was a touching thing,' Rye Brook Lt. Joseph Ciccone said. 'You've got two people in love, and one can't live without the other.' . . . 'They loved each other,' 'They did everything together. They just needed to be with each other. It's a powerful statement. They had been married their entire adult lives. They'd been together for a long time.'

(Lipka 1998)

The premeditated and carefully executed exercise of choice in these circumstances shows the autonomous (or isolated) nature of people in contemporary society, insofar as they were able to ignore the potential constraints of kin, community and law, and realize through their joint suicide the ultimate value they placed on their relationship. Suicides by senior citizens tend to be less impulsive and more likely to have preparations made to resolve financial and other issues which would result from the death. Such suicides may include the meticulous accounting for what will happen to their possessions. The same paper reports an elderly couple calling the police prior to shooting themselves and then leaving insurance policies and financial information nearby for the police to give to their daughter. In practice it seems that numbers of older people are exercising lifestyle choices over life and death.

Euthanasia and the right to die

Extreme cases are often used to illustrate the moral choices involved in life and death decisions. There are those people in a 'persistent vegetative state' – effectively brain dead who none the less have bodies that remain alive as long as they are fed and nursed, which raise issues of authority and moral responsibility for others. These issues are significant when in old age dementia robs people of decision making faculties. There are those in the final days and weeks of terminal cancer where pain makes people's quality of life unbearable but where nevertheless they retain their full rational capacity for autonomous decision making. The case for euthanasia is usually presented by starting with examples of people whose quality of life is appalling – great pain for example – but whose medical prognosis is death within a very limited time. One procedure through which such choice might be given effect is through the 'living will'. The living will or advance directives can be made by people as to their wishes if they become too incapacitated and unable to make decisions about their own treatment and can specify the circumstances under which they wish to be helped to die. This is conceived as giving choice to the active moral agent and apparently avoids the life and death decision being placed in the hands of others. The US state of Oregon has pioneered euthanasia legislation, but even here it is reported that fewer than 15 per cent of the dying have prepared such written instructions and these wills are not always acted upon. Giving effect to living wills requires appropriate institutionalization in the practices of caring institutions.

> One Portland nursing home came up with a clever solution for alerting paramedics to a patient's wishes: Patients who did not want resuscitation had flowers painted on their front-door nameplates. That worked well for paramedics, notes Jerry Andrews of Multnomah County Emergency Medical Services, until another nursing home started painting flowers on the doors of residents who did want to be resuscitated.

(Shapiro 1997)

The range of circumstances in which self-control is lost, situations whereby people can no longer achieve the capacity to take action about their quality of life, include not only physical, but also mental disease. Suicidal thoughts are in many circumstances treated as symptoms of mental illness. Most people would wish to prevent those with mental illness, such as an organic-based depression, from being driven by that illness into taking their own lives; such circumstances which might lead to suicide are not seen as suitable examples for euthanasia. However, given the possibility of use of mood changing drugs and the contested nature of mental illness the concept of the rational, freely choosing, individual is undermined. The moral position of individualism – moral choices being merely or solely a matter of individual decision – is highly problematic when the socially constructed nature of individuality is brought into the equation. A key question concerns the circumstances in which choice is exercised. Choices are always made in a context of power relations. The idea of completely free choice is an intellectual construct similar to absolute vacuum or absolute zero for temperature. In other words, it is a useful theoretical concept but not practically achievable: it can be approached only in highly unusual and carefully constructed experimental situations. The politics of euthanasia are probably best illustrated by taking case examples and looking at the contested nature of legal and medical practice.

The staff and inmates of hospitals, nursing homes, hospices and old people's homes are confronted with issues of power and autonomy for older people. Should older people, close to death, have the right to decide how to die? Who, if anyone, should make the ultimate lifestyle choice, the choice to end life? Moody (1994) presents us with an archetypal case:

> Theresa Legeurrier, a resident in the Good Samaritan Nursing Home in upstate New York . . . was in her eighties but not suffering from any serious medical problems . . . began to refuse food and water, expressing a wish to die of starvation. Staff in the nursing home were divided in their opinions about what to do. The nursing home administration claimed that by refusing food a resident might make the home vulnerable to legal penalty for assisting suicide. Against this view, a physician and a social worker involved in the case maintained that Theresa Legeurrier was rational and competent to make her own decision in the matter. The nursing home petitioned a court to institute artificial feeding but the court eventually agreed with the patient's right to refuse treatment in this case.
>
> (Moody 1994: 102)

In the UK euthanasia has been subject to pressure group activity. The Euthanasia Society campaigns for changes in the law and has been supported by particular interest groups – for example some of those associated with AIDS. The society tends to have been opposed by religious-based 'right to life' groups, again supported by particular groups such as some members of the hospice movement, who would prefer to see greater priority given to palliative care for those dying in difficult circumstances.

A survey on attitudes to euthanasia was conducted in the UK undertaken by one of the leading market research organizations, NOP. The research was undertaken during 14–16 November 1997 among a representative sample of 961 adults aged 15 years and over in Britain. Among its findings NOP states that:

> More than four in five (84 per cent) of all Britons interviewed in an NOP survey published today support euthanasia – the practice of deliberately allowing a person who is terminally ill a painless death – both in principle (84 per cent) and in practice (83 per cent).
>
> (NOP Research Group 1997)

The survey also reveals that there is most support for euthanasia amongst the younger age groups. Almost nine out of ten respondents aged 15–34 are in favour of euthanasia for themselves compared with three out of four of the over-55s. Similarly, a significant majority of those younger respondents (85 per cent) believe that euthanasia should be legalized in the UK compared with only two-thirds (63 per cent) of the over-55s. There seems to be decisive public support for the right to make a choice about one's death. Key findings from the research include that amongst those who support euthanasia:

- Almost four out of five feel that they would be able to make the decision on euthanasia on behalf of a terminally ill relative.
- More than eight out of ten men (83 per cent) feel that they would be able to make the decision on euthanasia for a terminally ill relative, compared with three-quarters (74 per cent) of women.

The NOP researchers comment:

> In the wake of a number of recent high profile cases in the media, it would appear that there is overwhelming public support in Britain – particularly amongst younger people – for not only the principle but also the practice of euthanasia. It is clear that many people would like to see a change in the existing law which does not currently permit euthanasia.
>
> (NOP Research Group 1997)

Euthanasia has been contested in the legislative realm in a number of places, some of which have introduced more permissive/liberal laws. These places include northern Australia, the Netherlands and the US state of Oregon. In each case the key move has been to establish a legal framework within which the medical profession can make end of life decisions. The Oregon Death with Dignity Act was passed in November 1994. After extensive consultation and a referendum, the Act enabled physicians to prescribe a lethal dose of medicine to terminally ill but mentally competent patients who had made multiple requests to die. Doctors in Oregon faced the dilemmas of legalized physician assisted suicide. This was studied by Lee *et al.* (1996) who looked at the attitudes and practices of Oregon physicians in relation to assisted suicide. They conducted a cross-sectional mailed survey of all doctors who might be eligible to prescribe a lethal dose of medication if the Oregon law (which was being challenged in the courts) was upheld. A clear majority, some 60 per cent of the respondents, thought that physician assisted suicide should be legal in some cases and nearly half (46 per cent) might be willing to prescribe a lethal dose of medication if it were legal to do so. However, a significant minority, 31 per cent of the respondents, would be unwilling to do so on moral grounds. Medical practitioners are trained to preserve life, so despite the importance in control over life and death the law grants to doctors, they do not necessarily have the skills or knowledge to be effective in this field. Half the respondents were not sure what to prescribe for the purpose of assisted suicide. The doctors also expressed concern about medical complications that might surround suicide attempts and were presumably concerned about the incompetent or ineffective assisted suicide. The lay public's confidence in doctors and scientific medicine is not necessarily held by doctors themselves and this sample had doubts about their ability to predict survival at six months accurately and thus the appropriateness of their decisions to assist in a suicide (Lee *et al.* 1996).

Shapiro (1997) usefully illustrates the issues and dilemmas of euthanasia legislation from the Oregon case by quoting the example of changed thinking by a local radiation oncologist, Dr Nancy Boutin. Like most physicians who deal with terminal cases, Dr Boutin had seen at first hand the long, often painful, dying process that is an unintended consequence of modern medicine's ability to keep patients alive. Her initial support for the right-to-die law sprang from the suicide of one of her patients. The man, who seemed to be clear minded and not depressed despite a brutal, two year struggle with cancer, gathered his family around his bedside for an emotional ceremony of loving goodbyes and then took a fatal overdose. When his wife called police to take the body, officers cordoned off the house with yellow crime-scene tape and took the grieving family members off to the police station. The death was investigated as a potential homicide. Though no charges were brought the cancer specialist referred to felt that legislation would protect such families.

However, after the legislation was passed, Dr Boutin began to have second thoughts. The most dramatic challenge to her views came when she cared for an elderly woman dying of ovarian cancer where the medical administration resisted meeting the bill for expensive prescriptions for anti-nausea drugs. Given the choice, the dying woman would have quickly sought suicide because her symptoms were so bad. A health care system intent upon cutting costs could give subtle, even unintended, encouragement to a patient to die. Doctors in the Oregon survey also had doubts stemming from the high cost of medical treatment in the USA and 83 per cent cited financial pressure as a possible reason for requests for assisted suicide (Lee *et al.* 1996). There is a perceived danger that older people see the expensive medical care as a drain on family expenses and, because they wish to pass something on to their children or grandchildren, will feel a duty to die rather than see their last savings go on drugs and medical care. Burnt out carers or flawed relationships may produce subtle or not so subtle pressures for older people to opt out of life. Pictures may be conjured of mercenary relatives undermining an older person's will to live in order to collect an inheritance. Alternatively, one partner in a deeply committed and loving relationship may, through trying to do their best for a terminally ill spouse, become exhausted and, in response, the sick partner might then choose to show commitment to the carer by committing suicide. In these circumstances a better option might well be improved carer support.

The hospice movement is particularly concerned about the demand for euthanasia. Even if we set aside the religious arguments and the links between many hospices and religious beliefs and institutions, the movement has valid concerns about the proper management of pain for dying people. Hospice care, which started as a movement to create refuges where people could die in dignity, now also tries to help terminally ill people live out their final days alert and pain free in their own homes. In the USA, the national average proportion of people dying in hospital is close to 60 per cent. Even before the assisted suicide law, Oregon had topped all states in the per centage of people who die in their own homes. Only a reported 31 per cent of Oregonians die in hospitals, 7 per cent less than in 1994 (Shapiro 1997).

Conclusion

Social movements are becoming more powerful and prevalent (cf. Touraine 1985) and reflect the lifestyle politics which profoundly shape old people's lives and their opportunities for a fulfilling old age. The examples discussed above also reflect a difference in political organization between the UK and USA. There is a greater tendency for the formal organization of lobby groups in the USA, while politics in the UK has been more ideological. For example, anti-gun control and anti-abortion lobbies have considerably more power in the USA; however, single issue politics are becoming more important in the UK. These issues will be dealt with at length in Chapter 7.

Although there is a legal and legislative framework in which the politics of gender and the right to die currently take place, the pace is being set by people in their daily lifestyle decisions. Greater diversity of options on moral issues such as gender and the right to die is to be expected. Given the force of social trends we can expect these issues to become more and more acute. More medical control over biological survival, increasing ability and willingness of people to negotiate new forms of domestic, sexual and family relationships will see greater conflict rather than resolution and moral consensus.

5

Professions and institutional politics: the medicalization of old age

Health politics and professional power

This chapter is about the relationship between old age and ill-health and disability. The questions that will be addressed concern the relationship between the medical profession and the institutions of health care on the one hand and elderly people on the other. Who has the power to control what is considered to be a natural old age and what is considered to be normal ageing? Who decides what constitutes pathological ageing that should be subject to medical or other kinds of intervention? To what extent are the stereotypical associations between old age and ill-health cultural and/or ideological and thus involve questions about power.

The first set of questions is about the history of the medical and allied professions and their relationships in terms of knowledge, power and control with respect to other institutions – for example poor law institutions, families and the state. There are a subsequent set of questions which will require an examination of the political processes within the institutional structures of the modern health service. Currently, it is the health services to whom most elderly people, who are experiencing difficulties, turn to for assistance or remedies. Given a growing set of medical and scientifically based techniques for modifying people's health status and quality of life, who should get those benefits that are available? What are the political processes by which resource allocation decisions are made? Should the medical resources available for the older members of society be rationed to favour those who could be expected to live longer? Further, demographic change and the greater use by older people of health services have called into question the extent to which society can in the future afford the costs of medical care for ageing populations. This last question will be addressed in Chapter 8. The prime purpose of this chapter is to examine the ideological basis on which services for elderly people have come to be allocated.

Therefore the politics considered in this chapter is about struggles on both local levels and national levels between interests of

- older people (who in these circumstances might be differentiated between those who are potentially old, fit older people and those people with chronic illnesses or disabilities)
- professionals (who may be differentiated into medical professionals, those professions ancillary to medicine, social care professionals and the associations which represent the interests of these groups)
- entrepreneurs and capital (differences between economic sectors and size and form of firms are of importance, e.g. family run care homes, international for profit hospital providers, very large multinational drug producers, insurers to the medical profession, may have common or opposing interests)
- institutions of the state (and thus the various interests of state administrators, politicians, civil servants, state sector workers and the organizations through which they organize).

Thus the decision about how much of the nationally available health care resources are devoted to older people will impact on a variety of groups, not simply older people themselves. We are also likely to see a difference of interests between professionals expanding the definition of those elements of ageing which are pathological, and thus within their range of treatments, while managers of health services attempt to reduce costs by defining frail elderly people as untreatable or suitable for 'nursing only' and consequently as not the responsibility of their budgets. Politicians will have to balance imperatives for not raising taxes with satisfying demands for health care to stay in office. These people make claims and explain their actions with reference to knowledge, expertise and authority. Medical knowledge is particularly powerful in defining what is appropriately done for older people.

The medical model and professional power

The growth of professions in the modern world is based around control of knowledge. The twentieth century has seen the steady growth in power of those who claim medical knowledge as justification for their actions. The 'medical model' is a way of looking at illness and using science to control it. The medical model organizes knowledge around the view that medical practitioners have patients who they diagnose, treat and cure. The success of this process is thought to depend on scientific knowledge – knowledge that classifies all conditions and enables physicians to diagnose them and select appropriate interventions which will cure, or at least ameliorate, the patient's condition. This knowledge is about the body as an object on which scientific experts using experimentation and verification can determine cause and effect.

The medical-engineering model of health (Estes 1979; Estes *et al.* 1984; Hall 1990) is in reality concerned with illness. Health is not defined positively but seen as the absence of symptoms. The medical model, which dominates public policy, starts with the biological mechanism of the body and looks for causes of illness within the context of the body's cellular and biochemical systems. This approach sees medical care as the primary determinant of good health and thus investment in medical personnel and plant as the prerequisite for better health. An alternative, broader conception of health would in addition emphasize the importance of social, economic and political factors in determining the health of populations. The medical model tends to segment health problems and locate them in specific parts of a single organism. 'Whole person' approaches to health reject this over-concentration on biological subsystems, which are only to be addressed by mechanical or chemical interventions, in favour of promoting well-being of a person in all aspects of their humanity. What Estes and Minkler (1984: 18, citing Renaud 1975) would call an 'ecological' approach to health would stress that humans are both biological and social beings, and should be understood in relation to the entire political and social environment.

The ascendance of the mechanistic approach to improving health has a history which extends over at least three centuries (Powles 1973). The medical model legitimizes medical practitioner's specialist technical knowledge about the functioning of the body as an organism and the things that might go wrong with it. Further, because of this knowledge, only doctors are in an authoritative position to judge the efficacy of what should be done in face of a particular disease or trauma. Power to control individual patients and the priorities of medical policy follows. Robertson argues that in addition to a biomedicalization of health there is a 'gerontologization' of the experience of ageing. The emphasis on physical and psychological aspects of ageing and the accompanying search for scientific laws and theories tend to project old age as an observed phenomenon rather than a lived experience, turning old people into specimens for study. As a result elderly people are increasingly subjected to professional scrutiny, definition and management (Robertson 1991: 137). Armstrong (1983), following Foucault (1979) suggests that the social survey, and its ability to uncover large amounts of chronic illness in the community, legitimizes the extension of the 'clinical gaze' over the domestic and social life of older people.

Professional relationships

The power of this knowledge system has a series of consequences for medical practitioners' relationships with patients, with fellow practitioners, with political elites and with commercial elites. The specialist and esoteric nature of this medical knowledge means that the patient–doctor relationship has to be a professional one: the professional regulation of the relationship assuring the patient of the standard of knowledge, ethics and thus trust necessary for patients to surrender power over their bodies to the medical practitioner. Thus, for example, the definition of the relationship as a professional one, enables breach of codes of personal privacy and modesty and leads to privileged rights to confidentiality for practitioners. The relationships between members of the profession, because they are seen as the only ones competent to test and evaluate the knowledge required, have to be collegial. Professions have to be organized around institutions which validate those able to practise and who satisfy the ethical standards required. However, for these professional institutions to gain exclusive control they require the support of political elites and the state. The state provides a legal framework through which a profession can monopolize the right to practise. Not all aspiring professions gain the power to effectively control who enters their field and expel those not up to standard. In the real world, claims to knowledge and the right to control are contested and so the relationship between a profession or an aspiring profession to the state and its legislative and legal structures are crucial. The medical profession has, for example, successfully established control over surgery, by excluding barbers, childbirth, at the expense of midwives, and the treatment of madness, from the clergy.

Political elites when regulating professions have a variety of considerations; these might include not only contending professional groups but also public opinion, and perhaps economic and commercial interests. In the modern world, scientific research on which technical competence is based tends to be located in commercial organizations and to some extent in universities and similar state-supported research and educational institutions. The control of knowledge and, in particular, the speed and direction of change in knowledge involves a relationship between commercial elites and professions. The nature of this relationship can be illustrated by considering those members of the professions who do not work directly with patients or clients but are employed by a commercial organization. For example, when testing or evaluating a drug therapy, professional scientists may be forced in such a context to choose between their professional duty to the welfare of patients, the obligation to their employers and their own career prospects. Which therapies become researched and available depends not only on scientific knowledge but also on commercial opportunities. Individual patients who are sick have a specific relationship with their medical practitioner, and the public also has a general relationship with the medical profession. The general population face a variety of hazards and have interests in protection from both health risks and exploitation by powerful professional monopolies. People will be interested in the extent to which the state, commercial organizations, professions or others can limit the potential risks to their health. They may well, for example, seek regulation by the state in order to limit their risks, even though such regulation may be seen as a burden on professionals and to restrict the success of entrepreneurial activity.

Knowledge and power

There has been growth in the power of the medical profession over old age. How has that been achieved and how has this impacted on older people? The definition of ageing as largely a physical and biological process of decrement and decline has a history. The biomedical model of ageing has not always been dominant. The rise of the power of the medical profession is associated with the tendency to equate ageing with disease and is associated with the hegemonic idea of old age as a process of individual, biological and psychological decline. Professionalizing activities and struggles to control particular areas of expertise have taken place not only between the medical profession and other interest groups but also within medicine itself. Thus medical definitions of, and control over, old age, have been accompanied by a history of struggle by geriatrics to establish its knowledge, credibility and control over the treatment of older people.

History of gerontology as an emerging profession

Von Kondratowitz (1991) provides an interesting insight into the medicalization of old age by examining the changing concepts of old age and ageing in encyclopedias in the formative years of geriatrics in Germany (1782–1920). He periodicizes attitudes into the eighteenth century, an early nineteenth century period 1800–40 and a period from the middle of the nineteenth century to past the end of the century. He reports that the characteristic features of attitudes towards age in eighteenth-century encyclopedias include a wholly positive view of the age of 'manhood' (30 to 50 years), whilst old age is viewed more ambivalently. There was an acceptance of the mature person's influential position in juridical and political affairs which is contrasted with criticisms of the allegedly typical group behaviours of older people. Von Kondratowitz suggests that the portrayal of the old often verges on ridicule of old age. He identifies the coexistence of two distinct approaches. On the one hand a strict system of classification into individual stages of life is developed. Each of these stages is almost hermetically sealed from the others and is assigned its own unchanging characteristics which have little claim to realistic description since they are often deliberately based on the classical authors of antiquity. On the other hand, the legal and institutional possibilities and exemptions from specific duties available to the old are emphasized. He suggests that this strictly institutional understanding of the stages of life gains ground in this first period.

In the second period he argues that developmental lines of reasoning make a breakthrough and the effect of the human psyche is 'discovered'. The tight boundaries around age classification are replaced by a tendency to greater flexibility. There is thus a new emphasis, both on social variability and on the existence of additional learning abilities in old age. The sequence of institutional age groups is excluded from consideration by the encyclopedias and treated more or less as a technical canon. He believes that it is significant that the more radical developmental approach is not connected in the texts with an increasingly negative image of old age. Instead, the principle of the infinite possibilities and alternative futures inherent in the developmental view appears to have encouraged a thoroughly optimistic attitude towards old age. Thus, there is an emphasis on individual capacities for action. Nevertheless, there is still, as in the earlier period, an acceptance of a vital social threshold between 'mature age' (usually between 45/50 and 65/70) and older, physically weakened, 'decrepit age'. The latter was called *decrepitae aetas* in the eighteenth century and identified with ages above 70/75 years. It was argued that physically unfit people in this late stage of life did not retain their capacity to act.

In the third period, from the middle of the nineteenth century, von Kondratowitz (1991) finds evidence of increasing homogeneity, indeed a structural narrowing, of the ideas used. There is a growing influence of biological and medical concepts in the texts and a reduction in the socially variable components. The standardization and impoverishment of the entries can be thought to be connected to the increasing dominance of particular explanatory frameworks which exclude alternative and contradictory views. The presentation of the lifecourse becomes schematized and standardized as regards linguistic expression and reduced to purely biological and physiological factors. The content of these examples of medical thinking in this third phase reveal a preoccupation with purely negative perceptions of old age. The degenerative aspects of ageing are accentuated and there is an implicit denial of the learning potential of people in old age. The key point here for our discussion is that von Kondratowitz (1991) is able to demonstrate that the concepts with which geriatric science works have a social history. The distinctiveness of illnesses in old age and the extent to which they should be examined and treated differently was an issue and indeed remains controversial even today. It is contested in the politics of hospitals and health services and manifest in the activities of professional organizations.

In Britain geriatrics developed as a hospital based discipline, which was responsible medically for old people and the kind of treatment they received, and historically reflected the changing structures of the health service. Jefferys (1992), in a paper defending the need for a specialized medical service which deals specifically with older people, discusses the short history in UK of geriatric medicine. Before 1939, the voluntary hospitals, particularly those in large towns which had medical schools integrally attached to them, sought to avoid the admission of those who were labelled 'chronic sick' or 'aged poor'. Older patients were unwelcome because they blocked beds and were not 'good teaching material'. The illnesses which led to admission of old people were seen as intractable and chronic. Jefferys argues that the highly prestigious consultant doctors who, to further their lucrative private practice outside the hospital, gave their hospital services free, wished to be seen as concerned predominantly with aggressive interventions leading to a cure. The chronic sick and aged poor, therefore, tended to end up in the huge wards of the old Poor Law infirmaries, which, from 1929, had come under the control of the local authority medical officers of health.

The contested development of geriatric medicine in the UK can be illustrated from a case study by Isaacs *et al.* (1972) of the services for ill old people in the East End of Glasgow. They report that, before the advent of the NHS, Glasgow in common with other large cities had a dual hospital system. There were the great voluntary hospitals like the Glasgow Royal Infirmary with long traditions and large endowments, which were prestigious centres of teaching and research. Isaacs *et al.* (1972) tell us that to obtain an honorary appointment in a voluntary hospital was the mark of professional attainment and a route to 'material and social success'. Glasgow's industrial and professional elites served on the hospitals' committees of management. In contrast, there were hospitals which belonged to the Public Health Department of the Corporation of Glasgow. It ran two large and two small general hospitals, and had the sole responsibility for infectious diseases and tuberculosis. These hospitals had less qualified staff, lower levels of staffing and lower social status.

The voluntary hospitals exercised the right to choose patients. They were always ready to admit the young and the acutely ill, but were reluctant to accept too many chronic sick and elderly patients. Isaacs *et al.* (1972) suggest that this was in order to protect their function as centres of teaching and research. The corporation hospitals were open to all and elderly and chronically ill people formed a high proportion of their patients. This division was manifest in the administrative arrangements for admission. A general practitioner (GP) had to convince the receiving house physician in the voluntary hospitals to admit a patient by showing not only need but also suitability. Isaacs *et al.* report that:

> A question always asked was, 'How old is the patient?' and some general practitioners of considerable standing were made to feel, by a freshly qualified house physician, that they had committed a social misdemeanour in applying for the admission of a patient over the age of sixty.
>
> (Isaacs *et al.* 1972: 9)

In contrast, a doctor wishing to have a patient admitted to a corporation hospital simply gave the name, age and diagnosis to the clerk at the 'Bar' and some doctors merely scribbled a note and told the relatives to take it down for admission. The difference between the two systems was institutionalized by the practice of transferring patients who required long term hospital care from the voluntary to municipal hospital wards. The corporation hospitals included Barnhill, 'a grim Poor Law institution', which was looked upon by the general hospital as a suitable place for the terminal care of elderly people. In a pattern reminiscent of many cities across Britain, psychiatric services at this time were provided by immense Victorian mental hospitals in isolated positions on the outskirts of the city. The admission of old people to these wards was arranged by the duly authorized office of the local authority on the application of the general practitioner or the family, and Isaacs *et al.* (1972) suggest that this was 'usually on the basis of socially unacceptable' behaviour with no precise medical diagnosis'. Once admitted, elderly people usually stayed until they died.

Jefferys (1992) identifies the Second World War as crucial for the development of geriatrics. She argues that the expected military casualties were many fewer than anticipated. Beds which were to receive them were, therefore, often left unoccupied. Consultants from some of the best known voluntary hospitals were redeployed in the emergency of the war. Some were sent to emergency medical facilities and some to the local authority municipal hospitals, where they encountered great numbers of elderly patients for the first time. A few of those who thus found themselves responsible for the medical care of the chronic sick and aged poor began to question whether all their patients were inevitably bedridden and beyond discharge. Sometimes against the wishes of well intentioned nurses, who thought their regimes cruel, they instituted schemes for reactivating patients whose disability and incontinence they considered had been caused by, rather than been the cause of, their immobility (Jefferys 1992). In the years immediately following the Second World War and in preparation for the introduction of the NHS, the Ministry of Health became aware of the success which they were having in their treatments. Importantly, these new treatment regimes seemed to prevent the apparent chronic decline of some old people. The hereditary peer, Lord Amulree, at first a medical officer in the Ministry of Health and later a consultant at University College Hospital, London, encouraged other doctors to visit the pioneering institutions, and a Medical Society for the Care of the Elderly was formed to promote the provision of posts in the new speciality of geriatric medicine. It subsequently became the British Geriatric Society.

Following the establishment of the NHS, the newly formed regional hospital boards were at first wary of creating new consultant posts in geriatric medicine because the specialists in other branches of medicine and surgery were often opposed. Other senior medical staff saw the new development as giving undue status and resources to erstwhile superintendents of the despised local authority hospitals, or likely to recruit to its ranks those who could not compete for the more popular specialities. However, during the 1950s and early 1960s, much of the opposition from the elite of the consultants was diminished as it became clear that the geriatricians who admitted older people directly to their wards could prevent their own beds from getting blocked. Additionally, at a time of considerable increase in health service resources, the geriatric speciality was not likely to be too competitive in that its expansion was not likely to lead to too great a reallocation of resources, nor attract the brightest of the young medical graduates to its ranks.

In Glasgow, as elsewhere, the establishment of the NHS brought all the hospitals into a single framework. However, the specialization in acute medicine in the former voluntary hospitals continued and, increasingly, ex-corporation hospitals drew patients from their own new outpatient clinics or through direct contact with general practitioners. Their research traditions placed the prestigious Glasgow hospitals in the front of new specialist 'high tech' units for cardiological surgery, acute coronary care, renal dialysis and intensive care. The role of 'geriatrics', the label of the new proto-specialism, was discussed in the early years of the Glasgow NHS. Professor Noah Morris, the first occupant of the university unit at Stobhill Hospital (a corporation hospital), had been 'an early and powerful advocate of the establishment of acute geriatric units for the precise diagnosis and treatment of disease in old age' (Isaacs *et al.* 1972: 11). The first geriatric unit was set up in Glasgow in 1949. There followed pressure for 'the provision of scientific and humane treatment for the aged and chronic sick' and amelioration of conditions in the old poor law institutions. In 1952 the regional hospital board created a new post of consultant for the hospital which 'warehoused' the chronically sick, elderly patients and gave the incumbent the job of regional adviser on diseases of old age and chronic sickness. Isaacs *et al.* date the development of a systematic geriatric service from this time, pointing out that 'geriatrics as a branch of general medicine was in its infancy' and that few people had a clear idea of its function. The strategy developed in Glasgow was to provide diagnosis and treatment for older people in the same facilities as other people and long stay wards to be reserved for patients who 'failed to benefit after a full trial of treatments in an admission ward'. This plan saw the city divided into sectors with a geriatric unit in each, linked to a general hospital, and providing services for the local community. Resources to develop these services came from two sources: the economic boom experienced in post-war Britain, and from success in combating infectious diseases and tuberculosis which, in particular, freed beds in the old municipal sector. By the 1960s Glasgow and most of Britain had an established hospital-based geriatric service.

By the mid-1960s geriatrics was well established across the UK with consultant posts in all regions. By the mid-1970s, nearly all medical schools had set up chairs in geriatric medicine or the care of older people. Training of undergraduate medical students included at least a minimum of attention to the medical care of older people. A new sub-speciality of psycho-geriatrics had begun and both it and geriatric medicine had been reasonably successful in securing training posts to support the consultancies. As a result of these changes and of the allocation of increased resources to the 'cinderella' services, including those for older people, geriatricians were beginning to detect an improvement in the interest and quality of medical personnel applying for work in the specialty. This period also saw the development of social services based on a voluntary service tradition and a developing role for local government in supporting older people in their own homes (Isaacs *et al.* 1972: 106–108). The 'Seebohm' reorganization brought old people's welfare departments into a single local government generic social service organization. It also played its part in establishing the profession of social work by boosting the qualification and training expected of the expanded numbers of people working in the new departments. During the 1980s, although still a time of considerable uncertainty, geriatricians had developed multidisciplinary teams which tended to make a point of liaising closely with community-based service workers ranging from the general practitioners to the local authority social service departments and voluntary agencies concerned with the care of older frail people. Thus at the present time geriatrics and psycho-geriatrics are firmly established in the list of specialisms through which health care is organized in the UK. Although the precise role and level of resourcing for geriatric medicine is fiercely contested, and it has been significantly affected by the moves which have closed most long stay wards for older people, medical practitioners remain in the dominant position in defining the nature of old age in contemporary Britain.

Critiques of the medicalization of old age

The definition of ageing as a biomedical problem tends to both individualize and medicalize the ageing process. As a result it obscures the understanding of how health in old age is related to one's location in the social structure. The distribution of healthy living is related to income, sex, race, social class, type of work and to the social and economic conditions of contemporary society. One of the most important consequences of the biomedical model of ageing has been the priority given to hospitals, doctors and medical services. This priority has sometimes been at the expense of crucial developments in other major areas such as income maintenance, pensions, employment and housing. The dominant perception has been that medical services, rather than income or employment, can address the major problems of older people. The hegemonic typification of ageing as a physiological process results in the treatment of the problems of older people, their illnesses and their needs in a manner which is separated from their social causes. The resolution of the problems of old people are thus naturally seen to be through the consumption of medical services. There is a strong case to be argued that it is not increasing numbers of older people which are placing a strain on medical services. Rather, it is the medically dominated way of thinking about old age and the resulting pattern of service provision that has created the dilemma. Estes (1979; Estes *et al.* 1984) argues that the dominance of the medical model has facilitated the expansion of human service technologies industries and professions and the economic growth of biomedical research industries. She argues that the effect of current health policy, with its focus on western scientific medicine, has been to transform the multiple needs of the aged into medical problems amenable to government funded and industry developed interventions for specific economic markets (Minkler and Estes, 1991; Estes and Swan 1993; Estes *et al.* 1996). Further, it has been argued that the medical model supports the idea that the origins of problems in old age reside within the individual thereby putting the blame on the victim. It also diverts attention from problems generated by a society that may reject or impoverish older people or make them ill. This view therefore strengthens the conservative notion that the best interventions and policies are those aimed at the individual level rather than at collective social change.

Apocalyptic demography and Alzheimer's disease

Two examples will show how the dominant modes of thinking derived from the medical model can form an ideology which acts to give power to some people and diminish it for others. The first looks at the development of Alzheimer's disease as a diagnostic category and the second at the concepts of old age embedded in health economics. Robertson (1991) presents a social history of Alzheimer's disease suggesting that in the 1980s it became identified as the 'fourth or fifth leading cause of adult deaths in the United States'. Estimates of the prevalence of AD varied widely, some leading to suggestions of an epidemic-like scenario amongst the old population. Studies estimating the prevalence in the over-65 population produce figures ranging from less than 5 per cent to slightly more than 11 per cent, with estimates of the prevalence in those over 85 averaging between 15 and 20 per cent but reaching as high as 40 per cent (Robertson 1991: 136). However, the statistical basis of the findings need to be examined carefully. Do the upward adjustments of the prevalence rates of AD have anything to do with real underlying disease rates in the population, or is something else going on? Robertson (1991) convincingly demonstrates how 'the politics of Alzheimer's' has contributed to the creation and expansion of a diagnostic category of uncertain boundaries. She quotes studies which indicate that increases in hospital use by those over 65 were spread over a small number of diagnostic categories (Hertzman *et al.* 1989). Between 1969 and 1985/6, 500,000 patient days of increase to the over-65 population were attributable to behavioural, thought and mood disturbances (lumped together in the diagnostic category 'dementia'), and

80 per cent of those days of increase were for women over 65. In the same time period, there was no evidence for an increasing temporal trend in the prevalence of dementia (Robertson 1991: 145). Robertson's explanation for this rise in the diagnosis of AD lies in changes in medical thinking and the social construction of problems of old age. She argues that a diagnostic category was formed with fuzzy edges. Although Alois Alzheimer identified the syndrome which carries his name in the first decade of the twentieth century in 'pre-senile' adults, senile dementia as a normal ageing process became identified with Alzheimer's disease by post-mortem identification of brain condition (the presence of plaques). A consequence of identifying senility with the label Alzheimer's disease meant that it became a pathology, a disease amenable to management by health professionals. Some people see the benefits which flow from this in terms of the research funds and effort directed towards the disease and look forward to developing new therapies and even a 'cure'. Others see old age devalued by attachment to a fearsome, progressive, irreversible illness with no cure, which leads to dreadful degradation and loss before an inevitable undignified death (cf. Harding and Palfrey 1997).

The implicit assumptions of health economics

Medical professionals are not the only 'experts' with claims to knowledge necessary for the formulation of policies for elderly people. Health economics is a growing discipline, stimulated by the significant proportions of national income which are now spent on health care. I. R. Jones and Higgs (1992) argue that the methods of economic evaluation used by this new branch of economics contain hidden value judgements about the form of care that should, or should not, be made available to certain groups at a given cost. They suggest that an anti-geriatric bias inevitably results from purportedly objective data because of the conceptual framework used to solve the problems as they are predominantly formulated within the discipline of health economics. The attraction of health economics for administrative and political elites is that it promises to solve difficult allocative decisions by means of 'a standardized set of algorithms' as well as fitting in with the expansion of the corporate sector of health care. These consequences arise because, in borrowing neo-classical ideas and models to operationalize the philosophy of utilitarianism, much of health economics simultaneously brings into its work the assumptions about productive worth on which these models are based (Jones and Higgs 1992: 120).

Scientific models require mathematical precision, but numbers can all too easily appear to be value neutral while concealing value judgements. For example, it becomes a simple matter to assume that ten years of life are worth the same as two five year periods, without realizing this is a value judgement. However, ascribing a numerical value to life based on years of expected life will tend to discriminate unfairly against older people. The converse assumption that the more years already lived the more valuable the successive years is not made. Jones and Higgs (1992) argue that the methods of valuing human life for planning within such a health economics framework, have, embedded in the numbers, a lesser value attributed to older people. They discuss three different criteria for patient selection and evaluation used by health economists when attempting to assess planning priorities and see them all as unacceptable. The 'human capital' approach involves strategies of health care which bring most benefit to the national economy from health expenditure and thus make judgements of human worth derived from people's economic potential. These judgements are not necessarily generally accepted by the population at large and discipline based definitions of 'economic potential' will tend to undervalue people who have retired and are towards the end of their lives. The 'willingness to pay' approach to uses markets or quasi markets to order priorities. The consequence is to decide which treatments are most desirable on the basis of access to personal wealth and resources and must therefore involve the creation of an even less equitable health care system. Insofar as older people have fewer resources with which to pay for health care, such an approach would be discriminatory. The 'QALY' (Quality Adjusted Life Years), which Jones and Higgs see as the most commonly adopted method, does ostensibly involve the use of medical rather than social criteria. However, they argue that it is still at root a system of social rationing because of the value judgements embedded in the numerical evaluation of different lives. In practice then all these methods are contentious because rather than leading to accurate unbiased construction of priorities they end up reflecting particular dominant images of old age (Jones and Higgs 1992: 130–1).

Where the claims of the policy evaluation tools developed within health economics to be scientific and value neutral become accepted and established, then these ideas can bring pressure to bear on policy makers, clinical practices and may regulate older people's access to care. Professional power is bound up with resource allocation methods and ideology is embedded in procedures which fundamentally devalue those sections of the population whose contribution to society is inappropriately measured by their future work potential, the size of their bank balance or a doctor's assessment of their capacity for autonomous action. Explicit or implicit policies which ration health care by age tend to treat old people as the nearly dead. It pressures not only health care providers but also elderly people in the form of appeals for them to cut their demand for health care so that the young can benefit more. Indeed Churchill (1988: 647) argues that: 'such a gesture should not appear to us as a sacrifice but as the ordinary virtue entailed by a just, social conscience.' These ideological pressures are not a product of historical accident. Estes (1989) while discussing cost containment policies in the USA shows that one of the major consequences of *laissez-faire* economics for health care was a shift in responsibility from corporate bodies to the individual. According to this dominant ideology, which became increasingly powerful in the UK from the 1980s onwards, older people have got to take more responsibility for their health and well-being. The key point from this discussion of the conceptual basis of resource allocation models in health economics is to emphasize the inevitably political nature of all rationing procedures and how apparently value neutral mathematical procedures have ideological features built into them.

Socially constructed dependency

Various writers have considered ways in which professional power has worked against the interests of old people. Illich (1976) iconoclastically questioned the loss of freedom associated with control by the medical profession as part of his more general critique of professional power. In the 1980s Phillipson and Walker (Phillipson 1982; Phillipson and Walker 1986; Phillipson *et al.* 1986; Walker 1987) pointed out how dominant professional groups structured the lives of elderly people. The idea of structured dependency highlighted the ways in which professionally defined relationships were both financially advantageous to the professional and were controlling of and restricting to the lives of older people. This radical anti-professional critique had the objective of liberating clients and giving them back control of their own lives. However, this work has to be juxtaposed to the Thatcherite demolition of all (trade union and professional) collective organization in the labour market which happened contemporaneously. This was done with the objective of liberating capital from barriers to profit so that the loss of professional power has not necessarily had a corollary in the empowerment of clients.

There have always been points of tension, both structural and cultural, between medical professions and social work and allied professions. This is particularly true where people working within different knowledge bases have sought to care for the same clients. Those trained within a medical model tend to see social workers as unscientific, imprecise and ideological. Those trained in social work tend to see those working within the medical model as inflexible, impersonal and dogmatic. These tensions have been manifest in recent changes whereby residential care of elderly people has moved from being hospital based towards community care. Given the institutional structures in the UK, hospital care is medical based and community care is local government based and run by social workers. The associated transfer of resources from the NHS budget to local authorities not only involved political decisions and development of new administrative structures, but also required professionals to work more closely together. This has been happening at a time when there have been strong pressures from the private and commercial sector to take a larger share of the care of older people.

Local government: professionals v. entrepreneurs

The development of a private market in the provision of residential care for elderly people and its corollary in the withdrawal of the NHS from the provision of long term care for elderly people is one policy development which has been fuelled by the ideologies of individualized health care. It is possible to examine the relationships between professionals and entrepreneurs through the example of private residential care for elderly people in Devon. By looking at the relationships between the proprietors of the new care homes and the other interest groups in Devon, we can see how the power of capital and the power of professional expertise manifest themselves. In Devon, as elsewhere, the numbers and standards of private old people's homes have been a controversial issue. Who in Devon make up the interest groups with a stake in this issue and how do they seek to enhance their interests?

Private residential care in Devon

Devon's population has a high proportion of older people, particularly in the resort areas. Although the expansion of the market for private residential care since the late 1970s has been stimulated by changes in government policy, Devon has had a long-standing tradition of private care. There existed in Devon a relatively large private and voluntary sector providing residential care for elderly people. However, as in the rest of the UK, up until the mid-1980s residential care was largely the responsibility of local authorities under Part Three of the National Assistance Act 1948. As a result of a series of changes initiated by the Conservative government, primarily through the use of the Social Security budget to pay the fees of residential care for old people in private residential homes, there was a rapid expansion in such provision. In the late 1990s this form of residential care is now predominant. The entrepreneurs trying to convert these new opportunities into profit making enterprises formed a growing interest group. They came in conflict with various established groups and organized themselves both locally and nationally to pursue those interests. The state provided the framework for these opportunities and entrepreneurs had to find their way through national benefit agencies, local planning processes and the regulatory regimes for residential care. Professionals in local government, largely drawn from social work backgrounds, staffed the regulatory regime. Planning considerations brought home owners into conflict with other property owners. The tourist industry felt that increases in the presence of stigmatized groups such as the frail elderly might damage their trade. Domestic property owners feared that concentrations of homes would undermine the value of their property (Vincent *et al.* 1988).

David Phillips, Sarah Blacksell and I (Phillips *et al.* 1988) conducted a survey of home owners and, amongst other things, we asked about their attitudes to the various people with whom they had to deal. How did those involved in running the private sector of care see those with whom they have to interact to establish a successful business? The complexity and changing structure of relationships which private homes have had with local authorities, health authorities and central government departments inevitably produced a fairly mixed response. Asked about their overall satisfaction with outside bodies, 48.3 per cent of home owners or managers interviewed expressed satisfaction and 51.7 per cent felt dissatisfied. Responses to enquiries about specific types of professionals were very generalized, but not always entirely as might be predicted. For instance, homes advisers, in charge of registration of homes to ensure minimum care standards, were seen as helpful rather than draconian figures. They were identified as amongst those who had given the most practical assistance in the early days of setting up the homes. This, perhaps, reflects the limited powers available to local authority social services departments to take any really firm action against homes which are substandard. They therefore very sensibly take the strategy of trying to work with home owners, particularly inexperienced ones, to secure their agreement to care standards by providing information and advice. Similarly, but not surprisingly, The Department of Health and Social Security (DHSS) officials who arranged funding for residents were seen as supportive. Local authority planners were seen in a negative light when they had delayed or refused permission to expand homes and, sometimes, because they were expected to control more effectively the numbers of new homes opening and stop competition getting 'out of hand'. Social workers were widely criticized. They were criticized for manipulating the supply of residents. Social workers had a tendency to rely on homes they knew and felt confident with and so were accused of not making placements in a sufficient range of homes and 'favouring' only a select group of homes. They also attracted criticism because they did not make return visits after placement of an old person in a home – 'out of sight out of mind'. The concern here amongst home owners was that there was not enough help with difficult cases and social workers would often do nothing to help remove 'difficult' residents from homes. These tensions reflect the key role of social workers, particularly hospital based social workers, in placing residents in homes. Doctors were also blamed for the sense of abandonment felt by home owners when hospital places for those residents who had become mentally infirm could not be found and for the limited help private homes could expect from district nurses. Home owners also felt insufficiently supported by services such as occupational therapy and physiotherapy which, at the time of the survey, were, in practice, not available from local authorities and which few homes had been able to fund privately.

The private sector has changed radically since the boom years of the mid-1980s. Our investigation took place in a period of rapid expansion for the private residential sector. Since then a number of important factors have developed to tighten the private market in residential care.

First, high interest rates have made servicing loans more difficult and expensive – the escalation in property prices in the 1980s was reversed in the 1990s, which removed many of the large capital gains that those who entered early in the boom were able to make. Indeed, most significantly, problems in the property market made it more difficult for entrepreneurs wishing either to leave the sector, or to expand, to realize their assets.

Second, government policy has been crucial: the key to the rapid expansion of private residential care in the 1980s had been the availability of DHSS board and lodging payments to pay the fees of many residents. However, in an attempt to restrict public expenditure, the Conservative government first placed ceilings on charges and then failed to raise those ceilings in line with inflation. These changes in funding levels created a situation where some elderly residents in private homes paid for by central government were no longer able to afford the increased prices charged. Subsequently, with the development of community care, payment of fees for residents in private care entitled to benefit was organized through local authorities. These local authorities, as a result of both a desire to sustain people in the community and a gross shortage of funds, have effectively rationed the number of clients that private homes could expect. Government moves are continuing to address the divided responsibility for community care between health, DSS and local authorities. The idea that there should be local managers responsible for community care budgets with which to support elderly people was meant to permit a genuine choice between residential care and continued support at home. This has not led to a slackening in the demand for residential care places. This has been partly because of a dramatic reduction in the availability of local authority homes and partly because of the changes in the NHS which have seen the removal of a large number of geriatric beds and the withdrawal of the NHS from continuing care for frail elderly people. The new Labour government in 1997 addressed the difficult and contentious issue of long term residential care of frail older people by appointing a royal commission to report in early 1999.

The introduction of market mechanisms as a principle for the provision of residential care for elderly people established new kinds of relationships between the local authority professionals and the private sector proprietors. There is a difference of culture between those who have been trained in the caring professions and continue to work as professionals and the entrepreneurial culture or petit bourgeois attitudes (Vincent *et al.* 1988). In the professional culture there are clients not customers, there is a body of expertise which has to be acquired before one can practise and there are methods of peer group evaluation on standards and on ethics. Professionals tend to try and take a detached objective role when assessing clients, often to the extent of explicitly taking a client-centred approach in opposition to the needs of the organization for which they work. For entrepreneurs there can be no distinction between their own attitudes and those of the organization. This is particularly true in the family-based enterprises which predominate in private residential care in Devon. Their value system is based on commercial success and they have customers not clients. They therefore seek to market their product and positively advocate their home. The existence of these contrasting sets of attitudes tends to make communication difficult between professionals, such as social workers on the one hand, and private home owners on the other. However, there are sections of the private sector which are trying to professionalize. It is possible to identify a move away from marketing on the basis of small, family, homely homes towards skilled, professional care. These homes are in part responding to professional community care managers and their attitudes to placement. These professionalizing home owners are also attracted by price differentials in care for clients classified as infirm and requiring nursing care and are thus prepared to take rather more difficult and dependent clients than the private sector in Devon has historically catered for.

Conclusion: science, Fascism and old age

The chapter has looked at the interests involved in the care of elderly people and the ideologies through which claims to control and resources are made. It is the characteristic of hegemonic ideas that they have a 'taken for granted' quality. However, it is important that we challenge those dominant ideas. The potentially corrupting power of ideologies through which old age is defined is all too evident in the historical research of von Kondratowitz (1989, 1990, 1991). His studies of the application of the ideologies of social hygiene and racial hygiene, and the subsequent fate of vulnerable older people at the hands of the Nazi regime in Germany, is chilling. In an extreme version of the desire for rational and scientific improvement, population policies were devised to remove the burdensome elderly people by killing them. These policies were partially put into effect in the crisis of the Second World War. Von Kondratowitz quotes documentary reports:

> After the bombardment of Hamburg in July and August 1943, on 6 August a transport of 284 old people confined to bed were transferred from one institution to the other, finally ending up in the small town Neuruppin, which was an 'ancillary post' for the killing institutions Bernburg and Brandenburg. Another example: in June 1944 a transport of almost 500 old women reached finally the notorious killing institution of Meseritz-Oberawalde where they were 'syringed' to death. These women came from the harbour town of Stettin (today: Sczeczin in Poland) where they were 'bombed out' as it was mentioned in the document.
>
> (von Kondratowitz 1989: 7)

He reports that in the confusion following air raids, doctors would readily declare old people, who were wandering around in the ruins looking for remains of relatives and personal belongings, as being 'confused' or 'insane' in order to have them transferred to institutions and to get them from the streets. Part of the motive for these actions was to ration scarce medical resources at a time of national emergency. To declare someone as being 'insane' meant that these people would be in danger of being killed. Further, von Kondratowitz suggests that this was widely known in Germany at the time.

The argument presented in this chapter is not some simplistic conspiracy theory. It is not that some badly motivated individuals sit in the committees of professions or on the boards of drug companies and think of ways to be nasty to old people. The argument is about the power of ideas which come to motivate powerful people and which develop a historical logic of their own, as the dynamics of the struggle between contending social groups work themselves out. People tend to develop ideas and theories which explain and justify their actions and provide a guide to what course of action to follow. People in similar social positions, who have common interests, tend to develop similar ideas. These ideas take on an obvious or 'natural' quality for those who hold them. They take on this quality because they 'work'. That is to say, provide effective practical solutions to dilemmas as they are experienced by the people who have internalized those ideologies. These dominant ideas can then motivate people to act in particular ways when confronted with new situations. The professional ethics of medical personnel can both motivate the heroes and heroines of Médecins sans frontières to provide assistance to the casualties of all sides in a civil war at great risk to themselves and yet also provide the motivation to organize the mass destruction of old people under the Nazi regime.

Foucault (1979, 1980) is a key figure in an intellectual tradition which has sought to understand the relationship between power and knowledge in the modern world. His work focuses historically on how we have come to constitute our 'knowledge of man'. This knowledge formed a rational medium for disciplining deviant people in institutions. He offers historical documentation indicating that disciplines like psychiatry, medical science and criminology were constituted as parts of the modern project of establishing a rational social order, and many other writers have extended his ideas in contemporary sociology. Medical science from this point of view is socially constituted to produce – in the form of scientific thought – definitions of health, normality and abnormality. The 'normal' individuals are investigated regularly to keep them in productive shape, the 'abnormals' are studied scientifically in order to treat the 'problems' of their conduct. Seen from this perspective the 'elderly' are not an objectively existing category about whom knowledge can be gathered. On the contrary the 'elderly' as a category are constituted by the intellectual strategies of gerontology which functions as a legitimation for social control in situations that deal with the 'elderly' (Baars 1991; Cohen 1994). The limitation of this kind of approach, which ties the exercise of power and control to social construction, is that, in the final analysis, it renders people incapable of action. In fact, power is contested and people do act to redefine their situation. The idea of power embedded in this approach is helpful in providing a critique of how older people are disempowered through monopolization of knowledge. However, these ideas themselves also need to be challenged and these themes will be taken up in Chapter 9.

_6

National politics 1: party politics and the electoral process

Are old people a force in national politics? If not, why not? If older people do not have the same standard of living as the general population and lack economic power (see Chapters 7 and 9) and if they do not have the cultural resources with which to gain influence and prestige (see Chapters 4 and 5) can they use their voting power within a democratic electoral system to have their interests as older people looked after? A number of commentators have suggested that the demographic changes associated with an ageing population will result in a shift in political power – that older people as a voting block will be able to dominate state controlled redistribution of income in their favour (Pampel and Williamson 1989; Dean 1990). We can examine these issues by pursuing fairly standard and straightforward research procedures. If we look at the content of the documentation produced by political parties designed to attract people to vote for them, we can gain an idea about how the party electoral machine regards different sections of the population, including older people. If we look at some of the many opinion polls which try to gauge people's voting intentions and the kinds of issues and policies that influence them, we can gain some insight into which issues older people see as important and the extent to which they will take some kind of action (e.g. vote) in pursuit of those goals. We can also look at systematic surveys of the electorate to examine people's reported voting behaviour and the extent to which this is patterned by age.

Election promises: where the political parties stand

In British politics party manifestos have a significance which is not necessarily given in other democratic political systems. They are formulated by the parties prior to a general election as a programme for government to be offered to the electorate. They have thus become seen almost like a contract between the party elected and the people, and the performance of governments are frequently assessed against the objectives they set for themselves in their manifestos. Although manifestos are not always delivered and are certainly not read by the majority of the electorate, they are useful documents in systematically comparing the priorities and objectives of parties over a period of time. Campaigning styles have changed over the period since the Second World War, particularly under the influence of electronic media and the dominance of the television in forming public opinion. As a result, the form and content of manifestos have tended to change and their role somewhat alter. They nevertheless represent each party's promises in terms of a programme for government. Manifestos formulated by parties when they are in government usually seek to defend their record in office and therefore look different from manifestos of parties seeking to present themselves as a credible, alternative government by setting out new plans and proposals. Party manifestos can be examined to see how they have viewed older people and sought their votes. This chapter is based in part on a review of all the general election manifestos of the major parties in all general elections from 1945 to 1997 which the University of Keele Department of Politics has usefully archived. This review reveals how political parties have changed their approach to voters and how parties differ in their characterization of age-based issues.

Images of older people in party political manifestos

The rhetoric of the deserving poor is central to the images of older people used by the political parties. This rhetoric is general to all parties – the manifestos conjure pictures of hard working citizens in reduced circumstances who deserve their share of national cake. Work is seen as particularly meritorious and an essential part of the necessary characteristic of those in receipt of state funds (cf. Bauman 1998). For example, in their 1950 manifestos, the case of working pensioners was taken up by both Conservatives and Liberals, both of whom were in opposition at this time. They proposed abolishing the means test on working pensioners. The two elements of the image are 'the deserving' and 'the poor'. Some special categories – widows, war pensioners, ex-service personnel in general – are seen as particularly deserving. The elements which are seen as deserving are citizenship and service. The idea that those who have contributed to the nation through their lives deserve consideration in old age, has been used to justify the pension in general, and particular kinds of additional pension.

> We have lowered the age at which increases in public service and armed forces pensions become payable, and we have further improved the position of war pensioners and their widows. Public service pensions, armed forces pensions and supplementary pensions are all now reviewed every single year, together with the main national insurance benefits.
>
> (Conservative Party manifesto February 1974)

The manifestos identify their opponents as either cheating these worthy people of their just deserts or of preventing them realizing the benefits of their own efforts.

Older people tend not to be differentiated in the social analysis implicit in the manifestos. They are collectively presented as poor – the case for food subsidies in the 1950s was made by an appeal for the interests of the old as a poor and deserving section of the population who should be defended. The manifestos can be deconstructed to reveal an implicit class analysis. Parties identify the key interests of older people and pensioners in specific ways which tend to be indicative of their more general approach to society. For example, Labour's 1997 view of social extremes in the UK is stated in its manifesto:

> We are a national party, supported today by people from all walks of life, from the successful businessman or woman to the pensioner on a council estate.
>
> (Labour Party manifesto 1997)

This statement carries within it an explicit denial of representing a class, along with an implicit acknowledgement of class difference and an assumption that old age and poverty go together. Over the post-war period, for Labour, pensioners are part of the mass of poor, they are part of an unequal society. For Conservatives and Liberals the issue of poverty in old age is, in contrast, a problem about fixed incomes, i.e. savings, value of money and capital. The Liberal Party (and its successors) likes to present itself as outside the class struggle of bosses against workers.

> The Conservative Party is clearly identified in the minds of the electors with employers and big business, and they cannot deal objectively or fairly with the problems continually arising between employer and employee. The Labour Party is in the hands of the Trade Union Leaders.
>   The return of a Socialist Government inevitably means that management is put on the defensive, for it does not know what is going to hit it next. The return of a Conservative Government means that the Trade Unions feel justified in going on to the offensive.
>   The whole nation is the loser from this crazy line up of power politics, and those who lose most in the struggle are those who live on fixed incomes, such as old age pensioners.
>
> (Liberal Party manifesto 1959)

This 'one nation stance' is a position which all major parties, in their attempt to appeal to the crucial middle ground of voters, have adopted. The image of pensioners as the deserving poor, which so dominates the party political thinking about older people, may be thought of as having both positive and negative effects. Insofar as old age pensioners are in conflict with other groups in receipt of state funded welfare, the very high levels of legitimacy given to pensioners as deserving and poor serves to protect their interests. On the other hand, the passive images of older people as receivers of handouts to the deserving poor on the basis of their past contribution to the nation, prevents them being seen as a positive and active resource for society in the present.

Issues in the manifestos addressed to older people

In the immediate post-war election in 1945 the welfare state was the major issue. The manifestos of all parties gave support to the Beveridge Report, which recommended setting up a national insurance to provide for illness, unemployment, disability, old age and death benefits. Although in its 1950 manifesto Labour claimed 'The conservatives . . . voted against the second and third reading of the National Health Service Bill', the 1950s saw a consensus on the benefits of public provision of welfare which, in particular, included a commitment to provision of a state pension. The issues which were taken up and debated in the manifestos were not about the principle of the welfare state and pensions but about how much was to be paid, and who could be trusted with economic efficiency which could deliver the most generous benefits. The Labour manifesto of 1959 promised a national superannuation scheme to end 'poverty in old age', and pensions again became an issue in the 1960s. All parties proposed various schemes which would relate individual pensions to a proportion of salary earned during the person's working life. These schemes were a response to the growing standard of living and increasing discrepancy between those on pensions and those benefiting from increasing wages. Labour governments in the 1960s and 1970s introduced first an earnings related top-up to pensions and then the state earnings related pension scheme (SERPS). Through the 1980s welfare was debated in the context of a New Right agenda of rolling back government including welfare provision and privatization. The Labour Party vision expressed in their 1983 manifesto was decisively rejected by a sceptical electorate:

Working time in Britain, over the life time of individual workers, is among the highest in industrial countries. We will work through collective bargaining to reduce working time; and this will include more flexible working arrangements, more time off for study, longer holidays, earlier voluntary retirement with adequate pensions – with progress towards our aim of a common pension age of 60 – and a 35 hour week.

The Conservatives' own assessment of their performance in government through the 1980s is expressed as follows:

The Conservative administrations elected since 1979 are among the most successful in British peacetime history. A country once the sick man of Europe, has become its most successful economy. A country once brought to its knees by over mighty powerful trade unions, now has industrial peace. Abroad, the cold war has been won; at home, the rule of law has been restored. The enterprising virtues of the British people have been liberated from the dead hand of the state. There can be no doubt that we have created a better Britain.

(Conservative Party manifesto 1997)

In 1997, like all manifestos in the post-war period, the concerns and issues affecting older people were not addressed directly in the manifestos of the major parties. In the Conservative manifesto the issue of pensions was largely addressed to the working population about their future pensions. The central points to their new proposals to attract voters were funded pensions not dependent on taxes, a personal pension which followed people through their employment career, a scheme which was to be funded by a National Insurance rebate and accumulated investments. In the Labour manifesto, in addition to attacking the government's record on pensions, the key points included a stakeholder pension designed to give all those in work access to good value second pensions and also suggested help for the 'poorest' and those who assume responsibility as carers.

Age Concern, the leading British charity concerned with older people in the UK, has taken a campaigning role in seeking to publicize issues which concern older people. Some local Age Concern groups held debates between the candidates in their constituencies. Age Concern's own 'election manifesto' – a list of desirable commitments it was seeking from political parties – was set out in a paper released in August 1996. At the time of the election it sought to influence voters by making a systematic comparison of its own list of desirable policies with the pledges made in the party manifestos for the 1997 general election. Age Concern included in its analysis the smaller parties, including the nationalist parties in Scotland and Wales, but did not include the Northern Ireland parties. The analysis paid as much attention to what was *not* said as to the commitments made. Age Concern suggested that legislation should be introduced to end age discrimination in employment. It reported that the Liberal Democrats and the Welsh nationalist party, Plaid Cymru, promised legislation to end all forms of age discrimination, while Labour attacked age discrimination but said nothing about outlawing it. The Conservatives and Scottish Nationalists were silent on this issue. Institutional ageism in the NHS was a concern and Age Concern looked for commitments that health care for older people should be provided on the basis of their medical needs, not their age. None of the parties made any specific commitment on this point, although Plaid Cymru mentioned 'equal availability' in the NHS. In line with support for such initiatives as the University of the Third Age, Age Concern emphasized that education and training should be available to people of all ages. No party explicitly covered this issue. However, Plaid Cymru's and the Liberal Democrats' promises of age discrimination legislation may be considered to have encompassed it.

Although Age Concern's agenda was not exclusively dominated by pension and welfare issues in the same manner as the political parties' appeals to older people were, it made key proposals in this area. It suggested that age limits on disability benefits should be removed. Plaid Cymru alone referred to this. On the state pension, Age Concern proposed that it should remain the bedrock of retirement income and enable the achievement of a modest lifestyle for all pensioners. Its analysis reports that the Liberal Democrats offered a top-up pension to replace Income Support, linked to increases in average earnings, and employer contributions to occupational or personal pensions for all. The Conservatives offered some improvements in the organization of occupational and personal pension schemes but no rise in the basic pension rate and its replacement for the next working generation. Labour promised a 'mixed economy of pensions' and improvements in SERPS, occupational and personal pensions but nothing on the basic pension rate. Plaid Cymru would restore the link between the basic pension and earnings. Age Concern highlighted the fact that many older people fail to take up the available state benefits that they are entitled to. The Labour manifesto promised more automatic help for the poorest pensioners, without specifying precise details and (as we shall see later in Chapter 7) Labour in power found pension reform a particularly difficult issue.

Housing, fuel and transport also featured in Age Concern's priorities. It said that a realistic provision for heating should be included in weekly social security benefits and that funding to make all older people's homes energy efficient should be restored, as part of a broader range of grants to make older people's homes fit to live in. Presumably in the knowledge of the climatic hazards faced by their voters, the Scottish Nationalist Party (SNP) promised a 'pensioners' package' to end fuel poverty, including higher pensions and a winter weather allowance. Plaid Cymru proposed to combine renovation and energy efficiency grants and give a boost for care and repair schemes. Labour promised a 'major push' on energy efficiency and an environment taskforce for the under-25s. The Liberal Democrats planned to end fuel poverty by launching a national homes insulation programme for 2 million households. Both nationalist parties responded to proposals that all new housing should be built to a standard which could allow access by wheelchair users and people with restricted mobility while the two largest parties remain silent on this specific issue. Older people are much less likely to have access to cars than the general public, so Age Concern proposed that public transport should be made accessible to people with limited mobility. Plaid Cymru, in line with its overall appeal to older voters, said it would set a date for all vehicles and bus stations to be accessible. Of the major parties, the Liberal Democrats mentioned a code of practice on accessible transport while Labour's pledge for comprehensive, enforceable civil rights for disabled people might be relevant to transport for older people. The new Labour government announced the setting up of a Disability Commission in the Queen's speech of November 1998; however, the extent to which it uses its powers in this field remains to be seen. The idea of a national scheme of uniform concessionary fares for pensioners available for all forms of travel was widely canvassed by pensioner's organizations. The Conservative manifesto did promise to protect concessionary fares on London Underground, a promise presumably made to acknowledge concerns expressed about their proposals to privatize that system.

Age Concern, like other organizations of and for older people, is caught in a dilemma. On the one hand it seeks to undermine the image of older people as sick and disabled and replace it with a positive image of ageing, while on the other hand it also seeks to ensure an appropriate level of care for the minority of older people who do need social care and medical services. It has made a number of proposals including reinstatement of NHS long term care for elderly people, stating that 'nursing care should be provided free at the point of delivery whether it is in hospital, in a nursing home or residential care' and 'the government must ensure that local authorities have sufficient funds to provide social services to disabled older people'. The Conservatives proposed to legislate to introduce partnership insurance that would protect older people's assets from means testing. The Liberal Democrats would have introduced national charging and eligibility guidelines for residential care and worked with other parties to agree a system for funding long term care. Labour has pledged to establish a royal commission on long term care funding, which in office it has done. While Plaid Cymru said it would 're-examine current practice' and would give extra funding for community care, the SNP committed itself to end means testing and also promised to increase funding for local authorities and voluntary organizations if their caring responsibilities increased (Age Concern 1996, 1997).

Older people's issues

What kinds of issues do older people themselves, as opposed to the political parties or pressure groups, suggest as important? We can look at the opinions and attitudes of older voters through opinion surveys – although of course we must bear in mind that power is also about keeping things off the agenda, as well as people's expressed and articulated interests. The Anchor Trust (Sykes and Leather 1997) published a survey entitled *Grey Matters*. This survey, conducted in the summer of 1996, was intended to influence the general election held in 1997. Over a thousand people aged over 55 were interviewed. The survey findings suggest a series of issues which older people consider important and might influence the way they vote. Three major issues stand out: crime and vandalism (mentioned by some 56 per cent of respondents), the NHS (48 per cent of respondents) and drug abuse (47 per cent of respondents). While pensions and social security were considered important, they did not come out of the survey as strongly as these three issues. Pensions, along with unemployment, education and schools, and Europe and the EU, were mentioned by between two-fifths and one-third of older people. Unemployment was a much stronger focus for older people's economic concerns than any of the other matters, such as inflation, which might be thought to concern them more directly. The survey reports that financial support for those in care, better local services and more suitable housing were more likely to influence older people's voting behaviour than better public transport or the abolition of inheritance tax. The British Election Studies panel study of opinions of a sample of the whole adult population before the 1997 general election recorded verbatim the responses to the question 'Which issue matters most to you in deciding how to vote in the general election?' The results were classified into 34 categories. The two most frequently mentioned issues were health and education, while pensions and the EU were close together in third place. The approach of the political parties and the opinions of the voters indicate diverging interests between current recipients of pensions and those of future pensioners (cf. Table 6.1).

The Anchor Trust survey showed that politicians as a group of people are not popular with older people, with high proportions feeling that politicians never listen to their views. The survey suggested high proportions of older people do not feel that their Member of Parliament (MP) represents their views and are less likely to trust their MP than ten years ago. A part of this finding may be due to the changing party allegiance and attitudes to incumbent Conservative members rather than any increase in the character defects of MPs. More generally, feelings of disenchantment with politics is growing. This sense of lack of political efficacy is a general characteristic of the population and indeed there is evidence from other sources (Heath *et al.* 1998) that the younger age groups feel even more distant from the political process than older people. There was agreement – from 84 per cent of respondents in the Anchor Trust survey – with the proposition that older people should stand up more actively for their rights; only 4 per cent disagreed. Support for this proposition peaked with those in their 60s and early 70s. At earlier ages, people tend not to regard themselves as older people, while in the late 70s and 80s most older people appear to take less interest in political issues (Sykes and Leather 1997: 46).

Most older people always vote for the same party, so policy developments like those above would not have much influence on them. Those who told the Anchor Trust that they would change their vote at the next election followed the overall national trend and were mainly Conservatives switching to vote for Labour. Respondents were also asked to indicate the extent to which polices beneficial to older people on a range of issues would influence their voting behaviour at a general election. More financial support for older people in long term care and increased local services for older people were the most likely policies to attract more votes (57 per cent of people said they would be more likely to vote for a party with these policies). However, almost two in five said this would make no difference to their voting behaviour. Just under a half of respondents would be more likely to vote for a party which offered suitable housing for older people. There was less response to policies for increases in rail and bus services (only 31 per cent of respondents were more likely to vote for this while 63 per cent said such a policy would make no difference). A proposal to abolish inheritance tax met similar percentages of respondents indicating that this would not influence their vote. Financial support for those in care and better local services were the main potential vote winners. The priority allocated to these issues clearly related to concerns over the availability of affordable residential care for frail older people, as the NHS has withdrawn from provision of long term care of elderly people and old people needing residential care have had to rely on private or means tested provision organized through local social services departments. Older people being required to sell their homes in order to pay for residential care has become increasingly controversial. It is argued that those encouraged to purchase their homes through government policy in the 1980s were in the 1990s having to sell those homes to pay for what they had thought was a free national provision.

Do older people act as a self-interested group when thinking about issues of pensions and benefits (and does this affect the way they intend to vote)? The *British Social Attitudes Survey* (Social and Community Planning Research 1996), which was also part of the panel study by the BES which looked at changing attitudes in the run up to the 1997 general election, asked questions which might help answer these points. Respondents were asked if the government had more money available to spend on social benefits to identify the one which they would give first priority. Nearly half (49.1 per cent) said the retirement pension, while 11.1 per cent nominated child benefits and 18.4 per cent disability benefit.

When we look at age groups, 62.9 per cent of those suggesting child benefits were between 18 and 34 (this age group made up 30.8 per cent of the sample), while 26.6 per cent of those supporting the retirement pensions

Table 6.1 First priority for spending on social benefits (percentages)

	All ages	*17–24*	*25–34*	*65 and over*
Child benefit	11.1	21.4	23.4	1.9
Retirement pension	49.1	17.1	35.4	70.0
Unemployment benefit	13.3	15.8	13.2	10.8
Other	26.5	45.7	28.0	17.3
	100	100	100	100

Source: Author's analysis of the *British Social Attitudes Survey* (Social and Community Planning Research 1996)

were over 65 (this age group made up 18.7 per cent of the sample). In fact 70 per cent of those 65 and over gave priority to pensions, compared to 35.4 per cent of 25–34-year-olds; 1.9 per cent of those 65 and over nominated child benefits while 23.4 per cent of the 25–34 age band also made that choice (see Table 6.1).

Walker and Maltby (1997: 62) report from data gathered by the EU Barometer that 56.6 per cent of the UK sample believe that pensions are too low and should be raised even if this means raising taxes; 20.7 per cent also think that pensions should be raised but believe they cannot because taxes should not be raised, while 14.9 per cent think pensions are about right. The equivalent figures for the EU as a whole are 43 per cent for raising pensions and taxes, 28.7 per cent agree pensions are too low but cannot be raised because taxes should not be increased, while 17.4 per cent think pensions are about right. Negligible proportions of British and other European people think that pensions are too high. There are, however, wide variations in pensions entitlement and opinions across Europe. US opinion polls also show a high level of support for benefits for older people, four out of five Americans opposing cutbacks in government spending for Social Security, Medicare and veterans' benefit (Vierck 1990). Older people believe pensions should receive priority, but so do a high proportion of the rest of the population.

The 1997 general election result and the role of older voters

The result of the British 1997 general election was to remove the Conservative government from office and leave the Labour Party dominating the House of Commons with a 178-seat majority. Patterns of voting by age are shown in Table 6.2. Those 65–75 were most likely to have voted. Those over 75 were most likely to have voted Conservative. Those 18 to 25 were least likely to have voted Conservative or to have voted at all. The Labour lead over the Conservatives was largest amongst the younger age groups.

Pensions and British national politics

The reason for the growing objective inequality between old people lies largely with what has happened to the pensions and benefit system. The two key political developments which affect today's British pensioners were the

Table 6.2 Reported voting in 1997 general election by percentage of age group

Age group	Did not vote	Conservative	Labour	Liberal Democrat
18–25	29.7	16.8	36.0	14.1
26–35	26.7	17.9	37.6	13.5
36–45	18.9	20.6	39.8	14.8
46–55	15.2	22.8	41.2	14.0
56–65	10.5	27.7	41.7	11.9
65–75	10.1	27.8	43.3	11.8
76 and over	15.8	35.0	26.3	17.3
All ages	18.6	22.8	39.0	13.7

Note: The percentages do not sum to 100% across the rows as the nationalists and minor parties and those who refused to disclose their vote are not included.
Source: Author's analysis of *British Election Survey, 1997* (Heath *et al.* 1998)

introduction by the Labour government in 1978 of SERPS, which superseded the graduated pension scheme (Arber and Ginn 1991: 86) and the removal in 1980 (Atkinson 1989: 233) of the Rooker-Wise amendment which linked pensions to both earnings and prices. Under the Thatcher government in 1979, amongst a series of measures to restrict the long term cost of benefits to the exchequer, the link with earnings was broken. Pensioners on the basic state pension have fallen steadily further and further behind the general standard of living of the UK. Conversely, those who have retired after long periods of steady employment paying earnings related contributions into SERPS or occupational pensions are now receiving substantial pensions. These pensions may not equate to those available in some places in continental Europe, but they represent a very substantial improvement on what might have been expected a generation previously. The consequence of these changes is to increase the levels of inequality amongst retired people. Those in the poorest sections of the elderly population have fallen relatively further behind the general population in their incomes. Around a quarter of all older people in Britain are either dependent on Income Support, or entitled to that benefit but not getting it. However, the most affluent sections of the retired population have experienced substantial relative improvement in their incomes compared to the rest of the population. There are concerns that this growing gap will become even wider as the consequences of increasing inequality in work opportunities for younger age groups have consequential effects on pension entitlement and produce yet greater inequality in old age.

Growing inequality among pensioners is a major challenge. In 1997 the Pensions Minister, John Denham, speaking to the Pensions Management Institute Conference, stated:

The pensions policies of the past failed to ensure that all retired people are able to enjoy their retirement in security, dignity and independence. While some have done well, too many today live in poverty. Over the last two decades we have seen widening inequality between the most well-off pensioners and those at the bottom of the income scale.

(DSS 1997)

It is clear that pensions have in the 1990s again become an important political issue. Pensions are a vital strategic point in locating political parties in the debate on the role of the state. Should governments be responsible for the redistribution of wealth, for the provision of welfare and for managing a framework for economic activity? Should the state resource pensions for all? Should it merely look after the people most vulnerable through poverty and infirmity? Should the state administer pensions schemes or should that be left to the private sector? Differences of emphasis between the British political parties have become clear over pensions. Conservatives see a reduced role for the state pension and have sought a greater role for the individual and private sector providers. Conservatives emphasize privatization, individual initiative and rolling back the 'nanny' state. A further principle of the New Right is the importance for economic prosperity of taking burdens off industry. This means deregulation, limiting the role of government in monitoring and enforcing standards, which the New Right believe could be done better through market mechanisms. It also means limiting tax burdens by reducing government expenditure. Thus the role of the private sector in pensions has become a conflict expressed as a party political issue. The New Right analysis would logically lead to the abolition of the state pension. The Conservative Party has always denied that this is its objective, and this attitude is not surprising given the popularity of the state pension with the electorate. However, the Conservatives did take a number of steps which had the effect of undermining the long term value of the state pension and introduced incentives for private pension arrangements.

The Conservative government in its June 1985 Green Paper proposed the abolition of SERPS (DHSS 1985: 24), although subsequently, in the pension legislation enacted later in that year, it changed tack away from a direct assault on the scheme. The legislation reduced the benefits under the state scheme and gave incentives to private personal schemes in a deliberate attempt to make private pensions more attractive. Nearly 5 million people took advantage of the incentives offered and transferred to personal private pensions, with the ironic effect of costing significantly more to the National Insurance Fund than it saved on future SERPS benefits (N. Johnson 1995: 34). This strategy to limit the state's involvement in pensions and increase the role of the private sector has met with considerable problems. It has become clear that many of those who changed their pensions were poorly advised, that they did not act in their own financial best interests and a number of pension and insurance companies may have to compensate 1 million people for this misleading advice, although estimates of the numbers vary widely.

Other scandals also prompted further legislation. The plundering of the Mirror Group employees' pension fund to support the financial problems of Robert Maxwell's business empire caused outrage. This scandal raised the issue of how to protect pensioners and, in particular, the beneficiaries of company pension schemes from fraud and incompetence on the part of trustees charged with the responsibility for pension funds. The Conservatives took a further pensions initiative by raising the female pensionable age to 65, which has the effect not only of limiting future government expenditure but also lessening the value for money of national insurance for women in the future. This was enacted in the parliamentary session beginning in November 1995. This change was covered by a rhetoric which sought legitimacy in an appeal to gender equality. Sara McConnell suggests:

> Unwelcome though it was at first, the Barber judgement provided a convenient alibi for the Government. In the name of equality, it finally announced last November that men and women would both have to wait until 65 for their basic state pensions, starting in 2010. Given that this will save £4 billion a year by 2035 at 1993 prices, there was never any doubt this was the Government's favoured option, top of the list of things it wants to include in a Pensions Bill.
>
> (*The Times* 6 May 1994)

In the 1997 general election campaign 'welfare reform', particularly in terms of the long term future of the pension, became a key issue. During the campaign, while it maintained that it would keep a state pensions system, the Conservative Party took the initiative in bringing forward pension proposals based around providing a framework for personal private pension schemes. Nicholas Jones (1997: 246) suggests that this was to demonstrate the continued dynamism of their New Right radical agenda and attract younger voters. The Conservative Party manifesto stated:

> We will make it easier for small employers to set up personal pension plans for groups of employees.
>
> We will create more flexibility for people who save in personal pension plans to continue investing in those schemes if they subsequently move to jobs with company pension schemes.
>
> We will also create flexibility for employees with savings in Additional Voluntary Contributions (AVC) schemes to take part of that pension earlier or later than their main company pension.
>
> But we believe the time has now come to plan for another important step in improving Britain's pension provision. Britain is already much better placed than many other countries to afford state pensions in the future, but we want even more people to be able to look forward to a properly funded pension that grows with the economy and is free from dependence on taxes paid by future generations. We now propose a practical way of achieving a gradual transformation of the state pension scheme.
>
> At the start of the next parliament we will set out proposals to provide all young people entering the workforce with a personal pension fund paid for through a rebate on their national insurance contributions. At retirement they would be entitled to the full pension earned by this accumulated investment. This could give them a pension significantly higher than they would currently receive from the state. But they will be guaranteed a pension at least equal to the current basic state pension, increased in line with inflation.
>
> . . . And eventually, the new policy will produce massive public expenditure savings.
>
> (Conservative Party manifesto 1997)

The comparison of the approach and thinking of Conservative campaigns of 1955 and 1997 is informative. In both they identified the ratio of workers to pensioners as a problem. They chose very different approaches to deal with the issue. In 1955 they emphasized economic growth – achieved through conservative virtues – and maintenance of the value of the state pension.

The nation has assumed very large obligations towards the pensioners of tomorrow; and tomorrow there will be very many more pensioners. For every 10 people of working age there are now 2 of pensionable age; but within a quarter of a century there will be 3. If during this period Britain can increase her national wealth and resources, by the policy of investment and enterprise which we advocate, these obligations can be met. But if wealth is dissipated, enterprise hampered and severe inflation brought about again by Socialist short-sightedness, the whole of our National Insurance scheme would be undermined and ultimately destroyed. In its first year of office the Conservative Government increased virtually all social service payments. This year it has again raised pensions and benefits, and fully restored the purchasing power that Parliament intended they should have when the main rates were fixed after the war.

(Conservative Party manifesto 1955)

In 1997 the recipe for dealing with the same issue was to reduce the state pension to a minimum safety net and sponsor private savings and investment schemes.

The Labour Party is also not satisfied with the pension status quo. It made what it called 'the reform of welfare' an important part of its proposed programme, and introduced the idea of 'stakeholder' pensions. The new Labour government in office has struggled with the issue. It developed plans for a stakeholder pension but has encountered opposition from within the pensions industry. Opponents of the scheme feel that the system proposed will be expensive to administer and that an indication of government approval, given to policies meeting their proposed criteria, might mislead customers into believing they are an appropriate purchase for their particular circumstances. The new government has adhered to a policy of giving top priority to keeping government spending down. It has therefore avoided proposals which might have significantly increased pensioner incomes. It has not as yet found a solution to the dilemmas of, on the one hand, the attractions of a universal non-means-tested benefit which retains the power and legitimacy and support from the general public, and on the other hand targeting resources at the least well off, thus limiting tax demands on the working population. Indeed difficulties over policy on pensions and benefits led to the departure of the ministerial team of Harriet Harman and Frank Field in the first Labour reshuffle. The Green Paper finally published in December 1998 contained modest proposals including stakeholder pensions, a new second tier pension and carer's pensions (DSS 1998). The Prime Minister in the foreword says:

Our partnership approach will deliver:

- an assurance of a secure and decent income in retirement for all through the new minimum income guarantee. This will be increased year by year as resources allow. Over the longer term our aim is that it should rise in line with earnings so that all pensioners can share in the rising prosperity of the nation;

- dramatically better pension provision for those on low incomes, and those unable to work because they are caring for children or a relative who is ill or disabled; and
- a better deal for middle and higher income earners through low-cost and flexible personal stakeholder pension schemes backed by extra government support and better regulation of pensions as a whole.

(DSS 1998: iii)

Pensions mis-selling scandal

Fears for the future of the state pension have been successfully raised and these fears, together with tax and legislative changes, have meant that many people in Britain since the late 1980s switched from public to private pension schemes. However, there remains a large outstanding scandal of over-selling these pensions whereby customers were advised to buy schemes which left them worse off than if they had stayed in SERPS or equivalent occupational pension schemes. The slow speed at which compensation for this mis-selling has been dealt with has itself become an issue. *The Independent*, five days after the Labour general election victory, under the headline 'Treasury summons for pension firms', said:

'The heads of the 20 largest pension companies have been called to a meeting with Treasury economic secretary Helen Liddell on Wednesday, at which she will tell them to speed up compensation for the pensions mis-selling scandal or face action. Of the 600,000 people who were identified as having been wrongly persuaded to switch from their company schemes to less favourable private pensions, only about 7,000 have so far been compensated. A Treasury spokesman said: 'Mrs Liddell is making pensions mis-selling her first priority. She is coming from the consumer's point of view and is determined to meet the pension firms and find out how they intend accelerating and improving compensation'.

(*The Independent* 12 May 1997)

The origins of the specific scandal lie in the New Right policies of the Conservative governments of the 1980s and their desire to remove the state wherever possible from economic life and open up areas for private entrepreneurship, initiative and profit making. These changes were driven by ideological considerations but had practical consequences of leaving hundreds of thousands, possibly over 1 million people, worse off. Sales staff sold over an extended period, 1988–94, pension schemes to many people who would have been better off staying with their company schemes. It might, perhaps, have been anticipated that an emphasis on deregulation, on individual initiative and the view of pensions as a financial service supplied for a profit, would lead to a lack of objective advice on the part of those with a financial interest in the sale. However, the intention was not for such a headlong ill-advised rush into private pensions, which has in the long term undermined the credibility of the private sector in administering the nation's pensions.

When the scandal was revealed in 1994 the scale of the problem was daunting and no firm numbers of people involved were available. It has been suggested that up to 1 million people and £11 billion of compensation are involved. At this time the financial regulators insisted on compensation but they were part of a complex and divided regulatory system. The companies and pensions advisers involved took a very long time to identify cases and work out compensation. The government of John Major and financial regulators were very desultory in pushing the issue, which was highly embarrassing to the then Conservative government, as it undermined its position on such an important issue in which it and the financial institutions had common cause. In 1996 some financial advisers were made an example of and fined. The fines, totalling £405,000 plus costs for rule breaches in pension transfers, were the first imposed by the investments regulator (*The Independent* 15 October 1996). The pace of compensation was exceedingly slow. In March 1997 the Personal Investment Authority (PIA) came under severe criticism by a Commons Select Committee for its handling of the 'mis-selling' review. Three years after the review was started, more of the 570,000 'priority cases' of mis-selling had died than had been offered compensation. It is reported that the PIA's internal Pensions Unit, set up to deal with pensions sold by firms that are no longer authorized or have gone bankrupt, had at that time awarded compensation to just one person out of a total of 300,000 cases to be dealt with (*Financial Times* 4 June 1997). The pressure on the regulators, advisers and companies to pay up received a substantial boost when Labour came to power under the lead of the new Treasury minister Helen Liddell. A new regulatory framework for the financial services industry was also set up which brought together the previous organizations dealing with the issue. Compensation payments have been speeded up but, at the time of writing, the process is far from complete. Indeed the relationship between the Labour government and the finance industry is at a crucial phase with Labour wishing to introduce its own pensions plans and personal savings proposals. Labour will require the cooperation of the pensions and finance industry in general to make its own plans work. Helen Liddell, the minister who proved effective in getting action on this issue, was moved to strengthen Labour in Scotland prior to elections for a Scottish Parliament and has been moved on again subsequently.

What interests are at stake and who are the protagonists in the conflict over the mis-selling scandal? If we look at the newspaper reports of the scandal and see who are issuing press releases and expressing opinions, it is possible to identify a range of people who are seeking to apply pressure. These include proximate parties; people who have a direct financial stake, for example, those people who have been mis-sold a pension; and more distant parties, who use the issue to campaign for tightening of legal regulation and to advance the interests of their members. Even those who are in line for compensation have diverging interests about which cases get dealt with first. The way the regulatory authorities have pursued the matter means that the younger victims of the scandal are treated as non-priority in favour of those who have already retired. There are also the estates of dead victims who have claims that need settling. Phase One was for people close to or past retirement who had been wrongly sold pensions. It is estimated that this group's compensation bill will total £4 billion to £5 billion. Phase Two is for people more than 15 years away from retirement and numbers up to 1.8 million people. Compensation in this tranche could reach £6.6 billion, bringing the final cost of the scandal to £11 billion. Thus age-based categories of people have come to have divergent interests with respect to this scandal.

The whole issue is extremely complex, which is perhaps one reason why it has not been pursued vigorously in the popular press. The different kinds of savings and pension products involved produce different liabilities and potential outcomes. The pensions industry, for example, sought to have 'rebate only' pensions removed from the list of cases to be reviewed on the basis that these people had opted out, not in order to increase their pensions, but as a manoeuvre to reduce contributions (by taking advantage of the subsidies available) and thus to increase their take home pay. However, it has been ruled that these cases must be looked at eventually. There are so-called 'orphan clients' where the financial advisers who sold them the pension have gone out of business and who cannot therefore make a direct claim against those most directly responsible. Occupational pensions schemes and those that represent them have taken a watching brief. Their interest lies in sustaining viable occupational schemes which were being undermined by the advantages being given to private personal schemes. The Trades Union Congress (TUC) and individual trade unions on behalf of workers have taken an interest not only in pensions in general as part of the social wage but specifically on behalf of members in SERPS and occupational schemes. The Consumers' Association has also taken an active interest in the issue, seeing it as part of its job in ensuring that consumers' interests in fair and accurate information, enabling them to make informed purchases, are applied in the area of private pensions. Also, the Labour Party saw the issue as one which (in addition to the ideological and welfare issues) it could use to undermine the Conservatives' image of financial competence.

There are equally a wide variety of interests on the other side – those who are required to compensate the victims and who more widely are adversely affected by the steps taken to redress the scandal. There is the financial industry in general, with a range of interlocking commercial and financial interests. This industry not only has an interest in short term profitability but also has a need to retain the integrity of financial institutions and the confidence of the public. The balance of interests for particular firms shifts, depending on the extent to which institutions are involved specifically in the pensions business. Even companies directly involved differ in the extent to which they are liable and thus, for example, the speed at which they wish to proceed in processing claims. The pensions were mis-sold not only by companies who themselves provided the pensions product, but also by independent investment advisers. Again the size of firm affected their interests and their priorities in dealing with the problem. Some of the small independent investment advisers were in danger of being bankrupted by compensation claims and the larger firms in the industry set up a fund to bail out small advisers. They saw it as essential to maintain both the reputation of the industry and a sales network. The employed and self-employed insurance sales staff found themselves at risk from the scandal, some lost jobs (even though they had not necessarily behaved disreputably) and some faced legal and even criminal liability. It has been argued by some, including the pensions companies, that those people currently paying premiums are in effect paying for the compensation. Ironically it is not salespeople who gained commission, nor executives who received bonuses, nor the Treasury and its political masters who encouraged sales, who will pay for the compensation to victims.

How these conflicting interests become manifest can be illustrated by an example of a specific exchange of views. The Institute of Actuaries who, in response to the Financial Service Authority (FSA) consultation about how to proceed on the second wave of compensation, argued for more targeting. They were opposed by the public sector trade union, Unison. The institute governs the UK's actuaries, who have played a critical role in the pensions débâcle, including assessing the compensation due to the victims of mis-selling. The *Independent on Sunday* (14 June 1998) reported that the Institute of Actuaries criticized the FSA for potentially wasting money and resources – and depriving urgent cases of speedy compensation – unless its plans to deal with the second wave of pensions mis-selling compensation were improved and targeted directly on the most needy cases. If the investigative resources (i.e. actuaries' time) were spread too thinly this would mean that victims, who needed help most urgently, might have to wait a long time before they knew what compensation they would receive. The institute wanted to see the FSA concentrate on employees who opted out of occupational pensions and joined a private pension scheme and who also had left jobs or had been made redundant. The institute estimated there were 154,000 people in this situation and their average losses ran at between £3,500 and £7,520 per person. However, a pensions officer at the public sector union, Unison, argued that all the cases should be addressed because in practice people are caught up in more than one category and there is no good reason why one group should carry less urgency than any other. Both organizations were seeking to assist the victims but Unison gave priority to the generality of its members in employment who were affected, while the professional association draws attention to the efficient use of its members' time.

It is also possible to look at the issue in terms of the personnel involved, to identify the extent to which there is an interlocking group of similar people who form a power elite (*The Independent* 2 November 1996). The same people appear to change jobs freely between the commercial sector; as managing directors and senior managers in pensions and finance, as top administrators in the regulatory authorities, civil servants and banking officials in both private and public spheres. From one side the petite bourgeoisie, the entrepreneurial class, resent this technocratic elite – a managing director of a Leeds-based group of independent financial advisers is quoted by the *Financial Times* as saying:

> The PIA is full of civil servants from the top downwards. What you need is practitioners, rather than Ms Bowe and her merry crew – if you have not been in the trenches, you do not know the job.
>
> (*Financial Times* 4 June 1997)

People championing the victims of the scandal are also wary of this elite. The all-party Treasury select committee accused both Ms Colette Bowe, the Personal Investment Authority's chief executive, and Mr Joe Palmer, the chairman, of taking a 'passive' attitude to their work (*Financial Times* 4 June 1997). Ms Bowe is a former civil servant with the Department of Trade and Industry. The Labour Party before the election criticized Mr Palmer's position as chairman of this key regulatory body given his previous role as head of Legal & General, an insurance company heavily involved in the problems of pension mis-selling. Another member of this elite, the chairman of the UK's biggest network of independent financial advisers resigned from the board of the Personal Investment Authority when his company, DBS Financial Management, was fined a record £425,000 for pensions mis-selling failures (*Financial Times* 2 September 1997).

Conclusion

Clearly the British electoral process only very weakly reflects older people's interests. The political parties do not appear to regard older people as a strategically important set of voters whose interests must be assiduously addressed. In Chapter 7 we examine the extent to which older people are effective in organizing around their own interests and pressing effectively to be heard. It is clear from the previous discussion that the politics around pensions has since the mid-1980s been largely about the pensions of future generations rather than the incomes of current pensioners.

7

National politics 2: participation, pressure groups and advocacy

Chapter 6 looked at why and how old age and pensions have become key contested areas in national politics. This chapter asks why do elderly people appear to play such a small part in that debate? If the argument in Chapter 6 is correct and that it is not possible to find systematic evidence of the influence of older voters on the democratic process in a manner which advances their collective interest, why is this? What explanations can be advanced for the relative lack of influence of older people on political parties and national politics? There are two kinds of explanations that will be explored in this chapter. The first is at root a social psychological explanation. This points to an innate conservatism in older people, a fixity in perspective and a lack of willingness to change attitudes and behaviour. The result of this rigidity of opinion, it is argued, is that politicians do not find it worthwhile changing policies and programmes to attract the votes of older people who will not respond but merely continue to vote the ways in which they have always done. The second is a structural argument about the organizations which represent older people. It seems to be difficult for older people to develop organizational structures within which to mobilize and through which their interests can be represented effectively. There seems to be a significant difference between the UK and the USA in the extent to which older people are an effective pressure group.

Patterns of voting by elderly people in the UK

We can examine the theme of the supposed conservative nature of elderly people, from a number of directions. Old people might be characterized as culturally conservative, old fashioned and less willing than younger people to adopt new styles; we explore this issue in Chapter 9. We can also ask 'are older people politically conservative?' Are they conservative, both in the sense of voting and holding beliefs which are to the right of the political spectrum, and in the sense of reluctance to change voting habits and patterns built up over a lifetime?

Using the series of British Election Studies conducted after each general election since October 1974, we can look at the relationship between age and the party that people voted for. Interpreting figures derived from such surveys must be done with considerable caution. The limitations of opinion polls tend to be well known. They are sample surveys and subject to sampling error. They depend on people's recollection of how they voted and their willingness to tell interviewers the truth about their voting behaviour. The overall result of the poll can of course be compared to the final results declared at the election. It has been shown that there has been an increasing reluctance on the part of Conservative voters through the 1980s and 1990s to declare their vote to survey organizations. Further definitions which allocate people into age bands and cohorts are also arbitrary and subject to reporting and other errors. When it comes to allocating people into social categories on the basis of occupation (or husband's occupation) there are further problems. There are distinct drawbacks to allocating an older widow to the occupational category of her husband when he worked 30 years previously. Nevertheless, the *British Election Surveys* are conducted in a highly professional manner, and represent some of the best available data with which to explore these issues of politics and old age. The surveys were carried out on large samples of the population over 18 and recorded their opinions, reported voting patterns and personal details on the general elections held between October 1974 and May 1997. The figures presented in Table 7.1 represent percentages of those in each survey who reported how they voted and reported their age or date of birth.

Voting behaviour, age groups and cohorts

Thus one can use, for example, the 1992 *British Election Survey* (Heath *et al.* 1993a) to note differential voting patterns by age. In the 18–25-year-olds category 24.5 per cent reported that they did not vote while in the 66 and over

Table 7.1   Age related voting behaviour from *British Election Surveys* 1974–97

Age group voting stability	1997	1992	1987	1983	1979	1974 (Oct.)
% of 18–25 voting Labour	32.4	28.4	40.2	22.3	30.7	36.2
% of 26–35 voting Labour	37.3	30.1	34.1	21.6	27.4	32.0
% of 36–45 voting Labour	39.4	27.2	27.5	22.3	32.4	38.0
% of 46–55 voting Conservative	21.6	44.1	46.4	37.4	40.5	31.4
% of 56–65 voting Conservative	25.4	37.4	43.9	38.6	41.3	35.8
% of 66–75 voting Conservative	26.1	40.8	41.1	39.4	42.9	36.2
% of 76 and over voting Conservative	32.2	51.6	55.9	47.0	49.3	46.6
Total % voting Labour	37.9	29.1	30.3	23.2	31.2	35.2
Total % voting Conservative	20.3	38.9	42.9	36.7	38.8	29.7

Source: Author's analysis of *British Election Surveys* 1974–97 (Crewe *et al.* 1981; Heath *et al.* 1983, 1993a, 1993b, 1998).

category only 8.8 per cent did not vote. Older people are more likely to vote and, despite the particular problems with the electoral role caused by the 'Poll Tax', which was reflected in the under-registration of younger people, this pattern appears to be more generally true in other elections and other western countries. On a simple basis it is possible to show a moderate association between age and the party voted for. Among the young age group, 18–25-year-olds, 30.2 per cent reported they voted Conservative, 28.4 per cent Labour and 12.9 per cent Liberal Democrat. Of the older age group, 66 and over, the proportions were 42.2 per cent Conservative, 29.7 per cent Labour and 11.6 per cent Liberal Democrat. As a proportion of the age group who actually voted, the survey suggests about 8.6 per cent more Conservative support in the older as opposed to the younger age group, while among the 18–25-year-olds there were 5 per cent more Labour voters and 4.3 per cent more Liberal Democrat voters than among the older group. This greater tendency for older people to vote Conservative is repeated over successive elections.

These figures show that older people are more likely to vote Conservative. Higher proportions of older people vote Conservative in successively older age groups. This pattern fits all elections except the 1987 election. In the majority of elections the youngest age group is most likely to vote Labour. Younger age groups appear to be more volatile in their voting allegiance. It is important to remember these are aggregates of people, different samples taken at different periods and do not necessarily reflect the changing voting habits of individuals. There are a variety of factors which could explain these voting patterns.

One possible view is that these features are cohort rather than age based. In other words, that today's older voters are only carrying through a tendency to vote to the right that they developed in their formative years. This seems a more plausible explanation than the idea that as they get older, voters are more susceptible to right wing ideas. With the data from the *British Election Surveys* we can look at cohort voting patterns. The cohorts used in Table 7.2 are defined in ten year age bands labelled by their mid-point, i.e. the 1905 cohort consists of those people with a birth date in the years 1900 to 1909, and the 1965 cohort consists of those people with a birth date in the years 1960 to 1969.

Table 7.2 Cohort voting behaviour from *British Election Surveys* 1974–97

Cohort voting stability	*1997*	*1992*	*1987*	*1983*	*1979*	*1974 (Oct.)*
1905 cohort % voting Conservative	60.7[a]	70.2[a]	58.9	55.8	54.5	41.6
1915 cohort % voting Conservative	35.1	53.1	46.6	47.8	46.9	41.5
Total % voting Conservative	26.4	45.7	44.0	45.2	46.9	35.9
1955 cohort % voting Labour	41.3	34.6	31.6	27.8	38.6	51.8
1965 cohort % voting Labour	40.7	36.0	40.7	31.8	39.4	too young to vote
Total % voting Labour	49.0	34.2	31.2	28.6	37.7	42.5

Source: Author's analysis of *British Election Surveys* 1974–97 (Crewe *et al.* 1981; Heath *et al.* 1983, 1993a, 1993b, 1998).
Note: [a] The small numbers of people in the cohort who survived and voted meant that the survey identified only 26 individuals in this category in 1992 and 17 in 1997

Table 7.2 shows a clear preference by the 1900–09 cohort for the Conservative Party, and they demonstrate the stability of voting patterns established at an early age. However, the increasing trend demonstrated in the figures (even discounting the very small numbers in the 1992 and 1997 survey) towards a greater proportion of the cohort voting Conservative over time could either be an ageing effect or, most likely, a cohort survival effect. In other words, their social and demographic characteristics give people who vote Conservative an increased chance of a longer voting life. Given the earlier mortality of manual workers and the greater longevity of women, this would seem a plausible explanation. In 1979, 61.1 per cent of voters in the 1900–09 cohort were women and 48.5 per cent of these voted Conservative compared to 39.7 per cent of the men. Women made up 65.8 per cent of the same cohort in the 1997 survey (when they were aged over 88) and despite the trend against the Conservatives, 48 per cent of them voted Conservative (although it has to be said the sample numbers are very small). Manual workers formed 52.5 per cent of the 1900–09 cohort for the survey in 1979, only 30.2 per cent of whom voted Conservative. In the 1997 survey manual workers formed 53.1 per cent of the cohort, 29.4 per cent of whom voted Conservative. The small numbers in this very old cohort make it difficult to draw firm conclusions. Nevertheless, the survival effect is also visible in the rather larger '1915' cohort (born 1910–19): see Table 7.3.

In the 1992 *British Election Survey* (Heath *et al.* 1993a) respondents were asked to indicate the strength of their opinions on a variety of issues. Some of these can be seen to be relevant to the debates about the extent to which elderly people use their votes to look after their own direct interests. Respondents were asked to grade their opinions on whether government should raise taxes and spend more on services or cut both taxes and spending on an eleven point scale. In response 64.3 per cent of all age groups indicated some degree

Table 7.3 Comparison of the 1910–19 cohort votes in October 1974 and 1997 general elections

Cohort born 1910–19	1974 election (aged 53–64)	1997 election (aged 78–87)
Number of respondents in cohort	1639	184
Proportion of managers in sample[a]	12.6%	22.8%
Proportion of managers who voted Conservative[a]	47.3%	40.5%
Proportion of manual workers in sample[b]	39%	26.7%
Proportion of manual workers who voted Labour[b]	58.1%	49%
All voters voting Labour	35.2%	37.9%
All voters voting Conservative	29.7%	20.3%

Source: Author's analysis of *British Election Surveys* 1974–97 (Crewe *et al.* 1981; Heath *et al.* 1983, 1993a, 1993b, 1998).
Notes: [a] Registrar General's classification of occupations into higher and lower managers
[b] Registrar General's classification of occupations into skilled, semi-skilled and unskilled manual occupations

Table 7.4   Government (A) v. individual (K) responsibility for standard of living (percentages)

	18–25	*36–45*	*Over 65*	*all*
A	40.1	36.1	38.1	37.8
A, B, C + D	82.9	77.5	67.4	79

Source: *British Election Survey* (Heath *et al.* 1993a)

of agreement with the ideas of increasing taxation in order to spend more on services; 65.5 per cent of 18–25-year-olds and 58.9 per cent of over 65-year-olds also expressed this opinion. Only 12.1 per cent of 18–25-year-olds compared to 23.3 per cent of over 65-year-olds expressed the strongest level of support for the 'tax and spend' option. In response to a similar question asked in 1997 on a three point scale, 69.9 per cent of all ages favoured increasing tax to spend more on education, health and social benefits. Both 18–25-year-olds (55.2 per cent) and over 65-year-olds (65.2 per cent) expressed less support than the middle aged for this opinion. A similar age group comparison can be made of opinions associated with the economic role of the state. Respondents in 1992 were asked to rank on an eleven point (A to K) scale between the views that the government is responsible for jobs and providing a good standard of living in contrast to the opinion that people should get ahead on their own (see Table 7.4). Young people show some trend towards being more receptive to the view of state responsibility and the older voters to more individual responsibility. These opinions, however, do not match with the idea of older voters acting as an interest group to obtain a redistribution through the state in their favour. They indicate a general support across the age groups for the welfare state.

A tendency to conservatism amongst older people might suggest that they change their views less frequently than young people. However, simply to ask how long people have held an opinion is not a sufficient measure, because obviously older people have been around a longer time than younger people. Nevertheless, when people are asked when they made up their minds how to vote, their replies show a distinct contrast by age. In the 1992 *British Election Survey* (Heath *et al.* 1993a) 27.7 per cent of 18–25 voters said they made up their minds 'a long time ago' while 29.4 per cent of the same age range made up their minds 'during the election campaign'. In contrast 69 per cent of the over 65 age group had made up their minds a long time ago while only 11.9 per cent said they made it up during the election campaign. Older people seem to have more fixed voting habits. This analysis then tends to support the view that the firmly held views of older people and their lack of change in voting behaviour limits their influence with politicians sensitive to shifting voting intentions.

Participation and representation by the older population

Party politics is only one way in which the interests of older people might get articulated in British politics. Single issue and pressure group politics are the methods by which various interests seek influence. Does the problem of older people articulating their interests lie in the structure of the British political system? To what extent are older people able to form their own organizations with which to lobby and campaign? There are a variety of groups which identify themselves with the interests of some, or all, elderly people. The major players in this form of politics include pressure groups on pensions and charities.

The National Federation of Retirement Pensions Associations calls itself 'Pensioners' Voice', which is also the name of its newspaper. It dates its origins from 1938 and was formed for pensioners to organize 'to alleviate the distress and hardship of those subsisting on a state pension to ten shillings weekly, a rate that had been fixed in 1919' (Pensioners' Voice nd). There are local branches which send resolutions to an annual conference. It sees itself primarily as a non-party-political campaigning organization. The National Pensioners' Convention was formed in 1979, encouraged by the TUC, Age Concern and Help the Aged, and sought to develop as an umbrella movement of national pensioners' associations to agree on representations to government. The bodies loosely linked initially were the Transport and General Workers' Union Retired Members' Association, British Pensioners and Trade Union Action Association, National Federation of Old Age Pensioners' Associations and the National Federation of Post Office and Telecom Pensioners. A variety of local groups and associations and trade union branches have also become involved (National Pensioners' Convention 1998). The Association of Retired Persons and those over 50 (which is abbreviated to ARP/O50) was formed in September 1988; it engages in anti-age-discrimination campaigns, for example on health and employment issues and for equalizing state pensions for men and women starting at age 60. It also emphasizes social activities and collective benefits. It has local 'Friendship Centres' and arranges, for example, holidays and insurance for its members. There are also the Campaign Against Age Discrimination in Employment which started in 1988, the British Pensioners' and Trade Unions Action Association and the Employers' Forum on Age founded by a series of 'blue-chip' British companies to promote the benefits of a mixed age workforce. There are also a large number of regional and local pensioners committees, often supported and promoted by local government and trade unions.

However, in terms of financial resources, staff and range of expertise and activities these groups are dwarfed by the two major old age charities Age Concern and Help the Aged. In terms of influence, when the media look for comments on older people issues, they usually turn first to these two major national charities for older people. Similarly, when consulting on proposed legislation or policy, governments will frequently turn in the first instance to these organizations. Help the Aged, at the time of writing, is sponsoring a network of self-help groups 'whose aim is to appeal for older people's interests in local and national policy-making' (*The Guardian* 13 October 1998) and Age Concern is running the 'debate of the age' urging people to have their say in the future of old age. Why are charitable groups such as Age Concern or Help the Aged so dominant in articulating the voice of elderly people whereas disabled groups or other minorities demand the right to represent themselves?

The 1997 British Society for Gerontology Annual Conference at Bristol held a session in which the possibilities and problems of combining the work of the disability movements and those of older people were discussed. From the point of view of those advocating older people's interests, the disability movement may seem like a model of self-advocacy. Disabled people have through the 1990s successfully taken control of the task of representing their collective interests. However, there are a number of problems for older people following this route and doubts have been expressed as to whether disabled people are an appropriate comparison. Certainly, many associated with the Third Age movement have sought to disentangle the image of elderly people from illness and disability. Neither disabled people nor older people are an undifferentiated interest group. They both, in order to form effective pressure groups, have to work hard to maintain unity of organization and purpose. For example, pensioners' lobby groups are seen as representing only currently retired, not future pensioners (Townsend 1997). Those with physical disabilities do not always make common cause with those with mental disabilities. Physically disabled people for example have been reluctant in some cases to incorporate those with mental handicaps within their organizations. Indeed, even within the disabled movement there are divergent priorities between those with differing disabilities. For example, those with a visual impairment, paraplegia or a muscle wasting disease would tend to rank priorities for aspects of transport and access, and hospital and respite care, differently; however, they would all agree about the importance of civil and legal rights, and the principles of self-realization for people with disabilities.

Charities, despite the best of intentions, may become dominated by professionals who form the full-time staff. These people have other interests of their own, over and above those of the people whose cause they seek to advocate. Critics of professional advocacy, as opposed to self-advocacy, suggest that those employed in such a capacity tend to reach an accommodation with existing power structures in a manner which does not disadvantage their own careers. This accommodation will mean that they limit their objectives and will avoid militant tactics. Some disabled activists believe that able-bodied advocates cannot represent interests of disabled people effectively and have advised older people to build their own self-help movement. All the major charities and groups who represent the interests of older people would agree with the desirability of older people organizing and representing themselves. To many the issues are seen as practical ones and the inability of some, particularly of disadvantaged older people, to represent themselves. To others, these attitudes appear patronizing and to gloss over key problems about who has the ability to set the agenda, and the potential for the advocates to become middle men and brokers with their own vested interests. Jack Jones's introduction to the National Pensioners' Convention pamphlet *Pensions not Poor Relief* states:

Should pensioners speak up for pensioners? The National Pensioners' Convention (a combination of most pensioners' associations and groups) says YES!

(National Pensioners' Convention 1998: ii)

Even leaving aside the issues about paternalism and advocacy, charities have a variety of other problems in actively representing the interests of elderly people. Their legal status creates a problem. The laws of charity in the UK prevent charitable organizations acting in a manner which might be described as political. A number of charities have sought to enter political debates, because they see the interests of those whose suffering they are seeking to relieve to be profoundly influenced by the actions of government. The Charity Commissioners have the responsibility to regulate the activities of charities, and in addition to attempting to ensure financial probity they also police the political non-involvement of charities. For example, Oxfam, which saw government policies towards Third World countries and aid policies as a key campaigning target, was warned by the Charity Commissioners about the implications of political involvement for its charitable status. In 1998 the Royal Society for the Prevention of Cruelty to Animals (RSPCA) had to re-examine a long-standing campaign against blood sports because of a legal opinion that it could be jeopardizing its charitable status. Charities like Age Concern and Help the Aged are engaged in campaigning on issues, and do seek to raise public awareness of issues affecting elderly people, but are limited to the extent that they cannot actively engage themselves directly in the political process. Charities value their political neutral role as this enables them to act as experts and consultants when not only government (in particular), but also other bodies, seek information about elderly people and their views. For example, when the new Labour government started the 'better government for older people initiative', Age Concern and the Carnegie Institute were invited to become involved, a role their directors and experts could not have played if they were directly involved in overt strategies for political or interest group objectives.

A further structural impediment for these charitable organizations to act as a political pressure group on behalf of older people is a financial one. These charities' prime initial purpose was to raise funds for the relief of poverty amongst the older population. Their income is in large measure raised through charitable donations (although increasingly their income is also derived from contracts and grants from national and local government in return for provision of services). Their financial viability, then, stems not from the interest group of older people whom they might seek to represent but from the wider donating public, grants and contract awarding authorities. There is at least a potential, if not an active, conflict of interest, between the requirements of an organization not to offend those who provide its funds and the needs of elderly people for significant changes to their social and political position. The history of disability charities reveals the extent to which the traditional disabled charities have been sidelined by activist movements of disabled people vigorously representing themselves.

Participation

There is a broad movement to encourage both participation by those who use the services of local government and voluntary organizations. Indeed participation has become part of the legislative framework for British local government and is reflected worldwide (Thursz *et al.* 1995). There are initiatives and some funding to ensure that the 'voice of the consumer' is heard in planning new health and social services and commenting on performance. There have been numbers of schemes to devise procedures through which the most disadvantaged groups, including elderly and disabled people, could be enabled to express their opinions. These schemes ranged widely. They included advocacy schemes, whereby people specially trained and designated to work with elderly mentally ill or young people with learning difficulties, collected and expressed views on behalf of their people to service providers. There were specialist forums established, for example under the 'better government initiative', sometimes based on localities, sometimes on actual or potential service users, in which local authorities committed themselves to listen and act on the opinions expressed. Although these schemes are in the most part valuable, it is important to understand that the driving initiative for them comes from the service providers and the professionals within them. They are consultation processes not decision making processes. As was found, for example, with the community development movement of the early 1970s, such consultation was empowering and beneficial in the short term and on a small scale, and thus not to be dismissed lightly as irrelevant, but did not fundamentally change power structures. They are a mechanism for improving service delivery, they do not reflect an increasing power of older people to assert themselves and set a political agenda.

This apparent lack of powerful lobbying and campaigning organizations run by elderly people for themselves is not because older people are reluctant to join and participate in collective institutions. Sainsbury's (1993) research on war and industrially injured pensioners illustrates the fact that people wish to integrate themselves into 'normal' society and not to separate themselves off into a special group. She reports that there was a reluctance on the part of war pensioners and industrially injured people to involve those outside the family in their day to day care, and this was matched by their insistence on achieving normality in their leisure time primarily through the family. These people, by and large, lived sociable lives. Pubs and clubs were highly popular and as many as three-quarters of war pensioners and industrially injured people had visited a pub or drinking club in the previous week.

> However, in many ways analysis such as this understates the formal commitment of war pensioners and industrially injured people to integration and normality: As many as three quarters demonstrated their integration by membership of formal associations of people which had nothing to do with disability, such as religious groups, clubs, political parties, trades unions, professional associations, and so on. And even among those who made no such claims there appeared to be a widespread undercurrent of feeling that is was desirable to join such groups.
>
> (Sainsbury 1993: 189–91)

By no means everyone actively participated in the organizations to which they belonged. Sainsbury states that 40 per cent of her informants were trade union members of whom two-thirds had been to at least one meeting in the course of the previous twelve months, while one-quarter usually attended meetings. This demonstrates not only a high degree of active support but also participation compared to able-bodied trade unionists. About one-third of war pensioners and industrially injured people belonged to religious organizations, of whom a little more than half attended a religious service at least once a month. Among members of political parties, active participation was less likely: about one-tenth belonged to a political party, and of these a little more than half had attended at least one meeting in the previous twelve months. Sainsbury (1993) reports club members amongst her sample as invariably involved in active and regular participation. In all, approximately one-third of war pensioners and industrially injured people belonged to clubs, including 11 per cent to those associated with hobbies such as model building, 2 per cent to sports clubs and most of the remainder to drinking and social clubs such as the British Legion, Working Men's and Conservative clubs. Although Sainsbury argues that it was membership, rather than involvement, which was crucial in staking a claim to normality, such figures also indicate that such pensioners are no less 'joiners' than the rest of the population. It is not organizational commitment or competence which lies behind the reluctance of older people to campaign in their own interests, it lies more in their attitudes and beliefs.

> They were prepared to pursue nominal involvement in mainstream organizations such as trades unions, professional organizations and drinking clubs to the exclusion even of interest groups of disabled people. Few belonged to such interest groups: although many belonged to the British Legion it was as a drinking club rather than a pressure group – in general war pensioners and industrially injured people showed little interest in or sympathy for its political role.
>
> (Sainsbury 1993: 219)

This ability of older people to organize rich collective lives for themselves is amply illustrated by the work of Myerhoff (1978) on a Jewish community of older people in California and also by the study of Merrill Court, a residential development for older people by Hochschild (1973). Merrill Court is described as the 'unexpected community' and Hochschild points out the irony involved in the fact that these 'fundamentalist widows from Oklahoma and Texas', who had retired to the shore of San Francisco Bay, should be among those least likely to talk about 'communal living' and 'alternatives to the nuclear family' even while they had improvised something of the sort. Their community is presented as a mutual aid society, as a source of jobs and fulfilling activity, as an audience, as a pool of models for growing old, as a sanctuary and as a subculture with its own customs, gossip and humour (Hochschild 1973: ix). Myerhoff's work, which in many ways was ground breaking in both social gerontology and social anthropology, demonstrated not only the ability of older people to run very full and rich community lives, but also the creativity of older people. The ability of the community she studied to invent new rituals clearly demonstrates that old people are culturally innovative. She recounts the example of the graduation ceremony of a Yiddish history class (Myerhoff 1977): it was a powerful symbolic construction, built from elements of Yiddish and American culture and woven into a performance, which expressed the specific values and dilemmas of their community.

There have been two primary sources of recruitment for activists for pensioners' organizations. These organizations have been based on people from both the trade union movement and ex-service personnel associations. These people's commitment has frequently stemmed from situations in which working people have had to organize to protect themselves and have drawn on the social solidarity engendered in their middle years as fellow workers or comrades in arms. As a result the organizations, even given the demography of older people, tend to be male dominated. Trade unions allow members who have retired to continue as members. They participate variously, according to the different union rules, in a separate retired section, or as full members of their previous branches. The trade union movement, both in its values and objectives on the one hand and its organizational skills and procedures on the other, has been the backbone of the active political organization of pensioners. At every Trades Union Congress in recent years there has been a rally of pensioners lobbying for a better deal. Their objectives have usually been formulated as a restoration of the link between pensions and earnings, and the reinstatement of the decline in the value of the pension in the period that it was decoupled from earnings and linked only to prices. Jack Jones, the former general secretary of the Transport and General Workers' Union, has been a leading campaigner (as was the former miners' leader Joe Gormley). Thus trade union organization and leadership have been mobilized to achieve improvements in income and living standards of the working class through the universal state pension. This left wing agenda is also reflected by former Labour leaders such as Barbara Castle, a former cabinet minister and MP for Blackburn, who has campaigned for restoration of the value of the pension and used her position within the Labour Party to speak out against a leadership unwilling to take on the financial consequences for the exchequer of these demands.

The treatment of ex-service personnel is a highly potent political issue. The role of the state in rewarding its military servants for services rendered formed a key part in the origin of the institution of the pension. The rise of the nation state saw the concomitant development of the citizen-in-arms. The conscript armies meant that most men had experience of national service. The duty to defend the nation could be linked to the duty of the nation to provide for its elderly. According to Achenbaum (1997), the Grand Army of Republic, the civil war veterans' organization, proved highly successful 'in getting its snout into federal coffers'. This organization started as a drinking club for soldiers, but then came to demand pensions and old soldiers' homes. The organization's influence in the key US state of Ohio, which held a particular importance in presidential elections at this time, led to extension of pension rights. These were successfully extended to all veterans over 65 and those with a disability had an automatic pension. Pensions for veterans ended up in 1914 as 18 per cent of the federal budget. These benefits were for the armies of the Union, the southern states had to look after their own. In the UK, those who fought in the First World War were promised they would return to a land 'fit for heroes'. A decent pension was seen as the necessary reciprocity of sacrifice in war. Thus ex-servicemen's associations of various kinds have taken a lobbying role in seeking to advance the level of payments made to pensioners. Not only the British Legion, but the British Limbless Ex-Servicemen's Association, the Burma Star Association and similar organizations have sought to ensure financial support for their particular constituency of pensioners.

Campaigning

Despite this demonstrated ability of older people, given the opportunity, to organize their community life to good effect, national organizations, at least in Britain, do not seem to demonstrate the same dynamism. However, we should not confuse the routine lack of interest by the media in their activities as a lack of commitment or ability on the part of such organizations. For example, on 2 December 1998 a campaign was launched in the Houses of Parliament to protect people against age discrimination at work. The campaign 'Equal Rights on Age' brought together, the National Association of Retired People and those over 50, Age Concern, the Campaign Against Age Discrimination in Employment, Carnegie Third Age Programme, Help the Aged, National Federation of Post Office and Telecom Pensioners, and the Third Age Employment Network. There are campaigning organizations and alliances of older people's organizations fighting for better pensions in Britain. These groups tend to be small and comparatively fragmented, but the most influential is the umbrella organization – the National Pensioners' Convention – whose best known activists include Jack Jones and Barbara Castle. The Pensioners' Party put up some candidates at the general election but obtained very few votes, and while there are a number of organizations with aspirations to the status of an older people's national campaign, there are no UK pensioners' organizations which can automatically command the attention of all leading politicians and set the terms for national debate on old age. While older people seem well represented in terms of local groups, this local participation of elderly people does not seem to get effectively channelled into a firmly based national movement.

Bornat *et al.* (1985) in their *Manifesto for Old Age* included an appendix for contacts, which listed two organizations of older people – the National Federation of Old Age Pensioners' Associations and the British Pensioners and Trade Union Action Association – and then 16 charities and foundations. The position remains similar at the end of the 1990s. There are increased numbers of older people, and the state pension has declined in value considerably since that time, but despite an increase in awareness of old age issues, there are few signs of a significant increase in activism amongst older people. Many of those supporting the pensioners' movement do so not to support a specific age group or cohort, they do so out of a sense of social justice or as part of a broader progressive social movement to produce a fairer or more equal society. Hence the difficulty in mobilizing sets of people defined by their age in a political context. This can be seen to be reflected across Europe by the opinions expressed to the European Barometer, where well over three-quarters of the population of most countries (including the UK) believed that 'older people should stand up more effectively for their rights'. However, only small proportions (22 per cent across the EU) of older people said they would join a political party formed to further their interests (Walker and Maltby 1997: 111–12).

Lobby organizations in the USA are much more developed than in the UK

Many political analysts and media accounts attribute substantial political power to elderly people in the USA. It is important to distinguish between the power of older people to veto changes which work against their interests and the positive ability of older people's institutions to effect social change. There has been a growth in the study of the history of 'elder power' in the USA and their influence on social legislation (Pratt 1976; Haber and Gratton 1994; Elman 1995; Achenbaum 1997).

In the period between the two world wars the US Federal government was resistant to the idea of an industrial pension. As in the UK, there was a lobby of liberal reformers and academics for social security programmes including old age pensions. These relatively small groups were dwarfed by the Townsend movement which mobilized up to one-tenth of the US elderly population (Elman 1995). The first Townsend clubs were founded in 1934 and in the 1934 elections several Townsend-endorsed candidates got into Congress and were highly vocal (Pratt 1976: 23). The depression was important in triggering collective action which crystallized around the ideas of Dr Francis E. Townsend for solving the economic crisis. It was his belief that, by giving pensioners 200 dollars per month on condition that they renounced employment and spent all of their allowance, the increased demand would lead to a revival in the economy and greater tax revenues with which to pay the allowance. Pensions were thus presented as a scheme which looked after the interests of everyone. The Townsend movement fell apart in 1939 surrounded with financial scandal. However, the Roosevelt administration did introduce the federal pension system as part of the New Deal policies of the 1930s.

Achenbaum (1997) presents a fourfold classification of old age interest groups in the USA after the Second World War but suggests they were all predominantly middle class in character. His first type were the professional organizations, then advocacy groups, interest group liberalism and finally mass membership organizations. Among the professional groups he includes the American Gerontological Society and the Western Gerontological Society which then became the American Society on Aging. Advocacy groups, in this typology, included the Gray Panthers organized by Maggie Kuhn and the National Caucus on the Black Aged and the Older Women's League (OWL). The mass membership movements included the National Retired Teachers' Association, which allied itself to the American Association of Retired People. In 1976 Pratt stated that there were ten organizations in the USA engaged in politics at the national level and more or less exclusively preoccupied with old age problems. Four of these were trade associations with a narrow focus – the American Association of Homes for the Aging, the American Nursing Home Association, the National Council for Health Care Services and the National Association of State Units on Aging (NASUA). Pratt lists the National

Council on the Aging as a loose confederation comprising specialists in the field and public and private social welfare agencies. In addition to groups mentioned above, he quotes the National Council of Senior Citizens and the National Association of Retired Federal Employees as mass membership organizations.

The most powerful and well organized lobby for older people in present day USA is the American Association of Retired Persons (AARP). It has a modern organization, membership payments are made by standing order, and a minimum commitment to the organization brings with it life assurance benefits and travel and drug discounts. It is a highly profitable organization of 35 million members, and is listened to and seen as a powerful interest group by the US political establishment. The AARP was founded in the 1960s by Dr Ethel Percy Andrus. Its leadership is democratically elected at biennial convention and members have a say in the formal policy decision making process. There is a continuous process of policy analysis and advocacy of the associations policies into the US legislative process. At the federal level, AARP's advocacy effort is managed and coordinated by the Federal Affairs Department and supported by the work of the Public Policy Institute. While much of the day to day lobbying is performed by the professional staff in Washington, members of the Board of Directors and the National Legislative Council, along with other association officers, regularly testify on Capitol Hill on behalf of AARP. The Department of State Legislation is responsible for the coordination of advocacy at the state level, but the volunteer state legislative committees, acting within nationally established policies, formulate and identify public policy goals for each state. State legislative committees and capital city task forces, where they exist, then actively promote the adoption of those goals by the state legislature or state agencies.

Elected politicians tend to be keen to respond to AARP because of its size and potential for mobilizing votes. The association has a direct electoral role in advising voters. It has an arm of the organization, called AARP/VOTE, that is charged with informing the public about where the candidates for public office stand on old-age issues. Through mechanisms such as sponsorship of candidate debates and dissemination of written voters' guides, AARP/VOTE can influence the electorate. Although the British Association of Retired People and those over 50 models itself directly on AARP, it does not have the same size and influence as its US counterpart. It claims about 100,000 members and 160 'Friendship Centres'. Perhaps one reason for this is the existence of the NHS, which means that medical costs are less pressing on older people and the benefits of collective insurance and organized medical consumers are less relevant in the British context. Further, in the UK there is not the same tradition of interest group politics. The British party system is organized historically around more ideologically based parties. Although the UK has a range and diversity of organizations of older people, these do not have the size and resources, even in proportional terms to the American situation. The UK has a strong voluntary service sector, and organizations *for* older people and charities are numerous and in some cases control considerable resources. Campaigning and lobbying organizations *of* older people do not seem to have the membership or influence of their US counterparts.

Street and Quadagno (1993) provide an important cautionary note to the general view that older people form an effective pressure group in the USA. They argue that it is necessary to question the views that age against youth is an explicit conflict, that elderly voters act self-interestedly and vote as a bloc. The preceding analysis has suggested that such views do not reflect the British context. The US attribution of senior power is usually made in the context of the politics of Social Security and Medicare. Street (1997) contrasts the conventional construction of elderly political actors as a special interest group successful in extracting the spoils of 'pork barrel' politics with a more critical perspective that views Social Security and Medicare as citizens' rights. She uses a political and moral economy framework to analyse the welfare state's role in creating age as a potential political cleavage. In her view, investigation of the politics of Social Security and Medicare reveal no undifferentiated politics of ageing in the USA. Rather, age interacts with a variety of other statuses, such as race and ethnicity, gender and class, to condition citizens' political mobilization. Welfare state policies – social insurance programmes like Social Security and Medicare, means-tested programmes like Medicaid, are targeted tax expenditures, and reflect the power of revenue contributing groups. Similarly access to private pension and health insurance differentially empower particular subgroups of elderly citizens and routinely disadvantage the most vulnerable elderly including minority elders, women and the oldest old. Thus, the essence of Street's (1997) argument is that the fragmentation of elderly people means that older people do not have the unity of interests, or the self-perception of themselves as a group with a common interest, to sustain an effective solidarity.

Conclusion

Older people tend not to act collectively or vote together, even though many share common experiences of dashed expectations of income and support in old age. Achenbaum (1997) argues that in the USA old people do not vote differently than the rest of population, although they tend to vote more. As we saw in Chapter 6 this is also true for the UK. Voters in both the USA and the UK do not tend to vote as an interest group. The reluctance of older voters to shift their votes deprives them of the political clout they might otherwise expect. Achenbaum (1997) questions whether the 'baby boomers' generation may behave differently and to show less historical party allegiance. Both Achenbaum and Street emphasize that, in the USA, social security issues fragment older age groups. If their characterization of 'grey power' as a myth is true of the USA, with its tradition of interest group politics and highly organized lobby system, how much more is it true for the UK. Older people's collective interests do not get reflected through the political process in the UK. Even for the USA, Palmore (1990: 32) says: 'politicians do not usually behave as though they were strongly influenced by senior power.'

Contrary to the argument that there is a problem of age inequality, which all experience in later life in modern societies, numbers of writers have sought to identify the upcoming generation of elderly people as privileged compared to future generations. The discussions of generational equity which have been particularly powerful in the USA have focused on whether, rather than elderly people being a disadvantaged sector of the population, they are consuming more than their fair share of society's resources to the detriment of younger groups, particularly children. These propositions are premised on assumptions about older people's numerical importance as voters and their effectiveness as an interest group. The image of self-interested elderly people who, as a result of demographic changes taking place in the contemporary west, have created a bloc of older voters who by their size can dominate the agenda, seems (on the evidence presented above) not to be true. On the contrary, there appears to be a need to combat ageism, in order to sustain political pressure in favour of effective welfare programmes, including provision for our old age, it is necessary to stop fragmenting sections of the lifecourse into rival elements.

The burden of this chapter is to argue that older people do not seem to carry the political weight ascribed to them by others. It may be that statistical analyses by Pampel and Williamson (1989) and others (O'Connor and Brym 1986; O'Connor 1990; Pampel and Stryker 1990) suggest that where there are more older people, the greater the welfare state expenditure on older people. However, even if these correlations are valid, and there must be severe doubts about the concepts and data that are used in such studies, it may be that it is the belief of decision makers that older people do have electoral power that inclines them not to cut specific expenditures. However, this assessment of older people's electoral impact is wrong. I believe that it is possible to demonstrate that elderly people are not successful in setting a political agenda. They do not influence the party manifestos or the electoral debate, and do not set them terms for broader political competition. Further, older people do not act electorally in their own interests. They do not engage in tactical vote switching in order to gain either direct personal gain from welfare benefits or organize their votes in a way which benefits older people as a group. Thus not only do older people not think and act as an interest group, but also they do not organize effectively to focus objectives and achieve them. Compared to groups who are much smaller, for example farmers, gun owners or police officers, they are relatively ineffective. Even taking into account their difficulties of physical mobility and resources, older people do not mobilize militant support in the manner of road protesters, animal rights or disabled activists. While pensioners' organizations are able to hold mass meetings, marches and lobbies they do not attract the attention or the political clout that the numbers of older people in the community suggest they might.

8

Generational politics: population change and intergenerational solidarity

The central issue of this chapter is the question of generational politics. Does an ageing population – an increasing proportion of the population in the older age group – create problems for society? What is the significance of this demographic change? The image of a timebomb is used to suggest the fearsome nature of demographic change. Headlines such as 'Grey timebomb at the heart of the Western welfare state' (Ian Traynor, *The Guardian* 27 January 1996) or 'Wrinklies timebomb waiting to explode' (*Sunday Times* 23 February 1997) have become increasingly frequent. Neasa MacEarlean (*Observer* 23 June 1996) wrote: 'The IMF [International Monetary Fund] believes that the restructuring of labour markets is crucial to the long-term economic prospects of the EU. Developed economies also need to tackle the pensions, healthcare and general welfare issues raised by the "demographic timebomb".'

It has been suggested that the current generation of older people will obtain an unfair share of resources compared to the generations which follow them. The intergenerational equity argument centres around two aspects. One is the cost of income maintenance and the command that growing numbers of older people will have over a share of the available wealth. The second is the cost of medical treatment for an ageing population. It is argued that an older population is a sicker population and that this will create increased financial burdens on the rest of society. Is the conflict over resources in terms of medical treatment and income maintenance one in which age groups form genuine interest groups with conflicting interests? There is much talk about growing intergenerational inequalities and the possible breakdown of the so-called intergenerational contract (Walker 1996). Do people of different cohorts have conflicting interests which are becoming increasingly significant? An examination of the bases of social solidarity in contemporary society, and the suggested social fragmentation of society by cohort, age group and lifestyle, will be used to critically examine these questions. The first section of the chapter looks at the demography of the issue – the numbers and changes involved in an ageing population in the UK and across the world. We can also examine some of the associated issues over the health status of an ageing population. This discussion should provide a view of the social dynamics associated with population change. The second section of the chapter examines the ideas of equality, social justice and social solidarity which form the rhetoric within which the proper relationship between generations is debated.

Demographic concerns

Changing proportions of older people

The size of a population depends on three things: the number of babies born, the number of people who die and the numbers of people who come and go. Demography at its simplest deals with three variables, birth rate, death rate and net migration. Similarly, the demographic balance between the size of different age groups in a population also depends on these features. To explain the size of a particular age group, you have to be able to answer a series of questions. What was the size of the birth cohort which now occupies a particular age range? At what rate did the members of the cohort die from birth to their current age? How many of the cohort have emigrated and how many have replaced them?

The proportion of older people in the British population is growing and, as a result of declining fertility rates and increased longevity, is likely to continue to grow until at least the year 2040. Contrary to popular belief, it is not an increased life expectancy but rather a decline in the fertility rate which is the principal cause of the current population ageing. Between 1971 and 1991 the percentage of the population over retirement age increased by 2 per cent but the percentage aged 16 or under declined by 5.2 per cent (see Table 8.1).

One of the successes of modern society has been to improve the health and increase the life expectancy of people. People are now much more likely to live a full span and die in their 80s. Current British life expectancy at birth is approximately 74 years for men and 80 years for women. The difference in life expectancy is slightly less at age 60, when men can anticipate a further

Table 8.1   UK population by age group 1971–97

Population	1971	1981	1991	1997
UK population (millions)	55.9	56.4	57.8	59.0
Population aged under 16 (%)	25.5	22.3	20.3	20.5
Population between 16 and retirement age 59–64 inclusive (%)	58.2	59.9	61.4	61.4
Population over retirement age 60–65+ (%)	16.3	17.8	18.3	18.1
Population aged 75+ (%)	4.7	5.8	7.0	7.2

Source: Calculated from *Population Trends* 92: Table 6

18 years to age 78 while women can typically expect to have a further 22 years of life to age 82. The age of death and length of life appear to be becoming more standard, although as more people are living to older ages, there is a debate as to whether the maximum available lifespan has been reached (Victor 1991; Gilleard and Higgs 1998). Census forecasts in 1998 by the UK Office for National Statistics (*Population Trends* 91) suggest that the number of pensioners will have risen from 10.668 million in 1996 to 11.956 million in 2021 with 5.36 million aged over 75. However, this is affected by the raising of the pension age for women, and had it remained static at 60, the total population of pensionable age would have been projected as 14.0 million in 2021. At the same time the working population will increase from 36.035 million in 1996 to 39.229 million in 2021. This means that if the ages from which the state pension is paid are not changed again, that part of the dependency ratio which relates the numbers of people 'of working age' to the numbers of people over retirement age will fall from 3.38: 1 in 1996 to 3.28: 1 in 2021.

The demographic position for the UK is that its population will age less quickly and to a lesser extent over the next 40 years than much of the rest of the world and indeed of Europe. This is because, as a nation, the UK went through the 'demographic transition' earlier and at a slower rate than other countries. The number of people aged 65 and over per hundred people aged 15–65 in Europe stood at 15.1 in 1960 but is expected to double to 29.1 by 2025. In the UK the equivalent figure will change from 17.9 in 1960 to a predicted 29.7 in 2025. This changing ratio is a feature of all industrialized countries. It is most significantly a feature of those societies whose birth rates declined rapidly in the 1950s and 1960s (Hills 1993). In Europe, while Sweden has a relatively old population at the present time, countries like Italy, whose fertility rate has transformed much more rapidly, will in the first part of the twenty-first century see their population ageing even more dramatically. Ireland, Portugal and Greece, with relatively high proportions of rural population and strong religious attitudes on birth control, show signs of following a similar route of declining fertility rates followed by an ageing population but somewhat later than the rest of the EU (see Table 8.2).

The diversity within the world-wide pattern of population ageing is very large. Within this diversity, Europe has characteristically the oldest populations (Day 1992; Walker and Maltby 1997). The UK doubled the proportion of its population aged 65 and over from 7 per cent in 1930 to 14 per cent in 1975, a 45 year period. In contrast, in France and Sweden (with traditionally low fertility rates), the equivalent transition took 115 years from 1865 and 85 years from 1890 respectively. Japan has undergone the same doubling in 26 years from 7 per cent in 1970 to 14 per cent in 1996. It is projected that the world's largest country by population, the People's Republic of China, will make the same transition between the years 2000 and 2027. Both the historical timing and rate of change seem to differ significantly related to patterns of economic development and of attitudes to population and fertility (Kinsella and Taeuber 1993: 3, Table 2.2).

The demographic basis of the concerns over an ageing population is the so-called 'dependency ratio'. This standard index is the numerical relationship between the number of people of employment age and the number of people

Table 8.2   Population over 59 in European countries 1993 and 2020 (percentage)

Country	Population aged 60 and over (1993)	Population aged 60 and over (2020)	Increase
Sweden	22.4	26.3	3.9
Denmark	20.1	24.3	4.2
UK	20.6	25.3	4.7
Portugal	19.5	25.5	6.0
Ireland	15.3	21.8	6.5
Greece	20.8	27.3	6.5
Austria	19.8	26.5	6.7
Luxembourg	19.2	26.3	7.1
Netherlands	17.6	24.8	7.2
Germany	20.4	27.7	7.3
Spain	19.6	27.2	7.6
Belgium	21.1	28.8	7.7
France	18.7	26.7	8.0
Italy	21.3	29.9	8.6
Finland	18.8	28.2	9.4

Source: Modified from Walker and Maltby (1997: 10)

assumed by their age to be dependent. The ratio usually compares numbers of people in an age band defined as economically active (e.g. 16–60 years) with those who fall outside that range. A 'gerontological ratio' is sometimes calculated by comparing the numbers of those aged 16 to retirement age to the numbers above that age. As the population ages these ratios change. The gerontological ratio increases as the older cohorts get larger relative to the rest of the population. The dependency ratio also tends to increase but this is somewhat offset by the fact there are fewer children counted amongst the 'dependants'. Problems are thus assumed to arise because those in older age groups are seen as unproductive and a burden on society. Their growing needs for income and health care are seen to fall on a smaller number in the age groups assumed to be 'productive'. Some demographers (Kinsella and Taeuber 1993) have used a parent support ratio which compares the numbers of people in a population who are aged over 80 with those (sometimes only women) who are aged 50 to 64 years (see Table 8.3). This index seeks to measure the amount of family support available to older people who are most likely to need high levels of social care (cf. Qureshi 1996).

There has been relatively little analysis of the movement of older people. There has been interesting work on retirement migration (Warnes 1987; King *et al.* 1998; Warnes and Pearson 1998) but the intergenerational equity argument pays very little attention to such issues (Vincent 1996). Migration patterns (Ferris 1993; Weiner 1995; Williams *et al.* 1997) will have significant consequences for future cohorts of elderly people. The rural–urban migration of predominantly younger people has led to the ageing of the countryside across the world (Sen 1994: 10). The social significance of long distance and global migration has changed as a consequence of dramatic improvements in

Table 8.3   Parent support ratios: selected countries 1950–2025

Country	1950	1990	2025
Bangladesh	2.4	3.0	3.5
China	2.5	7.2	12.4
India	3.0	4.6	7.6
Indonesia	4.3	2.8	9.4
Japan	4.5	13.0	45.3
Brazil	4.1	7.2	10.5
Mexico	6.0	10.6	11.9
USA	8.0	21.5	24.6
Germany	6.0	19.9	43.3
Greece	9.0	17.1	36.7
UK	9.0	23.7	30.1
Sweden	9.3	28.8	38.2
France	10.1	25.9	31.6

Source: Extracted from Kinsella and Taeuber (1993: Table 9)
Note: Parent support ratio is the number of persons 80 years and over per 100 persons aged 50–64

transport with cheaper and easier travel. Thus, intercontinental migration may not limit generational interaction because expanding communications technology and the transport revolution may facilitate ongoing contact. However, the social barriers erected by cultural assimilation of migrants also disrupts intergenerational expectations of old age and the final part of the life-course (Askham *et al*. 1993; Blakemore and Boneham 1994).

Population projections, like all other forecasts of the future, are never precise and always prone to error. The projections are only as good as the assumptions on which they are based. This uncertainty about population projections does not seem to figure strongly in the arguments of those suggesting that there is a problem of intergenerational justice. However, it is precisely embedded in those assumptions about the direction of future change that the crux of the debate lies. One of the most crucial aspects is the period over which the projection is calculated. The selection of 30 or 40 year projections are important to creating the idea of a problem or crisis. Short term projections, say over 5 or 10 years, do not support alarmist scenarios, and the demographic changes anticipated do not look insurmountable. Projections for the period 2045 to 2060 and beyond show negligible increases in the over-75 population for major European countries (Day 1992: 16). Making very long term projections over 100 or 200 years, directs attention to other, particularly environmental, issues. Such long term projections could plausibly anticipate low and stable birth rates with concomitant stable proportions of younger and older age groups in the population.

Health and old age

The extent to which an older population can be thought of as problematic depends, to considerable measure, on expectations about the health of the population, about what is required to keep a population healthy, and about who bears the cost of health care. Stahl and Rupp Feller (1990: 30) state that equating old age with sickness is an 'ontogenetic' fallacy, and argue that adaptation during the last decades of life is an extension of successful strategies used throughout life to achieve positive and healthy lifestyles. Using data from the *General Household Survey* and from the *Health and Lifestyle Survey*, Victor (1991) explores both the health status of older people and their use of health and social services. This information suggests that the moral panic which has developed over population ageing and health is misplaced. Although chronic illnesses appear to be more prevalent with age, only a minority of the population is affected by acute and chronic health problems at any age. Indeed, Victor (1991: 67) emphasizes: 'ill health is not a universal feature of later life'.

The American physician, Fries, hypothesized about the relationship between health and age. He outlined two concepts about the health of older people, the 'rectangularisation of mortality' and the 'compression of morbidity' (Fries 1980; Fries and Crapo 1981). The 'rectangularisation of mortality' refers to increasing tendency for people to live their full natural lifespan. This stems from better nutrition, sanitation and ability to control infectious disease, along with an increased ability to prevent premature mortality at all ages. Fries made the assumption that the natural lifespan of the human species is of fixed duration; in his work he takes this as 85 years. The consequence is to greatly increase mortality at the end of the natural lifespan, creating an almost rectangular pattern to the graph of mortality by age. Fries's view is based on an approach to biological ageing which sees death resulting from the body 'wearing out' at the end of the natural span. It follows from this argument that the pattern of population morbidity will be dominated by chronic diseases. If infectious diseases are rendered relatively harmless and appropriate interventions can delay the onset of chronic diseases, then morbidity will be compressed in the final years of life. From this perspective, not only will more people live to the full extent of their lifespan but also the onset of disability will be confined to the last phase of life.

Victor's (1991) assessment of Fries's ideas is that they remain an interesting speculation rather than being conclusively established (although she does consider that they have been of considerable value in that they have challenged the assumptions of many gerontologists and policy makers and forced a closer examination of our knowledge about health and ageing in later life). There are alternative views of ageing which give more weight to social and environmental factors on the one hand and genetic factors on the other. One argument stresses that the median age of death continues to increase at an undiminished rate, whereas, following Fries, this rate would be expected to diminish as the median age of death and the natural length of life come closer together. Moreover, life expectancy in the very old age groups has also continued to increase (Gilleard and Higgs 1998). There are also problems with the compression of morbidity thesis, most notably the lack of any clear and rigorous evidence of decrease in morbidity and the non-availability of measures of morbidity with which to test his proposition which are reliably disentangled from cohort effects (Victor 1991: 42–3). Victor suggests that older people are more healthy than portrayed in popular stereotypes. It appears that acute health problems for older people are little different, in terms of prevalence, from younger age groups. Evidence appears to indicate an increase in chronic health problems with age. However, most of the evidence is based upon cross-sectional data, and therefore cannot be relied upon to separate out the consequences of age *per se* from the cohort effects of the lifecourse of the current older generation. If younger generations do have healthier lifestyles and store up less health problems than those who are now old, we need not expect an increased disability prevalence as the population ages (cf. Gilleard and Higgs 1998; Mheen *et al.* 1998). Can we expect, for example, the current significant gender, class and ethnic differences in health status to be maintained in future generations? The ageing of the population over the next decades need not automatically bring an increase in the number of people with health problems who require care (Stahl 1990; Victor 1991: 74–5).

This debate about the consequences on the resourcing of health care for an ageing population has to be linked to the issues associated with the medicalization of old age discussed in Chapter 5. Within the medical model and, following the imperatives of commercialization, new knowledge about illness will result in new expensive medical technologies. If the medicalization of old age is not assumed to be inevitable, then the alternative models of old age and health provide alternative answers to the challenge of demographic change. There are non-western models of medicine which make different assumptions about old age in particular and, more fundamentally, about the nature of the relationship between people, good health and medical practice. Even within the confines of conventional western medicine, it is possible to place very different priorities on sustaining good health and the prevention of disease than is currently the practice. It is a curious irony that the most accurate and readily available source of information about the 'health' of older people comes from statistics about the extent of death and illness from which they suffer. We know what people die from, but have to make inferences from this about the health status of the survivors. The medical model is particularly problematic in dealing with issues of mental health, and one aspect of this has been discussed in Chapter 3 with respect to Alzheimer's disease. Prevention of mental illness is a very undeveloped subject, yet the psycho-geriatric consequences of the older population are presented as a major source of concern. Nevertheless lifestyle changes are credited with improving health, for example: changes in diet and smoking have led to a decline in the incidence of heart disease in the USA, and changes in sexual practices have changed the distribution of HIV infection.

Redistribution between generations

Are the fears that society cannot afford pensions for all these older people real? It has been suggested that, if pensions are to keep in line with wages as the ratio of workers to pensioners declines, contributions in the UK will have to go up, perhaps by as much as 10 per cent by the mid-2030s (Ermisch 1989: 31). However, Hills (1993) argues, with respect to the upward pressures on

SERPS, higher basic pension entitlements and the ageing population that 'even if benefit levels kept up with overall living standards, the total net effects on public finances over the next fifty years would add up to an addition of about 5% of GDP – no more than the increase (mainly due to the recession) over the past three years' (Hills 1993: 4). Another estimate projects that 40 years ahead overall expenditure on health and personal social services would need to be 12 per cent higher than now to maintain present levels and standards of provision in the UK (Brodie-Smith 1993). However, because most British pensioners have opted out of the state pension scheme (only 17 per cent of employees belong to SERPS) and the benefits of the scheme have been linked to prices not wages (and are currently only about 15 per cent of average earnings) the UK does not face a serious long term problem of financing pensions (Budd and Campbell 1998). Indeed, if these policies are continued it is calculated that in future reductions in contribution rates will be possible.

The World Bank (1994) has been significantly more pessimistic for the rest of the world. Barr (1993: 46) argues that, averaged across the Organization for Economic Cooperation and Development (OECD) countries, pension spending is set to double from 10 to 20 per cent of gross domestic product (GDP) by the year 2040. Bosworth and Burtless (1998) made a comparative study which also suggests that the UK does not have the same difficulties in meeting pension commitments as other major industrial countries. However, Bosworth and Burtless (like the World Bank 1994) anticipate problems for state funded systems and advocate the need to build reserves in funded schemes to meet future pension expectations. The differing calculations and levels of alarm at the consequences of ageing population for government expenditure vary due to a number of factors. The pensions systems, how they are funded and the extent of their vulnerability to demographic change vary widely. Further, the geographical, fiscal, time and demographic parameters chosen for the calculations produce significantly differing views of the future. Because Britain's population aged earlier than other industrial countries and because it spends less on its welfare state than other industrialized countries (Hills 1993, 1996), there is a variation between British and continental European perspectives. Additionally, there are variations in which expenditures and compensating factors are included in the calculations; all welfare expenditures may be included, or only pensions, and sometimes increases in the costs of elderly people are offset against fewer young people and thus less educational expenditure.

> Date of birth is only one of the many characteristics determining how the welfare state affects people. For individuals, the differences in the net life-time effects of the welfare state that result from their income levels, gender and family circumstances may be much more important.
>
> (Hills 1996: 80)

This can be regarded as a sensible assessment and highlights the difficulties and inappropriateness of considering age as an isolated independent factor.

Although these differing estimation procedures are interesting and perhaps useful they are not the key to the issue. The real question is why is the issue being constructed in the way it is now? Population ageing has been going on for most of the twentieth century and the UK is not demographically in a new situation (Laczko and Phillipson 1991: 107). In fact, the rate of ageing of the British population was at its highest at precisely the time during which the British pension system was being established. The average age of the British population started to increase in the first decade of the twentieth century; the rate of increase in the proportion of people over retirement age peaked in the 1930s. Nevertheless, at the time when its population was ageing most rapidly, the British pension system was established and expanded, and proved very popular even though the working population was being expected to find larger and larger sums to support these schemes. This history would suggest that over an 80 year period a population could see a 15 per cent increase in the proportion of its population over retirement age and yet still substantially increase the value of the pension, provided of course that the economic growth equivalent to that achieved over that same period was repeated. However, a 'new ageism' developed in the 1980s and has been prevalent since the late 1980s, particularly in the USA. It identifies the current generation of older people as 'greedy geezers', who are well off and subsidized by poor families. The success of welfare developments, giving minimum security and comparative affluence to some older people, has been used to challenge the idea of the 'deserving poor'. These views grew from the New Right whose desire to 'roll back the state' includes taking away all economic and welfare functions from government.

Labour force participation

The identification of the changing dependency ratio as a problem automatically assumes older people cannot be productive and ignores trends in employment history. Patterns of work and the reasons for non-participation in the labour market have varied considerably over time, but elderly people have not always withdrawn from work. In Britain in 1881, according to Paul Johnson (1985), 73 per cent of the male population of 65 and over were in employment, but by 1981 the percentage had shrunk to less than 11 per cent. This major change in the distribution of work is not because the population has become physically less able and therefore less employable. Townsend (1986) argues that, as there is no evidence that these changes were caused by increased disability amongst older people, these changing employment patterns must reflect either differing employment practices and/or changing lifecourse choices by the older population. Pressures and opportunities for early retirement came with the recession of the early 1980s and have continued into the 1990s with down-sizing and restructuring. There has been a rapid decline in the numbers of older people in work (Guillemard 1989; Laczko and Phillipson 1991). In 1965, 90 per cent of men aged between 60 and 65 years were working but by the end of the 1980s this was down to 60 per cent. The working life has shortened as education has lengthened and the age of retirement fallen. The decline in the ratio of workers to pensioners will depend on the extent to which declining rates of economic participation among elderly people continue.

There is evidence that if employers are willing to recruit older people to work for them there are plenty of elderly people who would like the opportunity. Workers on incremental salary scales close to retirement are relatively expensive and unattractive to new employers, but many employers value older employees returning to work who are regarded as reliable and skilled but who are also willing to do less popular, lower wage or part-time jobs to supplement their pensions. Unfortunately employers also carry many of the ageist stereotypes found in the rest of the population and suspect (wrongly) that illness and inflexibility are characteristics of older workers. Elderly and disabled people in the workforce have been forced out because of absence of opportunity for employment, and many of the supposed 'retirees' did not perceive their retirement as particularly 'voluntary' despite official labels (Guillemard 1989, 1990; Kohli *et al.* 1992). Why should the projected shortage of workers in future not be met by the reversal of this trend with elderly people increasingly participating in the labour force again? Perhaps in the future the work skills of the older sections of the population will become more valued and ageist assumptions about their employability will decline. The intergenerational equity debate, and the affordability of social support for elderly people, have to be seen in conjunction with opportunities for meaningful and rewarding work. It is evident that there is not a current or potential shortage of productive workers, or of useful work to be done: the shortage is in paid employment. There is an all too prevalent social construction by which elderly people come to be viewed as economically unproductive. This idea is embedded in the term 'dependency ratio'. Non-employed does not mean non-productive; it may mean productive potential is being lost, or that useful work is not recorded in national statistics or not recognized by economists.

Even if we make the assumption that there will be no future increases in labour force participation by older workers with which to tackle the changing dependency ratio, labour migration remains a logical possibility as a method for addressing this 'problem'. However, few studies in the UK have ever considered the potential positive effects of immigration (S. Spencer 1994). Numbers of countries have a significant part, even a majority, of their working population who are non-citizens. Conversely, some countries have the majority of their working population working abroad, and in some cases contributing to the pension schemes of the host countries. The exclusion of an active consideration of migration in the discussion of these demographic issues is to tacitly collude in the view that immigration is a problem, indeed that it is so self-evidently problematic that it need not figure in the debate. The apocalyptic population projections (Robertson 1991) are based solely on fertility and mortality rates. They fail to take proper account of potential or even foreseeable trends in migration.

Thus there are many things that could reduce any problems in pension provision as the result of demographic change (Barr 1998: 226–7). These could involve changes in the workforce. For example, more elderly people staying at work rather than retiring early could increase the numbers of employed people paying into pension schemes. Further, a shortage of workers in the UK could be met by importing labour (because the world as a whole is not short of young people looking for work). In addition, a better educated and more productive workforce would mean that fewer workers could generate more wealth with which to share with pensioners. A smaller proportion of workers would not have a detrimental effect on the living standards of the population as a whole if those workers were able to increase their efficiency and produce more. If there is economic growth, the key issue will be one of power and who benefits in terms of increased living standards from such increased productivity. A frequent explanation for increases in unemployment rates in the late twentieth century has been that technological change was displacing labour. Optimists argued that modern automation techniques would provide a world free from want, with everyone gaining more leisure time. Now, those putting forward arguments about intergenerational inequities declare that there will be a chronic shortage of labour necessary to sustain British people in the standard of living (or at least the levels of pensions) to which they have become accustomed.

Redistribution

Several studies addressed the processes of redistribution involved with pensions (Estes and Minkler 1984; Johnson *et al.* 1989; Minkler and Estes 1991; Johnson and Falkingham 1992; Barr and Whynes 1995). Some (Schmahl 1989) have stressed the fact that most national public pension schemes are not funded, i.e. that they are not backed by independent investments but are dependent on contributions from the current workforce to pay for the pension rights of those currently retired. In these circumstances it is clear that if the ratio of pensioners to current subscribers changes, in order to maintain the level of pensions, so must the level of contributions. Private pensions, in contrast, are usually 'funded' schemes in that they represent savings on current income, invested to yield a return subsequently payable as a pension. Professional actuaries calculate the correct balance between the potential liabilities of a fund in terms of the life expectancy of its members and the fund's accumulated assets. The policy preference for each form tends to be couched in the classic collectivist versus individualist moral formulas; thrift, individual responsibility and the rights of property, versus the common good and social justice. However, it is the macro-economic and social level that should be stressed. For whatever the administrative mechanism or the particular pension scheme, from the point of view of the whole society, what is at issue is how the total social production created is distributed amongst different social groups. What proportion of the national cake should elderly people receive? The share of the total social product that elderly people as a group consume is logically independent of the mechanism by which that consumption is secured. When considering on a societal level the consequences of changing balance between age groups it is essentially irrelevant whether pensions are obtained through funded schemes or not. People cannot store goods enough for their retirement and cannot store any personal services they might require (Barr 1993: 49). They must in some way claim a share of what is available at the time.

One potential solution to the issue of funding pensions in the context of changing demographic structures would be to make changes to public expenditure, either to increase it or to redirect it. The UK could divert some of its national expenditure into better pensions. The UK devotes only 9.5 per cent of its GDP to pensions while Germany spends 10.8 per cent, Sweden 11.6 per cent, France 11.8 per cent and Italy 14.4 per cent (World Bank 1994: 358). If we take a wider view of redistribution than who pays and who benefits from various forms of taxation, we can also take into account issues associated with exploitation and non-financial contributions to society's well-being (see Chapter 9). In these terms, the debate about the standard of living of future pensioners becomes one about the rights and claims on a share of society's economic output. Pensions contributions now are essentially buying rights to part of the national income in future. The requirements for a comfortable old age cannot be set aside in a pile in the attic. Altering pension schemes now cannot increase the number of workers available in the future, only alter who in the future can obtain the benefit of the activity of workers in the future. One cannot, for example, store up nursing care and bring it out when needed. The ability of an individual to command the time of a nurse in the future will depend on the number of nurses around and the competition with all the other potential calls on those nurses' time. Nursing care will be rationed (allocated) through some mechanism. There are, however, a wide range of mechanisms through which that might be done. It might be done through a market by allocation to the highest bidder, by apportionment by a professional to the most needy, offered first to those who fought to defend their country or some other process. Savings in the form of pension funds now will not increase the number of active people able to be nurses in the future.

The key question for the living standards of future old people is, what proportion of total production they will receive? Their share of the available income may be conceptualized as due returns on investments, payments for services provided to society in the past, or minimum standard of living morally acceptable to society. Whatever the ideological rationale for particular forms of redistribution are, they do not change the ratio of older people to younger people. Ideologies are, however, important. Persuading people to forgo current consumption for investment or social welfare purposes is a powerful tool for policy makers; the legitimacy of claims to a share in the distribution of production is a central issue in political economy. In particular, the security of decent pensions and living standards for elderly people require an ideological commitment which is reliably reconfirmed from generation to generation. Satisfactory material lifestyles for elderly people depend on both productivity and economic growth and the distribution of the wealth generated by such growth. However, which unit, what kind of society or community within which that distribution, or redistribution, takes place is an open question. Most commentators assume that it is the nation, some argue that it should be the family; I should like to suggest a radical alternative perspective might be considered which covers the whole of humanity. It is essentially an ideological issue as to which social unit is considered to have mutual responsibility for the welfare of its members. How to promote an individualistic stance towards provision for old age, emphasizing choice in a market for pensions, is a key theoretical and policy problem for the Right. In order to successfully privatize pension provision it is necessary to undermine and undo the broader social solidarity on which national schemes are based. Therefore, the final section of the chapter examines some of the issues of social solidarity which underpin the whole intergenerational equity debate.

Intergenerational solidarity and the legitimation of pension schemes

The core of the intergenerational issue is one of social solidarity: what mutual obligations towards securing income in old age are felt by whom? Do different age groups and different cohorts have real conflicting interests? To what extent do age groups act like classes; do they form self-aware interest groups prepared to organize around issues of mutual benefit? In contrast, which groups feel a sense of commonality and an obligation to provide for their mutual support without too close calculation of individual self-interest?

From one perspective, social solidarity across the age range can be seen to be built around reciprocity between generations. This formulation will point to the efforts made by parents for the well-being of their children being repaid by the younger generation to their parents when they need support in old age. Many respondents, asked by researchers about their willingness to support their parents in old age, will cite the obligation felt to return the parental care they received while a child (Asis *et al.* 1995). There is an alternative formulation which sees a great chain, whereby the debt of care incurred by children growing up is repaid to the successive generation through care of the next generation of children. The nature of reciprocity between generations can be illuminated by the response of parents with the particularly agonizing problem of a child with a terminal illness. The fact they do commit themselves materially and emotionally to their children is a clear indicator of the power of the downward obligation, related to the asymmetrical reciprocity between generations (cf. Finch 1987). Life debts for the support from parents are repaid to children. It is children with little or no parental investment who are more likely, when they become parents, to neglect or pass the deficiency in care to their children. It is not parents who can anticipate no return from their children in old age, because their children will not live that long, who withhold commitment and 'investment' in their children. It is important, however, to note that these arguments about reciprocity are constructed within the metaphor of the family. The relationships between generations in families, because of the nature of social solidarity in families, are not subject to judgements about profit and loss. Similarly relationships between wider generations cannot simply be forced into the framework of economistic calculus of self-interest which is necessary to impute a money value to fairness between generations. A direct, specific or calculable reciprocity is thus not necessary for a general society-wide solidarity between generations. What is required is a sense of communal solidarity such that the precise calculus of self-interest is inappropriate.

Solidarity across the generations is essentially a political and a moral question. Cole (1992), Moody (1992), Laslett and Fishkin (1992), Norman Johnson (1995) and Phillipson (1996) have, amongst others, debated the question of generational equity. Many of these discussions start with Rawls's (1971) development of principles of moral philosophy including the idea of a 'prudential lifecourse'. The prudential lifecourse account suggests that we in the current generation, when making decisions about pensions in terms of contributions and benefits, should be careful and cautious about the future, rather than merely hoping for the best. These decisions clearly have to be made with a large degree of uncertainty about the state of the future economy and current decisions should deal with this uncertainty by risk sharing. Each generation should take an equitable portion of the risks involved in perpetuating a stable pension system, and the current generation should not load the risks forward to future generations. Following such a prudential lifecourse should involve keeping sensible reserves, making sensible investments and not raiding assets for short term consumption which would leave successor generations at greater risk of default on pension expectations. For the generational contract to be sustained, it is argued that there must be a measure of trust and solidarity across the generations and that, if the imperfections in the system are to be tolerated and seen as unfortunate rather than exploitative, justice must been seen to be done by each cohort.

These arguments taken thus far seem to me unproblematic. It is when there are attempts to reduce the issue to a technical question and quantify fiscal transfers between generations in a manner which excludes the moral dimension that difficulties arise. The advocates of cutting state pension entitlements in the name of generational justice fail to see that intergenerational solidarity is not achieved through some mythical compact between cohorts. Rather, it is achieved through very concrete interpersonal relationships between old and young in families, communities and other basic social institutions (Irwin 1996). We cannot talk about a 'contract between generations' without an understanding of the webs of interconnectedness within which bonds of social obligation are created and feelings of morality and fairness are sustained. There is a moral economy of pensions and an ethical dimension to the entitlements of older people (Hendricks and Leedham 1991; Minkler and Cole 1991).

The idea of the moral economy draws on the tradition of historical scholarship exemplified by E. P. Thompson (1971), who described how nineteenth-century food riots were seen by the participants as a morally just response to breeches in the concept of a 'fair price' for food. These 'fair' prices were based on custom and need. The idea of a just price has a long history, the clashes took place as the idea of a just price was being crushed and lost to market forces. The idea of non-market prices are also found in the anthropology of pre-capitalist economies, for example, in the work of Polyani *et al.* (1957). Kohli (1991) also uses the concept of moral economy to look at pensions issues and sees not a decline of the moral economy but a shift from a 'just price' to a 'just return for labour'. There is no doubt that the idea of 'a fair day's pay for a fair day's work' is a powerful one in our society. The idea of a moral economy becomes relevant to collective provision of pensions when associated with the idea of the moral lifecourse. A moral economy requires a fair return (in old age) for a fair life (of work and contribution). The moral lifecourse (Kohli 1986; Cole 1992) has clear religious roots but in the modern west it can be an entirely secular concept. It is also linked to the idea of older people as the deserving poor. Such values become a possible and indeed dominant attitude when living a full lifespan becomes a relatively predictable occurrence. It holds that if you live a 'moral life', that is one of hard work, diligence, using your abilities to the full, not idling or squandering your resources, then you deserve to live decently for the entire span of your life, including a comfortable old age and a proper burial. Thus the converse: to die unattended or in poverty at the end of a 'moral' lifecourse is seen as morally outrageous.

This 'moral lifecourse' as part of the modern moral economy is not the same idea as the prudential lifecourse. That concept is based on the notion of a contract or a bargain. It identifies that which reasonable individuals would have done to ensure their own financially secure retirement, as a standard by which to measure the equity of intergenerational transfers. The 'moral lifecourse' is the socially constructed expectation of standards of living for people with unspoiled social identities when they have finished their working lives. Note, for instance, the argument made for relieving elderly people from increased costs for heating due to the imposition of value added tax (VAT) on gas and electricity in 1996. Among others, Michael Heseltine – a senior member of the cabinet at the time – argued that elderly people living on pensions and savings could not work harder or save more to meet this extra cost and therefore they had a moral case to be shielded from the full cost of the new tax. He did not argue that they should have been prudent and saved for such an unforeseen event. The central moral concern contained in the idea of social justice is, for many people, both young and old, that they do not want to live in a society where some citizens are living in increasing poverty while others grow rich. This is a communitarian ideal. The problem of equity is not perceived as one of intergenerational justice, because most people do not think in terms of society as made up of cohorts. Rather it has to do with common humanity, people do not wish to live in a society in which there are others who are in poverty. More precisely the issue is one of moral economy – a set of moral precepts which form the basis of economic relationships.

Most of us experience older people not as an abstract category of the demographers or economists but through specific relationships with family, friends and neighbours. Although we may also, to an extent, experience ourselves and others through recognizing age groups and cohorts, the prime bases for social obligation are located in family and a sense of community. It is insofar as age groups and cohorts are manifest in local groups that genuine solidarity results. When people of a similar age belong to the same club, participate in the same generation linked cultural activities in their local community that such solidarity is strongest. However, sense of solidarity and mutual obligation is constructed culturally and expressed symbolically. Benedict Anderson (1991) calls the idea of nationalism and national solidarity the 'imagined community'. If supra-community groups – groups larger than mutual personal interaction – are to achieve common action and thus any kind of power, they require the successful establishment of a symbolic identity. By and large, in the modern world, age groups and cohorts have not produced powerful cohesive symbols. They, unlike class or ethnic solidarities, are manifest in local community groups as by-products not as the primary overt purpose of their activities. On a national, society-wide, or global level, a sense of identity is created symbolically. Are there such symbols which are effective in uniting age groups or cohorts? It is perfectly possible that age or cohort could form a basis of social solidarity and many argue that such bases are becoming more salient. I would argue in practice, as an empirical statement, evidenced by opinion polls, surveys, ethnographic observation of the behaviour of older people and documentary sources, that such age-based symbols, capable of mobilizing people on a widespread basis, do not exist. Family, kinship and community are much stronger than age in expressing a sense of mutual obligation.

This argument links to the case presented in Chapter 7. There it was argued that old people and disabled people place a high premium on being 'normal'. They do not want to be thought of as old or disabled and treated differently. This is expressed in community life through participation in clubs and social and leisure activities but it is primarily expressed through the family. Older people do not see their primary identity as 'old people' and do not act as if there were age-based social cleavages. The extent to which they identify themselves with an age group is most likely to be on the basis of symbols based in historical events or popular culture. As seen in Chapter 8, cohorts are not social categories which readily form groups and articulate interests. People very rarely identify a cohort to whom they are opposed. In the UK increased organization by pensioners reflects an erosion of their pension entitlement. However, many of those active in the pensioners' movement see the issue as one of class as much as of age. Further, there are no signs of organized opposition from younger age groups to the aspirations of these pensioner groups. On the contrary, opinion surveys indicate widespread support for the state pension, and indeed for improving the level of the state pension, across people of all ages.

Chapter 7 also suggested that it is difficult for age-based interests to be expressed or articulated. This inarticulateness is strongest, of course, for the unborn generations and it is in the name of these unborn generations that important current claims are being made. A sense of communal solidarity is always symbolic. Deceased members of the community (the ancestors) and the yet to be born members of the community therefore stand as particularly powerful symbols of the nature and continuity of the community. Thus claims about future generations are strong symbolic claims about the nature of the community we are or wish to be. There are, on the one hand, statements made about the environment and the obligation not to pass the consequences of our current generation's pollution and resource depletion on to future generations. On the other hand, some from the radical right have claimed to champion these future generations from avaricious current cohorts making unfair claims to a share of their income. Certainly the agenda established by the intergenerational equity debate has been highly selective, concentrating as it has on the cost of state pensions as opposed to the long term cost to future generations of, for example, disposing of nuclear waste. The current recipients of building society windfalls, who are cashing in their elders' prudence and mortgaging successive generations' opportunities for cheap housing loans, seldom consider generational equity.

There is another form of social solidarity: in Tönnies' ([1887] 1955) words *gesellschaft* as opposed to *gemeinschaft*, that is the solidarity of a contractual rather than communitarian nature. Those people who sign a commercial contract, who agree to exchange barley for beans, or pension rights for money, create a common interest in that bargain. Although it has to be noted that there must be a minimum of social order and trust for such exchanges to perpetuate and to build into social solidarity, it has been argued that this form of solidarity is stronger and more reliable for delivering benefits to the older generation in the future. The problem here is the issue of risk and uncertainty over the long periods associated with pension contracts. Given political, economic and social stability and an appropriate level of regulation to avoid fraud and deceit, it might be the case in the short term that a commercial contract is as reliable as a sense of social obligation. However, the experience of Europe through the twentieth century should serve as a cautionary lesson to those who do not question property rights, the value of money and savings and the continuity of private financial institutions. Consider the position of pensioners in Bosnia Herzegovina. Their pension system is a pay-as-you-go (PAYG) system derived from the German model (via the Austrian annexation of Bosnia in 1878). It has survived two world wars and the establishment of two new states, and its problems and durability are highly illustrative. Because the vast majority of people in Bosnia are not earning very much during the current conflict, the payments to pensioners are pitifully low and frequently not enough to sustain life. However, if and when order and a working economy is re-established, the reciprocal right enshrined in the system will again ensure that the elderly pensioners will be able to participate in the revived prosperity. A fully funded system, one which is based essentially on savings, would have been wiped out by the levels of inflation, currency changes and the destruction of physical assets experienced in the former Yugoslavia. It is perhaps not surprising that attitudes seem to differ between Europe, which has experienced wholesale destruction and economic collapse due to war, and the USA which has not experienced invasion, territorial redistribution and systematic destruction of economic infrastructure in war.

The rise of Fascism in Germany has been linked in part to the failure of financial institutions to protect the living standards of the older middle class. In the aftermath of the First World War, poverty in old age was increasingly considered to be a 'mass problem'. This was not only because of the consequence of demographic change, but also, and to a much greater extent, the result of the massive inflation that occurred between 1920 and 1924. In particular, for the first time the middle classes were forced to experience a dramatic worsening of their economic and social situation in old age. The group of pensioners most affected were *Kleinrentner*, (small-saver/private pensioner) whose savings and private pensions had completely lost their value. Indeed they were in a worse position compared to the *Sozizalrentner*, (National Insurance pensioner) who received pensions from the PAYG social insurance system (old age, invalidity, accident and survivors' pensions). The group of *Kleinrentner* consisted mostly of people who had formerly been self-employed, craft workers or rentiers. Even more important numerically were the widows and unmarried daughters of the formerly economically independent bourgeoisie.

These women had thought that they could depend in their old age on their savings and securities but instead found themselves destitute. The frustration and anger of these pensioners was enormous since the new Weimar Republic proved to be incapable of compensating them. They blamed the republic for actually trying to cheat them. In the early 1920s, a group of these *Kleinrentner* established a self-help organization (Deutscher Rentnerbund) which pursued an aggressive policy with strong right-wing inclinations (von Kondratowitz 1990: 15). The Weimar Republic did not survive. The Nazi regime which displaced it was defeated after the devastating Second World War. The German people have retained a high degree of concern over monetary stability and a loyalty to state pension schemes to the present day.

It may well be that in the long term and taking into account the full range of insecurities, relying on the social power of reciprocity and a collective sense of social responsibility is a stronger option than individual investment plans in funded pension schemes based on the concepts of private property. There is something very American about the generational equity debate which stems from the radically different North American experience, where there is very long political continuity and it is over a century since war crossed its territory. Their experience of social security is very new and limited, while the European experience is that pensions systems have frequently outlasted states and constitutions particularly over the course of two world wars. Given this history, it is not surprising that in the USA a greater proportion of people see their old age more reliably secured through private property, and leave unquestioned the political underpinning of those rights, than is the case in Europe.

Conclusion

Apocalyptic demographers have provided the New Right financiers with a rhetoric with which to convince people that current pension arrangements are unsustainable. As a consequence many people seek to protect their own living standards in old age by buying private pensions and there has been an enormous growth in the pensions industry. Pensions are one of the biggest issues on the domestic political agenda (as discussed in Chapter 5). It has been suggested that what is at stake is a fair distribution of society's resources between the generations. It is argued that the younger age groups are being disadvantaged by paying for the pensions of the current generation of older people, however, because of demographic changes they cannot expect to be able to receive a pension of equivalent standard from the succeeding generation. This inequity, it is alleged, will lead to a breakdown in the intergenerational contract – the implicit agreement that one generation will support the previous one in old age. An analysis of these questions has shown that despite the way it is frequently presented, this problem is not merely, or at all, a demographic issue. The issue is in essence one of redistribution and the role of the state in evening out unacceptable inequalities of wealth (cf. Day 1992).

The construction of the pensions issue as a demographic problem gives it the force of impersonal inevitability backed by the scientific knowledge of demographers. This is necessary because state pension schemes have a high degree of legitimacy. Entitlements and their levels are strongly morally charged issues. The terms in which the debate about the future of state pensions needs to be set is one in which social solidarity and the moral obligations to others is at the forefront. Attempts to generate insecurity about that collective provision will have the effect of a self-fulfilling prophecy. If a pseudo-scientific argument is constructed which claims that the state pension is not a moral issue but a technical one, in which the experts reveal that the state pension system is unsustainable, pensions can be privatized and large capital is able to control the necessary private savings and create new mechanisms of exploitation. If sufficient insecurity and doubt can be spread about the future of the pension it will succeed in undermining those webs of social support which currently sustain it. Constructing the issue of the demographic timebomb potentially leaves individuals vulnerable to the whims of the financial markets in the manner such that their arguments can become a self-fulfilling prophecy.

The key politics of intergenerational equity is about legitimacy. It is about the loyalty and commitment to different social groupings. As Phillipson (1996: 219) says, 'we should not "offload" the responsibilities for an ageing population to particular generations or cohorts'. The argument about the future of the welfare state and its relationship to private markets arises not merely out of trends in intellectual fashion, it reflects a balance of power in society. One of the features of capitalist markets is that they generate differentiation. This is sometimes extolled as choice and difference but it also means a wider gap between rich and poor, and increasing social divisions. The welfare state commanded widespread legitimacy because it limited risks for most citizens and provided a reasonable balance of costs and benefits for the majority of people. The effect of giving free rein to markets and modern capitalism is social division, represented not least by high rates of unemployment. There is now, consequently, such a large social distance that on the one hand, there are people who will bear few of the costs of the welfare state and will gain a significant proportion of their income from it, while on the other hand, there are those who pay taxes and contributions but who see their affluent lifestyles as protected by their private schemes for health and pensions. The welfare state remains the most efficient way of delivering the utilitarian principle of the greatest good for the greatest number, but its universality has been undermined by social change. In the UK, the proposed private top-up pensions cannot provide an adequate replacement for a basic state pension set at a reasonable level. The problem with the proposals are that they are limited by what people can afford. In a society which is growing more unequal, to institute a social mechanism for pension provision which depends on individual lifetime earnings, will exacerbate those inequalities in later life.

The problems are, however, global in scale. Almost all discussions of these kinds of issue, around intergenerational equity and funding arrangements for pensions, treat individual nation states as the unit of analysis. Nations are not isolated populations or economies. An appreciation of both global demographic and economic change are necessary parts of a full understanding of the intergenerational equity issue. The major economic institutions of the world are multinational in character, be they multinational firms such as Ford or Phillips, or supranational institutions such as the EU or the World Bank. The extension of free markets across the world have lead to significant increases in economic growth and trade. The investment of pension funds are made on a worldwide basis. Pensions, savings and investment portfolios cannot be insulated from major changes in the global economy. Even at present, significant portions of British pension funds are invested abroad and accumulate value through the work of people overseas. Neither the contributions, nor the investments, nor the payments from a pension scheme are limited to the boundaries of the state. We live in a global economy and a global society and therefore to consider these demographic issues on the basis of individual countries and as single isolated economies is to manufacture an artificial problem (cf. Morris 1997). Looked at from a global perspective, the problem is not a shortage of workers willing to work and support pensioners, rather the significant problem is how to bring a modicum of financial security to people whatever their age in all parts of the world. The same relationships between demographic change, social solidarity, redistribution and a secure old age discussed above apply on a global as well as a national scale.

Globalization impacts on local economies, welfare states and pension schemes in two principal ways. First, it makes the return on investment on any funded schemes consequent on the success and failure of the global economy as a whole, and the ability of the institutions controlling the funds and their dispersal to extract a return on those investments. Second, there are social impacts, global free markets are even more divisive on an international level than they are on a national scale. The security of globalized market capitalism depends on solving the classic dilemma of giving the 'have nots' enough stake and interest in the system so that they do not disrupt it, but not enough that this reduces profitability, or over-taxes the 'haves'. An alternative short term solution is military repression. However, the reliability of pensions schemes tied to international financial markets depend on long term global political and economic stability. The supranational institutional structures with the requisite powers for ensuring such stability do not yet exist.

The conclusion to this excursion into futuristics is that in the long term market forces can deliver good secure pensions only by supporting some form of global welfare state which ensures the required worldwide social stability. Thus the key to a stable, enduring, prosperous old age – whether incomes for elderly people are delivered by private companies, state institutions, funded or PAYG schemes – is the level of social cohesion. There must be a minimum of social solidarity which confers legitimacy on economic institutions and thus enables people to trust that their interests will be sufficiently well protected so that they do not undermine the system by apathy, corruption or violence. This observation is applicable to both national and global levels of analysis. It is in the developing world, where the majority of people have no pension rights and whose future in terms of employment is far less secure than those experienced in the affluent west (even after down-sizing and growth of contract employment), where the majority of the world's working population will be located in the future. Global demographic trends and the access to pension rights will tend to produce a distribution of pensioners which follows the north–south divide. There are those who have suggested that it will be a problem to persuade the workers of the future to pay for the pensions of their co-nationals. But pension funds invested on an international scale, perhaps to circumvent the demographic problems of the developed countries, will require a continuing stream of repatriated profits. What will persuade the young workers in Asia, Africa or Latin America, that part of their productive effort should be diverted to support the living standards of older people in the states which were their former colonial masters? Class, race and generation divisions are not limited to, or even primarily based in, national political economies. If intergenerational solidarity is to be a problem for national societies in providing for the older sections of their populations then it will also be a problem on a global scale.

Cultural politics: consumers and consumption

Knowing older consumers – critical questions in gerontology

Where do older people fit into class politics? This chapter is an attempt to understand the position of older people in the totality of contemporary capitalism. We therefore examine the processes which structure exploitative relationships between social groups. Consumption is a dominant method by which people are integrated into contemporary political economy. What specific disadvantages does the domination of culture by selling, and society by consumption, create for older people? We know who we are by what we buy – what does this mean for older people? Further, the chapter is a debate between political economy and postmodern approaches to the study of society, and tries to locate the study of older people as part of broader agenda.

Consumption as a social process

The idea of political economy – society as a division of labour in which the dominant social groups are formed around the way in which the product of collective work is distributed through society – is the foundation of class analysis. From this perspective those who control capital, in the modern world, control society. The failure of the Soviet Communist Party to replace class politics with a classless utopia still leaves a world in which the dominant political conflicts are about the economy and who benefits from the way it is run. Understanding the nature of capital, and the particular division of labour associated with it, leads to a very powerful set of insights through which to understand contemporary society. The principal benefit of this approach is the totalizing perspective which tries to understand, in global historical terms, the development of different kinds of social systems. This benefit has also been a source of major criticism as the method has sometimes (too often) been reduced to a schematic simplification which purports to scientific status and predictive power. It is in this exclusive claim to knowledge that the post-modern critique of all 'grand theories' lies. This chapter works through a political economy of global capitalism in the late twentieth century to look at the specifics of the position of older people within it. It will be suggested that their particular position in relation to capital produces certain kinds of vulnerability and lack of power. We then move on to assess the postmodern critique and see what relevance this critique may be thought to have for older people and the purpose of social gerontology.

The idea of capital – on which capitalism is based – is not essentially or fundamentally encompassed by numbers in a bank account or even the machines, factories and bridges which might be seen as its material manifestation. Rather, capital is a social relationship. It is a social relationship which involves the rights and responsibilities of private ownership; the exclusivity of private possession against those who are not owners. The social division of society, into the owners and controllers of capital, and the host of changing technically skilled operatives and those who provide labour power, is necessary to make capitalist society work. Thus historically, the major social divisions in capitalism have been ones based on the conflicts of interest between the productive classes and those who control capital and, as a result, this is what political economists have tended to study. However, at the end of the twentieth century there are many other social cleavages embedded in the contemporary form of capitalism which dominates the world economy. The competitive nature of capitalism requires that it is socially dynamic. The technical and social organization of the economy changes and new divisions of labour constantly arise. Capital cannot stand still, it must continually circulate. Idle machines, factories, or unused bridges do not produce anything useful. For capitalist society to work, wealth must accumulate in the hands of capitalist entrepreneurs.

Although it is self-evident that useful things are produced only by people's work, it is very far from obvious in today's complex society how the benefit from useful work becomes distributed across society. The relationship between people's contribution to the collective effort and their rewards for their contribution is obscure. If a woman working in the chocolate factory takes home a bar for herself, she is likely to be accused of theft – she has no rights in the product of her work. She will probably take home cash wages, but will these be worth more or less than her contribution to the value of chocolate she helped to produce? If it is worth less, who gets the rest? If it is worth more, who has lost out? Is it the cocoa farmer, is it the owner of the factory, the owner of the land on which the factory is situated, is it the person in the corner shop who sells chocolate bars, or is it the street child who cannot afford to buy a chocolate bar? The more complex the society, the more complex the answer to such questions about production and distribution of surplus value. In modern capitalism access and control of markets is as much a problem as the historically important issues of the organization and control of labour. In political economy, exploitation has a technical meaning. It is not merely an accusation of unfairness but describes the accumulation of the value of other people's work. Such accumulation of capital is essential for a modern economy and is the basis of the investment from which people in the affluent west derive their standard of living. However, exploitative relationships can exist in many forms; for example, payment of dividends to shareholders, requiring bribes for production licences or charging monopoly prices for goods or skills. Class is crucially important in understanding the distribution of power in modern society. However, understanding class is not merely a matter of noting the relationship between occupational categories and measures of disadvantage. It is the processes of advanced capitalism which matter and understanding these cannot be reduced to simple class categories that are defined by relationship to production (cf. Turner 1989).

Where do older people fit into the patterns of exploitation in modern political economy? Elderly pensioners may be seen, in one sense, as consumers of surplus value; that because they are not working, but consuming, they are living on the productive capacity of others. Another view of the pensioners' position in the political economy is to see them as in receipt of deferred wages; as receiving, at a later time, part of the wealth that they created whilst in work. From this perspective, the balance of consumption and production should be looked at over a whole lifetime. Does this mean that a woman who has raised her children and kept house for her husband, but never entered paid employment, has a parasitic relationship to society? Clearly people's contribution to society's productive efforts are not limited to paid employment. Older women are amongst the poorest and most disadvantaged social groups in our society. This is because they do not receive a fair share of social production; to characterize them as receiving too much from society would be absurd. In capitalist society there is a problem for those whose social contribution is not mediated through the labour market in obtaining a just return for their efforts. Those people who are primarily connected to the capitalist economic system through their role as consumers can become disadvantaged. Can we understand cleavages in modern society on the basis of diverging interests, not only through the labour market and production, but also through different positions in the consumption process?

Exploitation

Modern industrial production techniques are highly automated. The demand for unskilled labour has diminished. Production and the division of labour is organized through a global market. Cheap labour in the developing world is one criteria (but not the exclusive reason) for such worldwide dispersal of production. Automation continues apace and a capacity for technical innovation is the key for a nation wishing to retain its position in the forefront of the world economy. Consumption is also organized on a global scale – the most powerful and profitable brands are multinational. Coke, Nike and even Shell are recognized the world over. Thus the key question, in that it is the most important one for a capitalist entrepreneur to answer, is not 'how can things be made cheaply?' Rather, it is knowing the 'where', 'what' and 'how' of selling profitably which is important. Successfully expanding capital is less concerned with the traditional view of the control and exploitation of labour but rather more with accumulating surplus value through being able to command a place in the market.

For exploitation through the market to take place, it must be structured in certain ways. Here we are talking about the market not as an abstract analytical idea but as an institutional structure and a concretely existing network of social relationships. Those who are able to influence markets require a source of domination. This domination can be institutional, economic, cultural, technical or military. The process can be readily identified where there are state regulation of markets, and where there are technological and other considerations which lead to a natural monopoly. Pricing regimes for essential public utilities, such as those that supply water, gas and electricity tend to have the characteristics of privatized taxation – they are seldom left unregulated by the state. Where there is an opportunity to monopolize technical knowledge, as with the arms trade, profitable opportunities exist. However, the process is also generally more applicable in today's highly complex global markets. Firms who have the knowledge and resources, backed up by sufficient vertical integration, that enables them to command a strategic place between relatively small scale suppliers and a mass market of consumers, have the power to command profitable pricing structures. Such economic institutions which, for example, know how to convert coffee beans on a bush into a jar on the supermarket shelf at the right place and time to make a sale, or can get a Korean-made trainer of the right style on the shelves of the right shops in Paris to catch transient youth fashion, can accumulate surplus value from both producers and consumers. Such firms are in a position to squeeze both ends of the production–consumption chain. They can realize profits both through powerful influence on the purchase price from alternative suppliers and charge high prices to consumers for desirable brands and styles.

Two specific contemporary examples of monopoly or restrictive practices issues, one British, the other American, can illustrate the processes which operate. In Britain, Rupert Murdoch's television company BSkyB proposed to take over Manchester United Football Club. The Secretary of State for Industry called the move in to see if the deal contravened monopolies and mergers regulations. The motive of Sky is to position the company in a powerful position in determining the price at which football will be supplied to a mass market via cable television. The logic of the take-over is to be able to influence both those selling the broadcasting rights to football and those purchasing them. Rupert Murdoch's ability to amass capital is not particularly at the expense of the well paid stars of Manchester United but through an ability to charge a high price to football followers wishing to see their favourite sport, and the most popular team, on cable television. In the USA, the Microsoft entrepreneur, Bill Gates, has been taken to court over the incorporation of his firm's Internet software into the operating systems which go into the majority of personal computers. The rapid accumulation of capital at Microsoft is not primarily due to exploitation of, or underpayment to, the talented scientists and engineers who produce the software, but rather to the ability of Microsoft to dominate the technology which gives access to the Internet and thus charge consumers for this privilege.

The key point to be made about this form of exploitation is that, insofar as prices are raised and capital accumulated through consumers rather than producers, those with fixed incomes and without the power to counter their exploitation are vulnerable to poverty. Some producers are able to protect themselves by increasing their incomes, by using labour market power to obtain wage rises, and taking a share of the increased profits. One indication of the shift in the balance of power between producers and consumers is the way in which governments have found it politically easier to increase indirect taxes (for example VAT) than to tax incomes directly. These decisions to move towards greater use of indirect taxation are taken despite the generally held view that income taxes are, in principle, more equitable. The issue is not one of legitimacy but of power. It does not matter what your contribution to society has been, if you are linked to the market only as a vulnerable end-point consumer. In the competition for surplus value it is only those who are powerless by lack of capital and of labour power who cannot pass on the market squeeze and lose out. Thus pensioners in particular, and older people in general, are likely to be vulnerable in this kind of economic regime.

Exploitation should be differentiated from social exclusion, although the consequences may look similar for those excluded. Exploitation is formally the extraction of surplus value. If this happens principally through prices, in the manner suggested above, those without work or reliant on benefits are disadvantaged and likely to end up poor. Exclusion refers to a marginalization, whereby the lack of access that some social groups experience, is the by-product, not the driving force, of economic structures. This exclusion may not even be conscious or deliberate, but rather the outcome of the way the system works independently of the explicit intentions of those participating in it. There are a variety of exclusionary processes through which older people can become disadvantaged. The argument here is that the dominant institutions of capitalism create a structure into which older consumers do not fit and that they are both exploited and marginalized. In the following sections I discuss how geographical and institutional considerations, and cultural processes, may exclude older consumers from their full share of the benefits of a modern capitalist economy.

Structural and geographical exclusion

Institutional arrangements can structure consumers' access to essential commodities. Consumption classes can be thought of in terms of the mechanisms by which people gain (or fail to) access resources essential to maintaining their standard of living. Who is able to obtain different types of housing, for example, is the result of complex institutional structures. In housing, access to accommodation in the UK and most other European countries is not provided entirely by the free market, and this applies to both accommodation available to purchase and to rent. Housing is provided, or subsidized, by public authorities and access is regulated through legal and administrative frameworks. Thus the consumers of housing not only experience the wide differences in quality of both public and private sector housing, but also are differentiated by a structure of opportunities for access to housing. For example, residential qualifications, means tests, waiting lists, age and disability criteria may be used to ration rights of access to public housing. Access to accommodation, both public and private, designed specifically for elderly people, is frequently rationed by non-market criteria. In the UK, older people tend to find it easier to make claims on public sector housing than the general population. However, this is not to say that such housing is easily or appropriately accessed. The point to note is the way in which consumption rights structure group interests. Saunders ([1981] 1986), Burrows and Butler (1989), Evandrou and Victor (1989) and Saunders and Harris (1990) have pointed to the development of a class of people dependent on inferior state provision for access to many necessities – from housing, transport, to income and health care.

The issue of access to health and social services support is of particular importance to some older people. Health care, in particular, has become an important part of the economy and is increasingly structured by commercial markets. There is a large body of literature, most from the USA, which has looked at the commodification of health. Estes and the critical gerontology school have since the 1980s documented the relationships between the medical establishment and the companies producing and selling drugs, and the complex relationships they have to the state (Estes 1979, 1989; Estes *et al.* 1984; Estes and Swan 1993). The core of her argument is that the power of commercial organizations is able to co-opt both medical practitioners and institutions, and political and administrative elites, in a manner which gives all these sets of people a common definition of appropriately funded health care.

> The social needs of the elderly . . . are defined in ways compatible with the organization of the American economy. The effect . . . is to transform these needs into government funded and industry-developed commodities for specific economic markets, commodities that are then consumed by the elderly and their 'servants.'
>
> (Estes 1979: 238 quoted in Minkler 1991: 81)

The most important political consequence of the wholesale adoption of the medical-engineering model (see Chapter 4) is that it transforms health needs into commodities for specific economic markets. It supports high technology medicine and manufacture of drugs and sophisticated equipment. It encourages specialization by experts who can thus claim premium prices for specific treatments. It gives priority to those problems which are presented by consumers seeking goods and services in the medical market place.

> What is most relevant to our concern with health and aging is that 'business and government have begun to look at medical care as more nearly an economic product than a social good' (Iglehard 1982: 120). Within this context, the incentive is to maximize profits rather than health. The consequence for the elderly, for all persons dependent on public policy and programs, is that social needs are turned into profit-making commodities (Scull 1977). The needs of the elderly are defined and processed by the medical industry in ways that merely serve to medicalize old age further and to exacerbate rather than alleviate the dependency of the elderly. The creation of what has been called 'the aging enterprise' (Estes 1979) reflects one aspect of this trend.
>
> (Estes *et al.* 1984: 19)

The current debate about rationing in the NHS is concerned with the conditions for non-market regulation of access to health care and greater introduction of market mechanisms. In the UK, the NHS is a highly popular institution and there is a widespread feeling that people's health should not depend on their ability to pay for treatment. The new Labour government has taken action to dismantle aspects of the 'internal market' introduced by the previous Conservative administration. In practice consumption classes for health care continue to exist. Consumption of medical services is structured by differential access through the institutions of the welfare state and the private market. The changing mix of services available through national and local government and private provision is of vital importance to older people. Changes to entitlement to free long term nursing care under the NHS, and the restricted access to this service that older people are now experiencing, have reinforced the common consumption class interests of older age groups over health care.

The geographical and institutional structuring of consumption applies generally and not merely to the examples of housing and health discussed above. The basic process of purchase in the market, usually known as shopping, is organized through institutions such as supermarkets, shopping centres, wholesalers and street markets. They are increasingly physically constructed with patterns of physical access which leads to shopping becoming dependent on car transport and electronic media. Institutions and technologies such as credit cards and telephone banking are part of the necessary prerequisites for modern shopping. In these ways shoppers' lives are structured, certain choices and options becoming restricted or unavailable. It is within these structures that elderly people's life chances are worked out. Consequently, shopping that is institutionalized to be convenient for those shopping monthly by car excludes or disadvantages some people. Those without cars, including many older people, and those without monthly pay check or other resources to pay large bills, are marginalized. Further, those whose physical mobility is restricted by disability or ill-health and who therefore cannot reach the large out-of-town retail estates are also excluded.

High proportions of older people live in single person households. People who are living on their own will tend to benefit less from the price reductions associated with bulk purchase. This is also true of poor households and those without ready access to credit and bank accounts. Supplies and services, particularly those for gas, electricity, water or telephone, whose tariffs are divided between a standing charge and a consumption tariff, are particularly disliked by older small scale consumers, who feel unfairly treated by such pricing arrangements. Those without a telephone lack access to price information and a range of consumption opportunities. Those who lack the tools and skills, or are too frail, cannot benefit from cheap home assembly furniture. Modern packaging, designed from the manufacturer's point of view for cheap transport and reduced assembly costs, may thus also disadvantage older consumers. It is possible to see that older people tend to share a collective disadvantage. As a certain kind of consumer, older people share some or many of the characteristics of other disadvantaged groups which are some times labelled as the 'underclass'. Looking at the processes of consumption enables us to look at diversity, as well as commonality, of people of a similar age. It is not the date on the birth certificate or the sex of the purchaser which is the cause of the disadvantage. Rather, that small purchasers with small incomes will, because of the institutional structures of consumption, find it harder to cover their daily outgoings than other types of consumers, whether they be widowed pensioners or single parents on benefit.

The modern structure of consumption does not always disadvantage older groups. For example, increasingly privatized consumption of home entertainment, and the institutions and technologies which deliver them, bring variety (literally) into the lives of older people. Entertainment becomes consumed by private individual households via television, video and other electronic media. This fits well with many older people's lifestyles (Riggs 1998). Those who wish to participate in mass public live entertainment – musical concerts, football matches – are the socially problematic, highly policed exceptions to the privatized consumption of entertainment. The image of a lounge in a residential home with old people arranged in chairs around the edge looking at the television in the corner may not be one which inspires many as a benefit. However, the television is a marked improvement on a blank wall (although it might be improved by being in charge of the remote control: cf. p. 38). Television is an improvement on the radio for the hard of hearing, and personal stereos and other entertainment technologies can improve the quality of life for older people.

Cultural domination and the market

The cultural undervaluation of old age and older people (cf. Chapter 3) impacts on the workings of the market. In some circumstances older people are not considered suitable consumers but in many circumstances they are simply not considered. In yet other circumstances, the image of pensioners as deserving poor leads suppliers to offer discounted access at off-peak hours to buses, cinemas or restaurants. Ageism is visible in marketing, particularly in the images of the advertising industry (Riggs 1998: 8). On the one level there is the absence of positive images of older people – although this may be changing at the margins with the growth of a more affluent group of pensioners. Minkler (1991) discussed 'gold in grey' – the business discovery of the elderly market. However, she cautioned on the mixed blessings of this discovery. On the positive side she welcomed the contrast to the earlier omission of older people from advertisements and other marketing strategies which she saw as forming part of the exclusion process which kept old people from the cultural mainstream. On the negative side she suggested that the efforts to develop and capture the old age market created needs where none existed, reinforced age separatist approaches and diverted attention from the needs of low income elderly people. She cited the marketing of age segregated housing development as such an example of separatism. Featherstone and Wernick (1995) also identified a commercial response to an increasing number of affluent older people:

> Hence when gerontologists argue for the need for positive images of ageing to combat the old models of decline and disengagement, perhaps

they should look around themselves in the everyday life of consumer culture where, for the middle classes at least, positive ageing is alive and well. Of course positive ageing does not provide the solutions to the problems of deep old age and death; its message is essentially one of denial, keep smiling and carry on consuming.

(Featherstone and Wernick 1995: 10)

The importance of power inherent in the consumption process is precisely demonstrated by the way in which increased disposable income amongst certain younger and middle class older people has generated a response from business.

Style is an essential part of consumption. The relative lack of market power of most older people is reflected in the range of design products available. This phenomenon represents disadvantage but not exploitation – which occurs only insofar as affluent older consumers may pay higher prices for their choice of design products. There is however a process of exclusion for older consumers. Production and marketing of, for example, clothes or furniture will give priority to more affluent and active consumers. These consumers are likely to be at a younger 'home-making' stage of life and prefer styles and fashions different from those of an older age group to whom the markets are less responsive. Marketing is about the need to stimulate demand through changing fashions and cultural, as well as technical, obsolescence of products (Packard 1951; Singh 1976: 59). The succession of youth cultures since the Second World War has been both a market and a resource for design-based industries. Young people have been interested in fashion and willing to purchase clothes and other style accessories (from Sony Walkmans to 4 × 4 vehicles). They also have been the source of cultural innovation which have launched new consumer styles. Youth cultures from Teddy Boys to Goths and 'new laddism' have taken bits of consumer culture and reassembled them into a new style which is itself then commercialized. Sociologists have identified this process as one of resistance and incorporation by youth into dominant capitalist consumer culture (Willis 1977, 1990; Hebdige 1979; Slater 1998). Youth cultures revolve around taste and fashion whereby they respond to but reinvent and rearticulate commercial components. These dominant dynamics of fashion, style and consumption fit oddly into the established worlds of older people. These people, who have established their own tastes and aesthetic judgements in their formative years, have as a result of their pre-existing cultural history become seen as culturally obsolete.

The attitudes of older people may also reflect the mores of the time in which they grew up. A range of questions in the *British Election Survey* series (Heath *et al.* 1983, 1993a, 1993b, 1998) sought to look at attitudes and to rank the significance of issues to the electorate. These questions provide the opportunity to examine this cultural conservatism in slightly more depth. For example, the question was asked in 1992 whether respondents agreed or disagreed with the statement 'People in Britain should be more tolerant of those who lead unconventional lives'. The response was strongly influenced by age as illustrated in Table 9.1. Although this is suggestive of a trend towards greater cultural conservatism in older people, it is wrong to think of elderly

Table 9.1 Attitudes to the unconventional by age group

More tolerance for the unconventional	*Agree or strongly agree (%)*	*Disagree or strongly disagree (%)*
Whole sample	48.4	15
18–24 year olds	52.7	10.7
65 and over	42.9	20.2

Source: Author's analysis of *British Election Survey* (Heath *et al.* 1993a)

people as a simple undifferentiated category. The interconnected influences of class, education and religious affiliation also strongly shape these kinds of opinions. It is not clear that these attitudes are merely a function of age.

Elderly consumers have a consumption history, which has economic, symbolic and identity components. Thus, from an economic point of view, some purchases are investments with a long duration, even a lifetime. Many older people tend not to buy large domestic items like beds or wardrobes; housemaking purchases were, for the older generation, more typically done on marriage and household creation. Older people have already made the investment into a repertoire of domestic equipment and clothing. But this is a symbolic as well as an economic investment. Older people do not tend to radically remake themselves anew in a different style. Older people, because they have lived longer, are more resistant to fashion; taste tends to be fixed and habitual. Thus older people are less malleable consumers and so constitute a problem for those wishing to manipulate the market. Older people appear to be culturally conservative. But we must be careful of this generalization and not assume that older people are, in general, inflexible. Popular musical styles are strongly linked to particular cohorts. 'Old fashioned' aesthetic judgements about music do not necessarily lead to fixed behaviour towards the music. When I attend a festival to listen to 'trad jazz', a pleasure discovered as a teenager in the late 1950s, it is possible to identify fellow fans through their age and appearance. However, such old tastes lead to new behaviour. With professional advancement and a grown-up family I now, along with other 'trad' fans, spend the time and money to travel across Britain and continental Europe to attend music festivals in a manner that I never did previously.

Cultural symbols play an important part in personal identity. However, older people have established and developed an identity over time, they do not change identity and hairstyle with the apparent ease of a teenager. We do seek, when we move home in our later years, to shape the new flat, bungalow or room in a home after our own image. There are particular pieces of furniture, domestic items, treasures and memorabilia which we use to impose our personal identity on the new home. In the context of residential care, which carries with it the dangers of loss of personal identity in the face of organizational imperatives of communal living, these treasures from our consumption history can play a vital part. It may even be possible to view these as expressing a counter-culture. Hanging on to furniture, pets, favourite diets and so on, even when they create problems for institutional management, are conservative symbols used to challenge institutional power. Older people do not always confirm to the malleable identity expectations of passivity and gratitude those controlling the institutional space might wish them to.

I believe that these cultural accounts are better explanations of the apparent conservatism of older people, than for example changes in psychological functioning akin to maturation which involves fossilization of personality or senescence of adaptability. However, this cultural conservatism experienced by some older people has consequences in a felt social isolation. They find a lack of meaning in contemporary culture and consequently feel somewhat beleaguered. Pickard (1995) reports:

> It has been suggested that many elderly people shelter themselves against these new values in order to feel that the rules by which they themselves played are not bereft of value and meaning.
>
> (Pickard 1995: 84)

This attitude has been termed 'moral siege' (Coleman and McCulloch 1985) and describes a process whereby elderly people actively compare the past with the present emphasizing differences between the generations rather than similarities and giving a high moral estimation to old people and a low one to the young. Coleman's analysis leads him to state that for some older people accepting the values of modern society is tantamount to denying meaning to their own lives as they have led them (Coleman 1990: 99–101). Some researchers have identified this inability of elderly people to share the values of succeeding generations as the principal factor in creating a sense of loneliness or of social isolation in their lives, commenting on the fact that the old are 'isolated' not because they lack the company of their children but because they are unable to share with them the same social and cultural beliefs (Rosser and Harris 1965). In a similar vein, Barbara Anderson (1972: 211) identified the phenomenon of 'deculturation' of the aged, whose lives are lived outside of and apart from the viable body of tradition that constitutes modern society, making a 'lost generation, carriers of a defunct culture'. In many cases it is not so much that they disapprove of these values for others as that they find them inappropriate for their own lives. Amongst the many values which have changed, Jerrome (1990) suggests, are sexual morality, duty, the importance of work (cf. Bauman 1998), patriotism, authority and definitions of family roles.

My own view is rather more optimistic. Many people of all ages feel a sense of moral disorientation in the rapid changes of the modern world. Even as the nineteenth turned into the twentieth century, it was Durkheim's concern that modern society was losing social cohesion and becoming more anomic (Durkheim [1895] 1982, [1897] 1952). The return to fundamentalism in religion, nationalism and other identities, is one response to such insecurity (Bauman 1991: 245; Davie 1995). While some older people may develop a siege mentality, others experience greater opportunity. For example, older people are taking up opportunities to travel in a manner that they were never able to do previously. I mention two examples to suggest that older people do not have to abandon long held attitudes and beliefs but can use them creatively in changed circumstances. The first was mentioned in Chapter 7, and is reported in the ethnographic studies of Myerhoff (1978). The Yiddish culture of eastern Europe, in which these Jewish older people had grown up, had been abandoned by their children; these older people had welcomed the opportunities that the USA had offered them and encouraged their children to succeed in American terms. The result was that (on the one hand) their learnt expectations of the relationship between adult children and their parents were not met, but (on the other) a positive response in creating a rich community life rediscovering and reworking the history, language crafts and ceremonies of the *shetl*. Myerhoff's account of the graduation class for the group studying Yiddish history is a heart warming and insightful view of how communities use symbols to create meaning for themselves. The second example is found in a block of old people's flats in Exeter, near where I live. On the landing outside a second floor flat, an older couple have created for themselves a garden. As this landing has very limited outside light and it would be impossible to grow anything there, the garden is made of green baize, plastic flowers, white picket fence and gnomes fishing in a pond. It is an extensive, elaborate and magnificent creation, which must have taken hours of work. It is produced within the typical aesthetic taste of older working-class people in Exeter but is an entirely original and unique solution to acquiring a garden for a second floor flat.

Older people, along with all others, are part of the consumption process of contemporary capitalism (Slater 1998). This discussion suggests that when we view older people as consumers we can see that they are liable to be subject to particular kinds of exploitation, and find themselves constrained by cultural and institutional frameworks. Many older people share with others the impact that those consumption processes have on small low income households. However, there is also a distinctive dimension given by age *per se*. By taking a lifecourse perspective – people as stories -we can see that, simply being an older person and thus having a consumption history and longer personal biography, places an older person in a particular position in the consumption process.

Postmodernity and ageing: cultural construction of consumers

It is possible to contrast class analysis/political economy with cultural analysis. The first looks at class interests differentiated by the structure of consumption and the second at the cultural process of consumption as the dominant meaning system of modern capitalism. Emphasis on transience and style is characteristic of postmodern analysis and their manifestation through consumption is seen as characteristic of postmodern society. Consumers are thus, from this perspective, to be understood as cultural phenomena. Baudrillard (1993) makes the case that consumption is the axis of culture. The term 'postmodern', while apparently simply describing an era which follows the modern one, carries with it a great deal of intellectual baggage – indeed a veritable jumble sale (or US rummage sale) of ideas. The term 'postmodern' can be used to denote both the current condition of society and a philosophical position on the methods (or lack of them) through which society might be studied.

As a condition of society it reflects the fragmentation of the modern bases of social order, with the concomitant breakdown in expected social patterns. Postmodernism can be represented in the economic sphere by increasingly unstable work patterns and 'disorganized capitalism' (Lash and Urry 1987). In the political sphere, the disintegration of class ideologies and coherent progressive programmes in favour of ephemeral scandal and short term issues can be used to exemplify postmodernity. While in the cultural realm, a kaleidoscope of shifting values and transient identities is noted. Specifically in social gerontology, postmodernity is associated with a breakdown in the standard expected patterns of the lifecourse. This is seen as a process of liberation from the iron cages of rationality and conformity, and offering the possibility of alternative lifestyles. Alternatively it is seen as creating new, unsolvable, dilemmas for people in an ultra-anomic world. Postmodernism revels in irony, contradiction and anomaly, and does not seek to reconcile or explain away these difficulties.

As an intellectual approach, postmodernity celebrates the end of the Enlightenment. This is an era characterized by progress achieved by the application of reason and logic in general, and science in particular, in order to transform social conditions for the better. The end of the modern era is associated with the end of grand theory and associated utopian programmes. The phenomenon of postmodernity represents the success of a radical epistemological position whereby a plurality of accounts are accepted and there is no valid criteria for accepting one view of the world as more plausible than another. Consequently, from a postmodern perspective, attention is directed not to the substance of accounts of the world but rather to the method by which they are constructed and in particular the linguistic form in which this account is rendered. As a direct result of this epistemological position such postmodern texts tend to be highly linguistically stylized and very difficult to follow. This is because the postmodern author's own version of reality is also deemed as only one of many possible accounts. In practice the method itself is not subject to the same deconstruction as the subject the author seeks to address. Language therefore becomes used in odd metaphorical and ungrammatical ways in order to construct an account of deconstruction. Postmodern titles are most frequently ironic. Nouns become verbs, adverbs become nouns, and first and second person constructions are elided. One might say in the jargon – 'In order to problematize the decentering of the self, the doing of being is narrated.'

On the first count, namely that postmodernity is a radically different new era, I am sceptical. Rapid social change and alienation are old experiences, they have taken place frequently throughout recorded time, and history is a catalogue of the rise and fall of civilizations (cf. Slater 1998). In the twentieth century new means of communication may mean the manifestations of change take on new forms. Further, patterns of global social and economic change have meant that western cultures, along with their languages and religions, have been profoundly undermined. The symbol of a white Christian male god who made people in his own image no longer embodies the economic and military dominance of Europe that it did in the nineteenth century. European views of the world are no longer hegemonic. Anthropologists have studied cargo cults and other millenarian activities manifested by native peoples following colonial subjugation. These cults were responses to the destruction of the meaning systems through which people made sense of their world and which provided them with possible routes to personal and collective salvation. Europe has not been colonized although it is losing its global political, economic and intellectual dominance. Nothing, however, in the current insecurity experienced by middle-aged European academics in a deprofessionalizing education industry can match the radical destruction of cultural certainty and meaning experienced by native people. But then postmodernism for all its pretensions to listening to other voices is profoundly Euro-centric and largely only meaningful to European intellectuals. The changes in global society at the end of the twentieth century are rapid, and may affect Europeans in new ways, but they are not of a different order than those of the past 200 years. Phillipson (1998) argues, using Beck and Giddens, that the political and economic structures of the 1990s create massive crises of insecurity which fundamentally change previous regularities of the welfarism and managed capitalism which preceded it:

> Labelling the new social ageing as 'postmodern' in fact raises complex questions about where old age has come from, and where precisely it is heading.
>
> (Phillipson 1998: 11)

He is in practice challenging postmodernism's pessimistic core theme, which is to reject that there is a trajectory to society and that we cannot meaningfully discuss where it is heading.

Postmodernity as an approach to knowledge can also be criticized. At its worst such writing becomes the substitution of style for method in academic attempts to understand the social world. Social theory needs to be more than a language game; it needs to be the basis not only of insight but also of action. Postmodernists are, quite correctly, aware of the limited and problematic nature of language as a communicator of meaning and how it is inherently embedded in a social context. However, their approach to knowledge results in reading and writing in certain ways. Whilst one level of reflexivity can sharpen our focus on the world, more than that creates confusion and thus inaction. If social science is a mirror to society, one image can help smarten ourselves up, two mirrors lead to infinite regression of images, and a postmodern hall of mirrors is a fairground.

To extend the fairground metaphor, postmodernism concentrates on language and performance not the sponsor and impresarios. In other words postmodernity tends to ignore the reality of power. Power is about social relationships, powerful people doing things to less powerful people. Power comes before language and interaction, it is the basis for them. Whose definitions of the situation become to be accepted as real, whose language dominates a discourse, are the consequences of power. Ageist language, like sexist language, is an expression of power, not power itself. It is the relationships of unequal power in domestic and economic structures which become embedded in language use. Thus, it is possible and desirable to give an account of the cultural construction of old age – how images of old age and elderly people are built up in specific contexts. However, this is not sufficient. We have to

ask not only 'how?' but also 'why?' Unless we believe ourselves to be hermetically sealed units unable to communicate with each other, the role of
social gerontology must be to communicate to others (including elderly
people themselves) new ideas which are also possible plans for action. We, as
academics, practitioners, or actual or potential old people, need not tell them
(other old people) what to do, i.e. impose our will through a claim to know
on some scientific basis what is best for other people. However, the alternative stance of offering some tools, which might help you work out what you
might do for the best, does seem to me to be a valid one. In other words, some
theories of social action and in particular some theoretical propositions in
social gerontology can be empowering for the older part of our society. To be
useful these theories in turn require to be based on an effective theory of
power. Social science cannot be value neutral. There must be a purpose
beyond the dilettante collection of words and images. This purpose must come
first; it is prior to intellectual activity.

Anthropologists have been dealing with these issues of cultural relativity for
longer than most social science disciplines. The study of 'other cultures' is their
stock in trade. However, only a few have looked at issues of old age. We can
look at the strengths and weakness of the postmodern treatment of the subject
by an anthropologist Haim Hazan whose first book *The Limbo People* (Hazan
1980) was an excellent ethnographic account about fieldwork in residential
and day care facilities for older people. He subsequently wrote *Old Age: Constructions and Deconstructions* (Hazan 1994) and I had anticipated that it would
be a seminal work. In the end I was disappointed. Where Hazan writes from
within the classic anthropology tradition, and based on direct fieldwork experience, he achieves good insights. I particularly like his discussion, on the basis
of ethnography, of the nature and meaning of time; how the limbo people,
dependent elderly people in care, experience time. However, many of his
points are drowned in linguistic circumlocution and while his objective may
be to celebrate ambiguity, this can lead to confusion and ultimately loss of confidence in the author. While sections of the book are dense with good ideas,
the overall effect of writing in multiple voices is hubbub. He values the possibility of holding ambiguous and contradictory positions and holds that this is
necessary for a full account of old age and older people. He then finds that
such a position cannot be translated into a meaningful conclusion. He moves
from insightfulness to being disempowered within a few paragraphs.

> Simultaneously context-bound and out-of-context, our society's various
> narratives on ageing are manifest in policy-making documents, social
> workers' reports, newspaper articles, fiction, ethnographic accounts, and,
> indeed, theoretical paradigms.
>
>   Deciphering such accounts involves the recognition of two contrasting
> codes, socio-cultural and existential. While the former captures the
> elderly as 'ordinary people', the latter projects some of the key dilemmas
> of being human onto the construct of the 'old' and the separation of the
> two renders any reference to ageing multivocal . . .
>
>   Old Age is best understood as a form of postmodern existence in which
> the mobilization of meaning is fluid and constant and confrontation with
> the self is continuous . . .

Knowledge of ageing, then, is a type of masking – often simply an academically celebrated form of necessary social ignorance. Whereas the endless pursuit of knowledge about ageing endows the phenomenon with the illusion of intelligibility, that very quest renders it unique and inexplicable . . . this book is another example of the potency of knowledge about ageing as a social construct and impossibility of pursing it as an intellectual enterprise.

(Hazan 1994: 92–4)

Hazan ends up in this negative position because his theoretical stance does not allow him to go behind the language and the conceptual frameworks embedded in the language to look directly at issues of empowerment. Hence, in practice, he treats as other postmodernists do, language as power, rather than seeing language as a reflection of power. He argues for multiple voices – emphasizing disunity rather than unity, fragmentation rather than cohesion, on the basis that by not giving any one voice priority in his text he is disempowering those who would otherwise be privileged. Further, he refuses to claim authority for his own views as this would silence those who are disenfranchised. But he refuses to develop a method for theorizing about these voices. As a consequence the voices which will be heard in gerontology and elsewhere are those of the powerful. Authoritative control of older people will, in practice, go unchallenged until alternative bases of power are found by the powerless. Critical gerontology in the mid-1980s did an excellent job of providing a critique of professional voices. This approach within social gerontology had the effect of giving pause to people who knew, all too readily, on the basis of their professional power, what to do to old people. That critical approach directed us to listen to and respect the voices of elderly people. In an unfortunate paradox, it also had the effect of assisting the radical right attack on public institutions providing care for elderly people. By undermining the legitimacy of professional knowledge to dispose of resources for elderly people's welfare it assisted with the domination by capital with the rhetoric of consumer choice.

We need, more than ever, analysis which suggests how elderly people's voices can become louder and demand more attention and be less likely to become marginalized. Bauman (1991), one of the best and most coherent writers within the postmodern genre, makes the case himself:

It is all too easy for postmodern tolerance to degenerate into the selfishness of the rich and resourceful. Such selfishness is indeed its most immediate and daily manifestation. There seems to be a direct relation between exuberant and expanding freedom of the 'competent consumer' and the remorseless shrinking of the world inhabited by the disqualified one. The postmodern condition has split society into the happy seduced and unhappy oppressed halves – with postmodern mentality celebrated by the first half of the division while adding to the misery of the second. The first half may abandon itself to the carefree celebration only because it has satisfied itself that the misery of the second half is their rightful *choice*, or at least a legitimate part of the world's exhilarating diversity.

(Bauman 1991: 259 original emphasis)

10

Conclusion: politics, power, ageism and social gerontology

We have established in the discussion of personal politics and lifestyle politics that there is a connection between the intimate and everyday lives of older people and the power structures of society. By looking at professional organiz-ations, pressure groups and political parties we can see how issues of ageing and old age are contended in national political processes. By looking at large scale issues of political economy, we have examined how patterns of domi-nance structure the lives of older people and we have examined the cultural processes which differentiate and define older people. These processes are con-tinuous and dynamic. They do not have beginnings and ends; social processes are long chains of mutual interaction. People take action in the position they find themselves in and their choices and responses set further frameworks within which yet other people have, in turn, to act. The issues discussed in each chapter of this book are tightly interconnected; the pattern of the book, moving from the micro- to the macro-level of analysis, is intended to aid the reader's 'sociological imagination'. C. Wright Mills ([1959] 1970) identifies this as the ability to see personal problems and dilemmas as part of broad patterns of social and historical change. Personal and cultural politics are not separate from the more formal organizational politics of national elections and welfare pressure groups.

Ageism and cultural construction of old age

Ageism is about acting on stereotypes about chronological age which prevent (older) people from having control over their lives and partici-pating fully and purposefully in society (Age Equality Action Group, LBH, 1991).

(Meade 1995: 7)

Ageism describes behaviour which is akin to racism or sexism. It refers to both prejudice and discrimination, the first being an attitude, the second being a behaviour. Negative stereotypes of people based on their age may refer to different age groups. Both young and old are subject to a variety of stereotypes. The negative image of old age is extremely prevalent and indeed getting older seems often to carry no positive connotations at all. A quick browse in any birthday card shop will indicate the disgust with which ageing is widely held. Palmore (1990) discusses both positive and negative stereotypes of old age. He lists negative elements as illness, impotency, ugliness, mental decline, mental illness, uselessness, isolation, poverty and depression. His positive stereotype includes romanticized elements and are listed as kindliness, wisdom, dependability, affluence, political power, freedom, eternal youth and happiness.

Discrimination on age grounds in Britain is not illegal in the same way as sexism or racism, although the practice of age discrimination with regard to employment is likely to change under pressure, not least from EU equal opportunities regulations. It is common for both young job applicants to find themselves passed over for older more mature applicants and for older people looking for work to find younger people preferred. It may be feared that training older workers will not be cost effective, or that older workers will be more prone to illness and absence. Reverse discrimination also takes place whereby older workers are offered dead-end jobs where it is thought by employers that younger people looking to further themselves would move on. Ageism is manifest in a large variety of ways. In this conclusion, I briefly present three examples.

Ideology of fitness

Sidell (1995) argues that, ironically, an increased ability to live a healthy old age, together with a 'fitness' culture which holds people increasingly responsible for their health and indeed body-shape and appearance, can lead to ageism.

> Chronic illness and disability are shameful, to be hidden away and not admitted to, not because they cause pain and suffering, but because they render people incompetent by the standards of fitness aspired to by the rest of society. The temptation in trying to counter ageist attitudes is to minimise the prevalence of chronic illness and disability in old age and emphasise the fit and healthy old people. This only serves to reinforce the worship of fitness and adds to the disadvantage of those who do experience chronic illness and disability.
>
> (Sidell 1995: 163)

Hepworth (1995) also takes up a similar theme when he discusses 'positive ageing'. He uses studies by Williams (1990) on Aberdeen and by Jerrome (1992) on Sussex to illustrate that older people in Britain have internalized a twofold distinction in old age between an active fit early old age and an old old age. The latter is seen as the 'real' old age associated with ill-health, lack of activity and social disengagement. There are strong moral imperatives to control the body and not fall into the second category. The sociology of the body and its significance for old age was discussed in Chapter 3. Hepworth (1995) sees this physically incompetent category of 'far old age' as a moral category, whose identification has consequences for surveillance and social control. To equate the Third Age with a positive expansion of human potential, it is necessary to invent a Fourth Age for those who cannot, or do not, aspire to an active healthy old age. Sidell (1995) argues that we need to accept the challenge that chronic illness and disability bring. It is necessary to try to prevent health problems in old age, but we should also concentrate on measures to directly relieve pain and suffering and help people maintain a sense of well-being even while chronically ill or handicapped. However, technical solutions, while highly desirable raise issues about who controls that technology, and do not address the fundamental cultural issue. As argued in Chapter 3, superficial appearance is related in part to the imperatives of modern urban living. To the extent to which older people have a personal history known by others, their appearance will be of less relevance than their biography. This is likely to be as true in a hospital as in a long-standing residential neighbourhood.

Stereotypes influence policy makers

In the context of discussing ageism in the construction of social policy, Victor (1991) argues that the strongest stereotype of the old are that they are all the same and that in policy terms they can be treated the same. She suggests that there are two consequences to the stereotype. First, that although elderly people may cover a 40 year period from age 60 to over 100, policy makers would not consider that people aged from 20 to 60 should be treated in a similarly undifferentiated manner. Second, dimensions of social stratification such as class, gender and ethnicity are no longer considered of importance in differentiating people as in the younger age groups. In fact, it can be argued that such divisions are exacerbated in old age. A key aspect of countering ageism is then trying to establish the diversity of old age and the variety of ways of living a satisfying old age, and identifying poverty and ill-health (but not old age) as conditions to be avoided.

New ageism

The third example I quote at length from an Internet website, in case it is thought that the 'new ageism' is an 'aunt sally', a fictitious enemy, raised for rhetorical purposes. The quotation summarizes the attitudes which link the New Right, anti-welfarism, with stereotypical images of old age.

I'm grateful to the older folks who saved the world from total tyranny. But I've got to admit, I'm getting pretty tired of paying them back for it. Sure, our nation owes a lot to the World War II generation, the one my parents belong to. No argument here on that account. After all, this was the generation that survived the Great Depression and went on to win the greatest war of all time, leaving the globe a legacy of democracy that will last for generations. But how many times must we repay my parents' generation before the debt is settled? This question is important to people my age and younger, because if the Baby Boomers and younger generations continue to pay back our elders at the current rate, there will be nothing left in the piggy bank when we retire. And that means the old-age poverty problem that was so common before and during the Great Depression (a condition that has been fairly well remedied by programs such as Medicare and Social Security) could be coming back with a vengeance. It will visit the Baby Boomers and younger generations when we get old. The Baby Boom generation, the so-called 'Me Generation,' is supposed to be hedonistic and into instant gratification . . . the cost of education and child care is so high that a second income is needed just to pay off student loans and day care. Saving money when there's nothing left is difficult if not impossible. Older folks who sit back, look over their half glasses and say 'tsk, tsk' to the Baby Boom generation for failing to plan for the future fail to remember something very basic: Their retirements were planned for and paid for by requiring future generations to subsidize their waning years. No retiree who collects Social Security or Medicare benefits paid into these systems anywhere near the amount of money they collect from them. Now that it's becoming publicly accepted that Medicare will be bankrupt by the year 2001, and Social Security by the year 2029, younger people like me are realizing that all the money we've paid into the system will be lost to us. So not only do we not save, now we've got no financial safety net for when we get old, even though we've been paying for one all our working lives. Talk about getting screwed.

(Fulks 1996)

These three examples of ageism reflect the dominant negative stereotypes of old age in western societies: all old people are the same, they are unhealthy and live off state pensions. Hummert (1994) explores the multiple stereotypes of old age by using trait analysis techniques developed by social psychologists. She correctly presents the case that not all stereotypes of old people are negative. Many people, particularly young people for example, hold images of benign grandparents or elders as pillars of respectability. The problem is that stereotypes, both positive and negative, can be disempowering for older people. The negative attitudes expressed in the jokes on birthday cards, when internalized by brutalized carers, leads to abuse. Even positive stereotypes of older women as benign mother figures can trap older women in the role of cheaply available informal care. The physical and sexual abuse of old people is not caused in any simple way by ageist attitudes. It is the interaction of the powerlessness of some older people with dominant ideas in specific circumstances which lead to abusive outcomes. The goals of rational pursuit of improvement in society may lead, when taken to extremes at times of crises, to the Nazi use of extermination to solve their problem with older people. Strapping old people in chairs in understaffed, poorly managed residential homes can be linked to a set of ideas about the worth of older people, which in turn are associated with lack of resources on a national level and objectification of old senile bodies on the interpersonal level.

Ideologies of normality, which define what is appropriate and acceptable and who is different and excluded, are constructed by powerful groups. Those oppressed by these ideologies will resist and develop their own ideas and seek to redefine the relationships in their own terms. But, of necessity, these counter-ideologies are a reaction to and a reflection of dominant ideologies. Bytheway (1995: 128) argues that it is a fundamental mistake to equate an anti-ageist stance with thinking positively. He states that there are ways of being positive which do not promote idealized scenarios and unreal beliefs.

Rather than claim that:

Most elderly people are really nice, absolutely fascinating once you get to know them . . . The things they say! . . . Working with them is really interesting . . . Some of them are real characters!

It is far less patronizing, far less self-righteous and far less ageist to state that:

The people I work with are pretty ordinary. They have lived long lives and survived many experiences. I like working with them because there are things I can do to make life more satisfactory for them. They tell me what they think and I listen to them and sometimes argue. You can learn a lot from ordinary people. I enjoy the work; it is worth doing.

(Bytheway 1995: 128)

Empowering older people

Empowering older people involves, amongst other things, overcoming ageism. However, I have argued throughout this book that ageism is the symptom of powerlessness, not the cause. The way in which the processes of modern capitalism generate cleavages in society are worked out in specific histories, whereby people struggle over the material bases of power and the social construction of the groups which result. On one level the metaphor of ageism as being like racism or sexism is useful in providing a model for action.

Like racism, . . . [it] is based on fear, folk-lore and hang-ups . . . Like racism, it needs to be met by information, contradiction and, when necessary, confrontation [Alex Comfort] (1977: 35).

(Meade 1995: 10)

However, it is not constructive to create an ever expanding list of disadvantaged and excluded groups on the basis of class, age, sex, ethnicity, race, religion, sexual orientation, disability and so on. What needs to be understood and changed are the social processes which systematically provide division in society and give power to some to exclude others. It has been my contention in this book (Chapter 8) that these divisive processes need to be understood and confronted on a worldwide scale.

Bytheway (1995) argues that definitions of ageism should not be based on parallels with sexism and racism. He prefers to understand each as a unique phenomenon with its own history and dynamics. He points out that it should not be presumed that old people exist as a group. As seen above, the simplistic stereotype of old people as all the same is false. They are as varied as the rest of the population and that labelling them with this single category is itself part of the problem. Separating out old people for special consideration (even special study as in social gerontology) implies a 'them' and 'us' situation in which the old are 'them', different from 'us', who are defining the meaning of the situation and who are not old. To illustrate his point, Bytheway (1995) takes a quotation and reformulates it.

> So, when Butler refers to 'discrimination against people because they are old', he is creating the same distinction: between a kind of ageless 'we' (ageless in the sense that our age is considered irrelevant) and 'them' who are old.
>
> (Bytheway 1995: 118)

His alternative formulation was:

> *Ageism can be seen as a process of systematic stereotyping of and discrimination against us when we are considered old.*
>
> (Bytheway 1995: 118, original italics)

Bytheway says that the problem with this alternative is that it implies a concern with ourselves and our future selves, rather than with older people currently suffering the consequence of ageism.

One way to overcome ageism is to work for a society in which age is irrelevant. An alternative goal would be to alter the balance of power between age groups. I have argued throughout the book that age based social solidarity is not particularly strong. I therefore see a greater prospect of lessening the impact of age than transferring power on the basis of age. It can be argued, in parallel to the postmodern analysis, that common social patterns determined by chronological age are becoming less critical to people's life experience. Periods of war and social upheaval affect the distinctiveness of common cohort experiences and mark them out from other 'generations'. There is evidence that the cohorts who had their early employment disrupted by the Second World War, carried the consequences of that disruption for the rest of their careers. Similarly, the marriage chances, and thus lifecourse patterns, of many women of marriageable age during the First World War, were structured by the slaughter on the battlefield, lifecourse effects that are still felt today by that cohort. Each of these consequences might be thought of as relatively minor perturbations in a stable overall system of lifecourse expectations. Refugees may been seen as an unfortunate minority deviating from standard patterns of lifecourse transition and ageing (Carey-Wood *et al.* 1995). However, it is claimed from the postmodernist perspective that there is a fundamental destabilization of social structures and previous bases of social predictability including that of the lifecourse. In this case the lifecourses of migrants and refugees may come to represent a new kind of norm. There is a danger that rather than being 'pioneers' (Silverman 1987) in the territory of old age, older people will be exiles in a strange land.

There are many ways to study older people (Peace 1990). Traditionally, sociological methods have used surveys and interviews which give snap-shot views and which treat people as social isolates with no past or future. People's identity, through the eyes of the questionnaire, becomes a mere collection of attributes. Older people are subjected to surveys and tests as if they were social atoms. They are labelled and identified by age categories. They come out of these studies ranked with attributes, so they are for example seen as conservative and resistant to change. However, if people are not atomized and looked at as having a whole life history, things appear rather differently. One way to avoid ageist stereotypes in research is to treat people as stories. In the context of a lifetime – a family career, an employment career, a housing career, a health career, a developing personality, an unfolding narrative – age is not a differentiating device but a thread which gives coherence to the story. Looked at from this perspective the choices elderly people make cease to be conservative and inflexible but can become seen to be rational, consistent and adaptive. An elderly widow, deploring the lack of sexual morality amongst the young, is not expressing an irrational psychological response ill-adapted to a changing world. As soon as a story is told of a woman who worked in service in a time before contraception, was betrothed and eventually married, kept house while she raised four children while her husband went to war, then has seen her daughter separated from her husband and is doing her best to help her raise the grandchildren, it ceases to be possible to devalue the older person's opinions with simplistic ageist categories.

Elias (1982) presents a theory of social change based on long chains of interconnectedness which work themselves out through history. Life histories are shorter versions of these extended chains of social interconnectedness. They have a similar 'unfolding character. Decisions made early in life have unintended and unanticipatable consequences for subsequent parts of the lifecourse. Youth cultures and the development of new styles are usually seen as processes of opposition, drawing on consumer and dominant cultural themes and refashioning them. Old people, in a similar way, do use cultural methods to resist ageist constraints on their situation. Examples of this resistance have been discussed throughout this book, for example in Chapters 3 and 9. However, the tools they draw on already have a history; a personal history of choice, whereby one choice is founded upon a previous one, and the consequences unfold through life. Simply by having more of a history, older people's reaction to disempowerment will be highly varied. In some cases drawing on gender or kinship bases for solidarity, in some cases class allegiances, and yet others on the basis of age-identified categories. In this way the study of older people can itself become less ageist by becoming less dependent on age categorization, and looking on ageing as a process which happens to people in all their humanity. This approach depends on seeing people as stories and considering them over their full lifetime, and not as an abstract concept of a slice of a person taken at one moment in time. In other words social gerontology should endeavour to make age insignificant.

Bibliography

Achenbaum, A. W. (1983) *Shades of Gray: Old Age, American Values and Federal Policies since 1920.* Boston, MA: Little, Brown.

Achenbaum, A. W. (1997) Elder power: a new myth for a new age. Plenary presentation to British Society of Gerontology Conference *Elder Power in the 21st Century*, Bristol, 19–21 September.

Age Concern (1996) Manifesto in *Reportage*, August. http://www.ace.org.uk/reportage/

Age Concern (1997) Election Special in *Reportage*, 21 August. http://www.ace.org.uk/reportage/

Allcock, P. (1993) *Understanding Poverty.* Basingstoke: Macmillan.

Anderson, Barbara (1972) The process of deculturation – its dynamics among U.S. aged, *Anthropological Quarterly*, 45: 209–16.

Anderson, Benedict (1991) *Imagined Communities*, 2nd edn. New York: Verso.

Arber, S. and Gilbert, G. N. (1989) Transitions in caring: gender, lifecourse and the care of the elderly, in W. Bytheway (ed.) *Becoming and Being Old: Sociological Approaches to Later Life.* London: Sage.

Arber, S. and Ginn, J. (1991) *Gender and Later Life.* London: Sage.

Arber, S. and Ginn, J. (1995) *Connecting Gender and Ageing.* Buckingham: Open University Press.

Arensberg, C. M. and Kimball, S. T. (1940) *Family and Community in Ireland.* Gloucester, MA: Peter Smith.

Aries, P. (1974) *Western Attitudes Towards Death: From the Middle Ages to the Present.* Baltimore, MD: Johns Hopkins University Press.

Aries, P. (1981) *The Hour of our Death.* London: Allen Lane.

Armstrong, D. (1983) *The Political Anatomy of the Body: Medical Knowledge in the Twentieth Century.* Cambridge: Cambridge University Press.

Asis, M. M. B., Domingo, L., Knodel, J. and Mehta, K. (1995) Living arrangements in four Asian countries: a comparative perspective, *Journal of Cross-Cultural Gerontology*, 10(1–2): 145–62.

Askham, J., Henshaw, L. and Tarpey, M. (1993) Policies and perceptions of identity, service needs of elderly people from black and minority ethnic back-grounds, in

S. Arber and M. Evandrou (eds) *Ageing, Independence and the Life-Course*. London: Jessica Kingsley.

Atkinson, A. B. (1989) *Poverty and Social Security*. Harvester Wheatsheaf: Hemel Hempstead.

Baars, J. (1991) The challenge of critical gerontology: the problem of social constitution, *Journal of Aging Studies*, 5(3): 219–43.

Barnes, B. (1995) *The Elements of Social Theory*. London: UCL Press.

Barr, N. (1993) Retirement pensions, in N. Barr and D. Whynes (eds) *Current Issues in the Economics of Welfare*. London: Macmillan.

Barr, N. A. (1998) *The Economics of the Welfare State*, 3rd edn. Oxford: Oxford University Press.

Barr, N. and Whynes, D. (1993) *Current Issues in the Economics of Welfare*. Basingstoke: Macmillan.

Barrett, D. (1997) Ageism and the sex industry, *Generations Review*, 7(3): 6–7.

Baudrillard, J. (1993) *Symbolic Exchange and Death*, trans. I. Hamilton Grant. London: Sage.

Bauman, Z. (1990) *Thinking Sociologically*. Oxford: Basil Blackwell.

Bauman, Z. (1991) *Modernity and Ambivalence*. Cambridge: Polity Press.

Bauman, Z. (1992) *Mortality, Immortality and Other Life Strategies*. Cambridge: Polity Press.

Bauman, Z. (1998) *Work, Consumerism and the New Poor*. Buckingham: Open University Press.

Beauvoir, S. de (1972) *Old Age*. London: Deutsch and Weidenfeld and Nicolson.

Bengston, V. L. (ed.) (1996) *Adulthood and Aging: Research on Continuities and Discontinuities*. New York: Springer.

Benson, J. (1997) *Prime Time: A History of the Middle Aged in Twentieth-Century Britain*. London: Longman.

Bernard, M. and Meade, K. (eds) (1993) *Women Come of Age: Perspectives on the Lives of Older Women*. London: Edward Arnold.

Blakemore, K. and Boneham, M. (1994) *Age, Race and Ethnicity*. Buckingham: Open University Press.

Bornat, J., Phillipson, C. and Ward, S. (1985) *A Manifesto for Old Age: A Radical Programme for Old Age*. London: Pluto Press.

Bosworth, B. and Burtless, G. (eds) (1998) *Aging Societies: The Global Dimension*. Washington, DC: Brookings Institution Press.

Brodie-Smith, A. (1993) A 'grey area': a critical deconstruction of the burden of elderly people, *Generations Review*, 3(2): 6–8.

Budd, A. and Campbell, N. (1998) The roles of the public and private sectors in the UK pension system. HM Treasury.www.open.gov.uk

Burrows, R. and Butler, T. (1989) Middle mass and the pitt – a critical review of Peter Saunders's sociology of consumption, *Sociological Review*, 37(2): 338–64.

Bytheway, W. (ed.) (1989) *Becoming and Being Old: Sociological Approaches to Later Life*. London: Sage.

Bytheway, W. (1995) *Ageism*. Buckingham: Open University Press.

Carey-Wood, J. K., Duke, V. K. and Marshall, T. (1995) *The Settlement of Refugees in Britain*. London: HMSO.

Carver, V. and Liddiard, P. (eds) (1978) *An Ageing Population*. London: The Open University and Hodder and Stoughton.

Chang Chiung-fang (1998) A silent protest-suicide in Taiwan, *Sinorama*, trans. C. MacDonald, Internet website.

Churchill, L. R. (1988) Should we ration health care by age? *Journal of the American Geriatrics Society*, 36(7): 644–47.

Cohen, L. (1994) Old-age – cultural and critical perspectives, *Annual Review Of Anthropology*, 23: 137–58.

Cole, T. R. (1992) *The Journey of Life: A Cultural History of Aging in America.* Cambridge: Cambridge University Press.

Cole, T. R. (1993) *Voices and Visions of Ageing: Towards a Critical Gerontology.* New York: Springer.

Coleman, P. (1990) Adjustment in later life, in P. Coleman and J. Bond (eds) *Ageing in Society.* London: Sage.

Coleman, P. and McCulloch, A. W. (1985) The study of psychosocial change in late life: some conceptual and methodological issues, in J. M. A. Munnichs, P. Mussen, E. Olbrich and P. G. Coleman (eds) *Lifespan and Change in a Gerontological Perspective.* Orlando, CA: Academic Press.

Colette ([1920, 1926] 1954) *Cheri and the Last of Cheri.* Harmondsworth: Penguin.

Comfort, A. (1977) *A Good Age.* London: Mitchell Beazley.

Connerton, P. (ed.) (1976) *Critical Sociology.* Harmondsworth: Penguin.

Crewe, I. M., Robertson, D. R. and Sarlvik, B. (1981) *British Election Study, February 1974, October 1974, June 1975, May 1979* [computer file]. Colchester, Essex: The Data Archive [distributor]. SN: 1614.

Cribier, F. (1989) Changes in life course and retirement in recent years: the example of two cohorts of Parisians, in P. Johnson, C. Conrad and D. Thomson (eds) *Workers versus Pensioners.* Manchester: Manchester University Press.

Dahlberg, F. (ed.) (1981) *Woman the Gatherer.* Princeton, NJ: Yale University Press.

Davidson, K. (1998) Doing good offices: the gendered nature of selfishness as articulated by older men and women. Paper presented to British Society of Gerontology Conference *Ageing: All Our Tomorrows,* Sheffield, 18–20 September.

Davie, G. (1995) Competing fundamentalisms, *Sociology Review,* 4(April): 2–7.

Day, L. H. (1992) *The Future of Low-Birthrate Populations.* London: Routledge.

Dean, M. (1990) Facing up to the forecasts, *Search,* 7(November): London: DSS.

Department of Employment (1987) *Family Expenditure Survey.* London: HMSO.

Department of Employment (1997) *Family Expenditure Survey.* London: HMSO.

Department of Health and Social Security (DHSS) (1985) *The Reform of Social Security, Volume 1.* Cmnd 9517. London: HMSO.

Department of Social Security (DSS) (1997) Press release 97/192 (2 October).

Department of Social Security (1998) *A New Contract for Welfare: Partnership in Pensions.* Cm 4179. London: HMSO.

Durkheim, E. ([1897] 1952) *Suicide.* London: Routledge and Kegan Paul.

Durkheim, E. ([1895] 1982) *The Rules of Sociological Method.* London: Macmillan.

Eisenstadt, S. N. (1956) *From Generation to Generation.* London: Collier-Macmillan.

Elias, N. (1982) *The Civilising Process.* Oxford: Blackwell.

Elias, N. (1985) *The Loneliness of the Dying.* Oxford: Blackwell.

Elman, C. (1995) An age-based mobilisation: the emergence of old age in American politics, *Ageing and Society,* 15: 299–324.

Eriksen, T. H. (1995) *Small Places, Large Issues: An Introduction to Social and Cultural Anthropology.* London: Pluto Press.

Ermisch, J. (1989) Demographic change and intergenerational transfers in industrialised countries, in P. Johnson, C. Conrad and D. Thomson (eds) *Workers Versus Pensioners: Intergenerational Justice in an Ageing World.* Manchester: Manchester University Press.

Estes, C. L. (1979) *The Aging Enterprise.* San Francisco, CA: Jossey-Bass.

Estes, C. L. (1989) Cost containment and the elderly, conflict or challenge? *Journal of the American Geriatrics Society,* 36(1): 68–72.

Estes, C. L. and Minkler, M. (1984) *Readings in the Political Economy of Aging.* Farmingdale, NY: Baywood.

Estes, C. L. and Swan, J. H. (1993) *The Long-Term Care Crisis: Elders Trapped in the No-Care Zone.* Newbury Park, CA: Sage.

Estes, C. L., Gerard, L. E., Sprague Zones, J. and Swan, J. H. (1984) *Political Economy, Health and Aging.* Boston, MA: Little, Brown.

Estes, C. L., Linkins, K. and Binney, E. (1996) The political economy of aging, in R. Binstock and L. George (eds) *Handbook of Aging and the Sciences.* New York: Academic Press.

Evandrou, M. and Victor, C. (1989) Differentiation in later life: social class and housing tenure cleavages, in W. Bytheway (ed.) *Becoming and Being Old: Sociological Approaches to Later Life.* London: Sage.

Featherstone, M. (1982) The body in consumer culture, *Theory, Culture and Society,* 1: 18–33.

Featherstone, M. and Hepworth, M. (1989) Ageing and old age: reflections on the postmodern life course, in W. Bytheway (ed.) *Becoming and Being Old: Sociological Approaches to Later Life.* London: Sage.

Featherstone, M. and Wernick, A. (1995) *Images of Ageing.* London: Routledge.

Featherstone, M., Hepworth, M. and Turner, B. S. (eds) (1991) *The Body: Social Process and Cultural Theory.* London: Sage.

Ferris, E. G. (1993) *Beyond Borders: Refugees, Migrants and Human Rights in the Post-Cold War Era.* Geneva: WCC Publications.

Finch, J. (1987) Family obligations and the life course, in A. Bryman, B. Bytheway, P. Allat and T. Keil (eds) *Rethinking the Life Cycle.* Basingstoke: Macmillan.

Finch, J. (1989) *Family Obligations and Social Change.* Cambridge: Polity Press.

Finch, J. and Mason, J. (1990) Divorce, remarriage and family obligations, *Sociological Review,* 38(2): 219–46.

Ford, J. and Sinclair, R. (1987) *'Sixty Years On': Women Talk about Old Age.* London: The Women's Press.

Forgacs, D. (ed.) (1988) *A Gramsci Reader: Selected Writings 1916–1935.* London: Lawrence & Wishart.

Foucault, M. (1979) *Discipline and Punish: The Birth of the Prison.* Harmondsworth: Peregrine Books.

Foucault, M. (1980) *Power/Knowledge: Selected Interviews and Other Writings 1972–7.* New York: Pantheon.

Friedan, B. (1963) *The Feminine Mystique.* Harmondsworth: Penguin.

Friedan, B. (1993) *The Fountain of Age.* London: Vintage.

Fries, J. E. (1980) Aging, natural death and the compression of morbidity, *New England Journal of Medicine,* 303(3): 130–35.

Fries, J. E. and Crapo, L. M. (1981) *Vitality and Aging.* San Francisco, CA: Freeman.

Fulks, T. (1996) Geezer rip-off: the older generation's greed is stifling the younger one, and Tom's mad, by Tom Fulks, 20 May. www.tomfulks.com

Giddens, A. (1989) *Sociology.* Cambridge: Polity Press.

Giddens, A. (1991) *Modernity and Self Identity.* Oxford: Polity Press.

Giddens, A. (1997) *Sociology,* 3rd edn. Cambridge: Polity Press.

Gilleard, C. and Higgs, P. (1998) The social limits of old age. Paper presented to British Society of Gerontology Conference *Ageing: All Our Tomorrows,* Sheffield, 18–20 September.

Ginn, J. and Arber, S. (1996) Gender, age and attitudes to retirement in mid-life, *Ageing and Society,* 16(1): 27–55.

Gledhill, J. (1994) *Power and its Disguises.* London: Pluto Press.

Goffman, E. (1961) *Asylums.* Harmondsworth: Penguin.

Goffman, E. (1968) *Stigma: Notes on the Management of Spoiled Identity.* Harmondsworth: Penguin.

Golander, H. and Raz, A. E. (1996) The mask of dementia: images of 'demented residents' in a nursing ward, *Ageing and Society,* 16(3): 269–86.

Gramsci, A. (1971) *Selections from Prison Notebooks.* Ed. and trans. Q. Hoare and G. Nowell-Smith. London: Lawrence & Wishart.

Gramsci, A. (1978) *Selections from Political Writings*. Ed. and trans. Q. Hoare. London: Lawrence & Wishart.

Gramsci, A. (1985) *Selections from Cultural Writings*. Ed. D. Forgacs and G. Nowell-Smith. London: Lawrence & Wishart.

Gubrium, J. F. and Holstein, J. A. (1995) Life course malleability: biographical work and deprivatization, *Sociological Inquiry*, 65(2): 207–23.

Guillemard, A-M. (1989) The trend towards early labour force withdrawal and reorganisation of the lifecourse: a cross-national analysis, in P. Johnson, C. Conrad, D. Thomson (eds) *Workers versus Pensioners*. Manchester: Manchester University Press.

Guillemard, A-M. (1990) Re-organising the transition from work to retirement in an international perspective: is chronological age still the major criterion determining the definitive exit? Paper presented to the 12th International Sociological Association World Congress, Madrid.

Guillemard, A-M. and Rein, M. (1993) Comparative patterns of retirement: recent trends in developed societies, *Annual Review of Sociology*, 19: 469–503.

Haber, C. and Gratton, B. (1994) *Old Age and the Search for Security: An American Social History*. Bloomington: Indiana University Press.

Hall, R. H. (1990) *Health and the Global Environment*. Cambridge: Polity Press.

Harding, N. and Palfrey, C. (1997) *The Social Construction of Dementia: Confused Professionals?* London: Jessica Kingsley.

Hardy, M. A. (ed.) (1997) *Studying Aging and Social Change: Conceptual and Methodological Issues*. London: Sage.

Hardy, T. ([1874] 1975) *Far from the Madding Crowd*. London: Macmillan.

Hareven, T. K. (1982) *Family Time and Industrial Time*. Cambridge: Cambridge University Press.

Hareven, T. K. (1994) Aging and generational relations – a historical and life-course perspective, *Annual Review of Sociology*, 20: 437–61.

Hazan, H. (1980) *The Limbo People: A Study of the Constitution of the Time Universe among the Aged*. London: Routledge and Kegan Paul.

Hazan, H. (1994) *Old Age: Constructions and Deconstructions*. Cambridge: Cambridge University Press.

Hazelrigg, L. (1997) On the importance of age, in M. A. Hardy (ed.) *Studying Aging and Social Change: Conceptual and Methodological Issues*. London: Sage.

Heath, A., Jowell, R. and Curtice, J. K. (1983) *British General Election Survey, 1983* [computer file] Colchester, Essex: The Data Archive [distributor]. SN: 2005.

Heath, A., Jowell, R. and Curtice, J. K. (1993a) *British General Election Survey, 1992* [computer file]. Colchester, Essex: The Data Archive [distributor], 15 April 1993. SN: 2981.

Heath, A., Jowell, R. and Curtice, J. K. (1993b) *British General Election Survey, 1987* [computer file] 2nd edn. Colchester, Essex: The Data Archive [distributor], 21 April 1993. SN: 2568.

Heath, A., Jowell, R., Curtice, J. K. and Norris, P. (1998) *British General Election Survey, 1997* [computer file] Colchester, Essex: The Data Archive [distributor], 2 July 1998. SN: 3887.

Hebdige, D. (1979) *Subculture: The Meaning of Style*. London: Methuen.

Hen Coop (1997) http://www.hens.org:80/

Hendricks, J. and Leedham, C. A. (1991) Dependency or empowerment? Toward a moral and political economy of ageing, in M. Minkler and C. Estes (eds) *Critical Perspectives on Ageing: The Political and Moral Economy of Growing Old*. Amityville, NY: Baywood.

Hepworth, M. (1987) The mid-life phase, in G. Cohen (ed.) *Social Change and the Life Course*. London: Tavistock.

Hepworth, M. (1995) Positive ageing: what is the message?, in R. Bunton, S. Nettleton and R. Burrows (eds) *The Sociology of Health Promotion*. London: Routledge.

Hepworth, M. and Featherstone, M. (1982) *Surviving Middle Age*. Oxford: Basil Blackwell.

Herskovits, E. (1995) Struggling over subjectivity – debates about the self and Alzheimer's disease, *Medical Anthropology Quarterly*, 9(2): 146–64.

Herskovits, E. and Mitteness, L. (1994) Transgressions and sickness in old-age, *Journal of Aging Studies*, 8(3): 327–40.

Hertzman, C., Pulcins, I., Barer, M. L., Evans, R. G., Anderson, G. M. and Lomas, J. (1989) *Flat on Your Back to Your Flat: Sources of Increased Hospital Services Utililization among the Elderly in British Columbia*. Vancouver: Health Policy Research Unit, University of British Columbia.

Hills, J. (1993) *The Future of Welfare*. York: Joseph Rowntree.

Hills, J. (1996) Does Britain have a welfare generation?, in A. Walker (ed.) *The New Generational Contract*. London: UCL Press.

Hochschild, A. R. (1973) *The Unexpected Community*. Englewood Cliffs, NJ: Prentice Hall.

Hockey, J. and James, A. (1993) *Growing Up and Growing Old: Ageing and Dependency in the Life Course*. London: Sage.

Hummert, M. L. (1994) Stereotypes of the elderly and patronizing speech, in M. L. Hummert, J. M. Wiemann and J. F. Nussbaum (eds) *Interpersonal Communication in Older Adulthood: Interdisciplinary Theory and Research*. Thousand Oaks, CA: Sage.

Iglehard, J. K. (1982) Health care and American business, *New England Journal of Medicine*, 306(2): 120–24.

Ikels, C., Diskerson-Putman, K., Draper, J., Fry, C., Glascock, A. and Harpending, H. (1992) Perceptions of the adult life course: a cross-cultural analysis, *Ageing and Society*, 12(1): 49–84.

Illich, I. (1976) *Limits to Medicine: Medical Nemesis, the Expropriation of Health*, new edn. London: Boyars.

Ingold, D. R. and Woodburn, J. (eds) (1988) *Hunters and Gatherers. Vol. 1: History, Evolution and Social Change. Vol. 2: Property, Power and Ideology*. Oxford: Berg.

Irwin, S. (1996) Age related distributive justice and claims on resources, *British Journal of Sociology*, 47(1): 68–92.

Isaacs, B., Livingstone, M. and Neville, Y. (1972) *Survival of the Unfittest: A Study of Geriatric Patients in Glasgow*. London: Routledge and Kegan Paul.

Jefferys, M. (1992) Is there a need for geriatric medicine? Does it do more harm than good?, in P. Kaim-Caudle, J. Keithley and A. Mullender (eds) *Aspects of Ageing*. London: Whiting and Birch.

Jenkins, R. (1996) *Social Identity*. London: Routledge.

Jerrome, D. (1990) Intimate relationships, in P. Coleman and J. Bond (eds) *Ageing in Society*. London: Sage.

Jerrome, D. (1992) *Good Company: An Anthropological Study of People in Groups*. Edinburgh: Edinburgh University Press.

Jerrome, D. (1993) Intimacy and sexuality amongst older women, in M. Bernard and K. Meade (eds) *Women Come of Age*. London: Edward Arnold.

Johnson, N. (1995) *Private Markets in Health and Welfare*. Oxford: Berg.

Johnson, P. (1985) *The Economics of Old Age in Britain: A Long-Run View 1881–1981*, discussion paper no. 47. London: Centre for Economic Policy Research.

Johnson, P. and Falkingham, J. (1992) *Ageing and Economic Welfare*. London: Sage.

Johnson, P., Conrad, C. and Thomson, D. (eds) (1989) *Workers Versus Pensioners: Intergenerational Justice in an Ageing World*. Manchester: Manchester University Press.

Jones, I. R. and Higgs, P. F. D. (1992) Health economists and health care provision for the elderly: implicit assumptions and unstated conclusions, in K. Morgan (ed.) *Gerontology: Responding to an Ageing Society*. London: Jessica Kingsley.

Jones, N. (1997) *Campaign 1997: How the General Election was Won and Lost*. London: Indigo.

Keenan, B. (1992) *An Evil Cradling*. London: Hutchinson.

Kemper, S. and Lyons, K. (1994) The effects of Alzheimer's Dementia on language and communication, in M. L. Hummert, J. M. Wiemann and J. F. Nussbaum (eds) *Interpersonal Communication in Older Adulthood: Interdisciplinary Theory and Research*. Thousand Oaks, CA: Sage.

King, R., Warnes, A. M. and Williams, A. M. (1998) International retirement migration in Europe, *International Journal of Population Geography*, 4: 91–111.

Kinsella, K. and Taeuber, C. M. (1993) *An Aging World II*. Washington, DC: US Department of Commerce, Economics and Statistics Administration, Bureau of the Census.

Kirk, H. (1992) Geriatric medicine and the categorisation of old age – the historical linkage, *Ageing and Society*, 12(4): 483–98.

Kitwood, T. (1993) Towards a theory of dementia care: the interpersonal process, *Ageing and Society*, 13(1): 51–67.

Kitwood, T. (1997) *Dementia Reconsidered: The Person Comes First*. Buckingham: Open University Press.

Kitwood, T. and Bredin, K. (1992) Towards a theory of dementia care: personhood and well-being, *Ageing and Society*, 12(3): 269–88.

Kohli, M. (1985) The institutionalization of the life-course – historical evidence and theoretical arguments, *Kolner Zeitschrift fur Soziologie und Sozialpsychologie*, 37(1): 1–29.

Kohli, M. (1986) The world we forgot: a historical review of the life course, in V. W. Marshall (ed.) *Later Life: The Social Psychology of Aging*. London: Sage.

Kohli, M. (1990) Plenary Address to the 2nd International Conference on the Adult Lifecourse, Leuwenhorst, Netherlands.

Kohli, M. (1991) Retirement and the moral economy: an historical interpretation of the German case, in M. Minkler and C. Estes (eds) *Critical Perspectives on Aging: The Political and Moral Economy of Growing Old*. Amityville, NY: Baywood.

Kohli, M. and Meyer, J. W. (1986) Social-structure and social construction of life stages, *Human Development*, 29(3): 145–49.

Kohli, M., Rein, M., Guillemard, A-M. and Van Gunstern, H. (eds) (1992) *Time for Retirement: Comparative Studies on Early Exit for the Labour Force*. Cambridge: Cambridge University Press.

Kondratowitz, H-J. von (1989) Old age under national socialism: strategies and experiences in the years 1933–1945. Paper presented to 14th International Congress of Gerontology, Acapulco, Mexico.

Kondratowitz, H-J. von (1990) Arguing with the 'burden of old age' – its historical genesis and present significance in the social and health policy of the modern welfare state. Paper presented to 12th World Congress of Sociology, Madrid, Spain.

Kondratowitz, H-J. von (1991) The medicalization of old age: continuity and change in Germany from the late eighteenth to the early twentieth century, in M. Peling and R. M. Smith (eds) *Life, Death and the Elderly: Historical Perspectives*. London: Routledge.

Laczko, F. and Phillipson, C. (1991) *Changing Work and Retirement*. Buckingham: Open University Press.

Lash, S. and Urry, J. (1987) *The End of Organized Capitalism*. Cambridge: Polity Press.

Laslett, P. and Fishkin, J. S. (eds) (1992) *Justice Between Age Groups and Generations*. New Haven, CT: Yale University Press.

Lee, M. A., Nelson, H. D., Tilden V., Ganzini, L., Schmidt, T.A. and Tolle, S. W. (1996) Legalizing assisted suicide – views of physicians in Oregon, *New England Journal of Medicine*, 334(5): 310–15.

Lee, R. B. and DeVore, I. (eds) (1968) *Man the Hunter*. Chicago: Aldine.

Lipka, M. (1998) Living longer and physically ailing, senior citizens number about 1 in 4 of local people who commit suicide, *Westchester Gazette* (Gannett Suburban Newspapers). Internet website.

Lukes, S. (1974) *Power, a Radical View*. London: Macmillan.

Macnicol, J. (1998) *The Politics of Retirement in Britain 1878–1948*. Cambridge: Cambridge University Press.

Mannheim, K. (1927) The problem of generations, reprinted in M. A. Hardy (ed.) (1997) *Studying Aging and Social Change: Conceptual and Methodological Issues*. London: Sage.

Meade, K. (1995) Promoting age equality, *Generations Review*, 5(3): 7–10.

Mercken, C. (1997) Partners in time: the impact of interaction between toddlers and elderly with dementia. Paper presented to British Society for Gerontology Conference *Elder Power in the 21st Century*, Bristol 19–21 September.

Mheen, H. D. van de, Stronks, K. and Mackenbach, J. (1998) A lifecourse perspective on socio-economic inequalities in health, in M. Bartley, D. Blane and G. Davey Smith (eds) *The Sociology of Health Inequalities*. Oxford: Blackwell.

Midwinter, E. (1991) *The British Gas Report on Attitudes to Ageing*. British Gas.

Midwinter, E. and Tester S. (1987) *Polls Apart? Older Voters and the 1987 General Election*. London: Centre for Policy on Ageing.

Mills, C. W. ([1959] 1970) *The Sociological Imagination*. Harmondsworth: Penguin.

Minkler, M. (1991) Gold in grey: reflections on business' discovery of the elderly market, in M. Minkler and C. Estes (eds) *Critical Perspectives on Aging: The Political and Moral Economy of Growing Old*. Amityville, NY: Baywood.

Minkler, M. and Cole, T. R. (1991) Political and moral economy: not such strange bedfellows, in M. Minkler and C. Estes (eds) *Critical Perspectives on Aging: the Political and Moral Economy of Growing Old*. Amityville, NY: : Baywood.

Minkler, M. and Estes, C. (eds) (1991) *Critical Perspectives on Aging: The Moral and Political Economy of Growing Old*. Amityville, NY: Baywood.

Minois, G. (1989) *History of Old Age*. Cambridge: Polity Press.

Moody, H. R. (1992) *Ethics in an Aging Society*. Baltimore, MD: Johns Hopkins University Press.

Moody, H. R. (1994) *Aging: Concepts and Controversies*. Thousand Oaks, CA: Pine Forge Press.

Morris, L. (1997) Globalization, migration and the nation-state, *British Journal of Sociology*, 48(2): 192–209.

Myerhoff, B. G. (1977) 'We don't wrap herring in a printed page': fusion, fictions and continuity in secular ritual, in S. F. Moore and B. G. Myerhoff (eds) *Secular Ritual*. Assen: Van Gorcum.

Myerhoff, B. (1978) *Number our Days*. New York: Dutton.

Naipaul, V. S. ([1961] 1964) *A House for Mr Biswas*. London: Deutsch.

National Pensioners' Convention (1998) *Pensions not Poor Relief*. London: National Pensioners' Convention.

NOP Research Group (1997) 'Euthanasia has wide public support' – survey findings, 27 November. Internet website.

O'Connor, J. (1990) Definition and measurement of welfare effort and its correlates in cross-national analysis: a reply to Pampel and Stryker, *British Journal of Sociology*, 41(1): 25–8.

O'Connor, J. and Brym, R. (1988) Public welfare expenditure in OECD countries: towards a reconciliation of inconsistent findings, *British Journal of Sociology*, 39(1): 47–68.

Packard, V. (1951) *The Waste Makers*. Harmondsworth: Penguin.

Palmore, E. B. (1990) *Ageism: Negative and Positive*. New York: Springer.

Pampel, F. and Stryker, R. (1990) Age structure, the state and social welfare spending, *British Journal of Sociology*, 41(1): 16–24.

Pampel, F. C. and Williamson, J. B. (1989) *Age, Class, Politics and the Welfare State*. Cambridge: Cambridge University Press.

Peace, S. M. (ed.) (1990) *Researching Social Gerontology*. London: Sage.

Pensioners' Voice (nd) *The Story of the National Federation: The Formative Years of the National Federation of Retirement Pensions Associations.* Blackburn: Pensioners' Voice.

Phillips, D. R., Vincent J. and Blacksell, S. (1988) *Home from Home: Private Residential Care in Devon.* Monographs in Social Policy. Sheffield: University of Sheffield and Community Care.

Phillipson, C. (1982) *Capitalism and the Construction of Old Age.* London: Macmillan.

Phillipson, C. (1996) Intergenerational conflict and the welfare state: American and British perspectives, in A. Walker (ed.) *The New Generational Contract.* London: UCL Press.

Phillipson, C. (1998) *Reconstructing Old Age: New Agenda in Social Theory and Practice.* London: Sage.

Phillipson, C. and Walker, A. (1986) *Ageing and Social Policy: A Critical Assessment.* Aldershot: Gower.

Phillipson, C., Bernard, M. and Strang, P. (eds) (1986) *Dependency and Interdependency in Old Age.* London: Croom Helm.

Pickard, S. (1995) *Living on the Front Line.* Aldershot: Avebury.

Pointon, S. (1997) Myths and negative attitudes about sexuality in older people, *Generations Review,* 7(4): 6–8.

Polyani, K. C., Arensberg, C. M. and Pearson, H. (eds) (1957) *Trade and Market in Early Empires.* Glencoe, NY: Free Press.

Powles, J. (1973) On the limitations of modern medicine, *Science, Medicine and Man,* 1(1): 1–30.

Pratt, H. J. (1976) *The Grey Lobby.* Chicago: University of Chicago Press.

Qureshi, H. (1996) Obligations and support within families, in A. Walker (ed.) *The New Generational Contract.* London: UCL Press.

Qureshi, H. and Simons, K. (1987) Caring for elderly people, in J. Brannen and G. Wilson (eds) *Give and Take in Families.* London: Allen & Unwin.

Qureshi, H. and Walker, A. (1989) *The Caring Relationship: Elderly People and their Families.* Basingstoke: Macmillan.

Rawls, J. (1971) *A Theory of Justice.* Oxford: Clarendon Press.

Renaud, M. (1975) On the structural constraints to state intervention in health, *International Journal of Health Services,* 5: 559–71.

Riggs, K. (1998) *Mature Audiences.* New Brunswick, N.J.: Rutgers University Press.

Riley, M. W. (ed.) (1979) *Aging from Birth to Death. Vol. 1, Interdisciplinary Perspectives.* Boulder, CO.: Westview Press for the American Association for the Advancement of Science.

Riley, M. W. (1986) The dynamisms of life stages – roles, people, and age, *Human Development,* 29(3): 150–56.

Riley, M. W. (1988) On the significance of age in sociology, in M. W. Riley (ed.) *Social Structures and Human Lives.* Newbury Park, CA: Sage.

Riley, M. W., Abeles, R. and Teitelbaum, M. S. (eds) (1983) *Aging from Birth to Death. Vol. 2, Sociotemporal Perspectives.* Boulder, CO: Westview Press for the American Association for the Advancement of Science.

Riley, M. W., Foner, A. and Waring, J. (1988a) A sociology of age, in H. J. Smelser (ed.) *Handbook of Sociology.* Newbury Park, CA: Sage.

Riley, M. W., Huber, B. J. and Hess, B. B. (eds) (1988b) *Social Structures and Human Lives. Vol. 1, Social Change and the Life Course.* London: Sage.

Robertson, A. (1991) The politics of Alzheimer's Disease: a case study in apocalyptic demography, in M. Minkler and C. Estes (eds) *Critical Perspectives on Aging: The Political and Moral Economy of Growing Old.* Amityville, NY: Baywood.

Rosser, C. and Harris, C. (1965) *The Family and Social Change: A Study of Family and Kinship in a South Wales Town.* London: Routledge and Kegan Paul.

Sabat, S. and Harré, R. (1992) The construction and deconstruction of self in Alzheimer's Disease, *Ageing and Society,* 12(4): 443–61.

Sainsbury, S. (1993) *Normal Life: A Study of War and Industrially Injured Pensioners.* Aldershot: Avebury.

Saunders, P. ([1981] 1986) *Social Theory and the Urban Question.* London: Hutchinson.

Saunders, P. and Harris, C. (1990) Privatization and the consumer, *Sociology,* 24(1): 57–75.

Saunders, P. and Harris, C. (1994) *Privatization and Popular Capitalism.* Buckingham: Open University Press.

Schaie, K. W. and Achenbaum, W. A. (eds) (1993) *Societal Impact on Aging: Historical Perspectives.* New York: Springer.

Schmahl, W. (1989) Labour force participation and social pension systems, in P. Johnson, C. Conrad and D. Thomson (eds) *Workers Versus Pensioners: Intergenerational Justice in an Ageing World.* Manchester: Manchester University Press.

Scott, M. (1996) Sexuality and aging: myths, attitudes and barriers. scottm@muss.cis.mcmaster.ca

Scull, A. T. (1977) *Decarceration.* Englewood Cliffs, NJ: Prentice Hall.

Searle-Chatterjee, M. (1979) The polluted identity of work: a study of Benares Sweepers, in S. Wallman (ed.) *Social Anthropology of Work.* London: Academic Press.

Sen, K. (1994) *Ageing: Debates on Demographic Transition and Social Policy.* London: Zed Books.

Shakespeare, W. ([1604] 1997) *King Lear,* edited by R. A. Foakes. Walton-on-Thames: Nelson.

Shapiro, J. (1997) Oregon reconsiders its pioneering assisted-suicide law. US News 1 September. Internet website.

Sherman, E. and Webb, T. A. (1994) Self and process in late-life reminiscence: spiritual attributes, *Ageing and Society,* 14: 255–67.

Sidell, M. (1995) *Health in Old Age: Myth, Mystery and Management.* Buckingham: Open University Press.

Silverman, P. (1987) Comparative studies, in P. Silverman (ed.) *The Elderly as Modern Pioneers.* Bloomington, IN: Indiana University Press.

Silverman, P. (ed.) (1987) *The Elderly as Modern Pioneers.* Bloomington, IN: Indiana University Press.

Simmel, G. ([1902–3] 1950) The metropolis and mental life, in K. Wolff (ed.) *The Sociology of Georg Simmel.* New York: Free Press.

Singh, N. (1976) *Economics and the Crisis of Ecology.* Delhi: Oxford University Press.

Slater, D. (1998) *Consumer Culture and Modernity.* Cambridge: Polity Press.

Social and Community Planning Research (1996) *British Social Attitudes.* Aldershot: Gower Publishing.

Spencer, P. (1990) The riddled course: theories of age and its transformations, in P. Spencer (ed.) *Anthropology and the Riddle of the Sphinx.* London: Routledge.

Spencer, S. (1994) *Immigration as an Economic Asset: The German Experience.* Stoke-on-Trent: Trentham Books.

Stahl, S. M. (ed.) (1990) *The Legacy of Longevity: Health and Health Care in Laterlife.* London: Sage.

Stahl, S. M. and Rupp Feller, J. (1990) Old equals sick: an ontogenetic fallacy, in S. M. Stahl (ed.) *The Legacy of Longevity: Health and Health Care in Laterlife.* London: Sage.

Stoller, E. P. and Gibson, R. C. (1994) *World's of Difference: Inequality in the Aging Experience.* Thousand Oaks, CA: Pine Forge Press.

Street, D. (1997) Apocalyptic demography meets apocalyptic politics: special interests and citizens' rights among elderly people in the US. Paper presented to British Society of Gerontology Conference *Elder Power in the 21st Century,* Bristol, 19–21 September.

Street, D. and Quadagno, J. (1993) The state and the elderly and the intergenerational contract: towards a new political economy of aging, in K. W. Schaie and

W. A. Achenbaum (eds) *Societal Impact on Aging: Historical Perspectives*. New York: Springer.

Sykes, R. and Leather, P. (1997) *Grey Matters: A Survey of Older People in England*. Anchor Trust.

Synge, J. M. (John Millington) ([1907] 1995) *Playboy of the Western World*, edited by M. Kelsall, 2nd edn. London: A. & C. Black.

Thompson, E. P. (1971) Moral economy of the English crowd in the 18th century, *Past and Present*, 50: 56–136.

Thursz, D., Nusberg, C. and Prather, J. (eds) (1995) *Empowering Older People*. London: Cassell.

Tönnies, F. ([1887] 1955) *Community and Association: Gemeinschaft und Gesellschaft*. Trans. C. P. Loomis. London: Routledge & Kegan Paul.

Touraine, A. (1985) An introduction to the study of social movements, *Social Research*, 52: 749–88.

Townsend, P. (1957) *The Family Life of Old People: An Inquiry in East London*. London: Routledge and Kegan Paul.

Townsend, P. (1979) *Poverty in the United Kingdom: A Survey of Household Resources and Standards of Living*. Harmondsworth: Penguin.

Townsend, P. (1986) Ageism and social policy, in C. Phillipson and A. Walker (eds) *Ageing and Social Policy: A Critical Assessment*. Aldershot: Gower.

Townsend, P. (1997) Social gerontology and the disability movement: time for joint action. Plenary paper presented to British Society for Gerontology Conference *Elder Power in the 21st Century*, Bristol, 19–21 September.

Turnball, C. (1984) *The Forest People*. London: Triad/Paladin.

Turner, B. (1984) *The Body and Society*. Oxford: Blackwell.

Turner, B. (1989) Ageing, politics and sociological theory, *British Journal of Sociology*, 40(4): 588–606.

Ungerson, C. (1987) *Policy is Personal: Sex, Gender and Informal Care*. London: Tavistock.

University of Keele (1998) Archive of party manifestos 1948–1998. Directly cited in text as Conservative Party manifestos 1955, February 1974, 1997; Labour Party manifesto 1997; Liberal Party manifesto 1959. University of Keele; Department of Politics Internet website.

Victor, C. (1991) *Health and Health Care in Later Life*. Buckingham: Open University Press.

Vierck, E. (1990) *Factbook on Aging*. Santa Barbara, CA: ABC-CLIO.

Vincent, J. (1995) *Inequality and Old Age*. London: UCL Press.

Vincent, J. (1996) Whose afraid of an ageing population? *Critical Social Policy*, 16(2): 3–26.

Vincent, J., Phillips, D. R. and Tibbenham A. (1988) Choice in residential care: myths and realities, *Politics and Policy*, 14(2): 189–208.

Walker, A. (1987) The social construction of dependency in old age, in M. Loney *et al.* (eds) *The State or the Market*. London: Sage.

Walker, A. (1996) *The New Generational Contract*. London: UCL Press.

Walker, A. and Maltby, T. (1997) *Ageing Europe*. Buckingham: Open University Press.

Warnes, A.M. (1987) The distribution of the elderly population of Great Britain, *Espace Populations Societes*, 1: 41–56.

Warnes, A. M. and Patterson, G. (1998) British retirees in Malta: components of the cross-national relationship, *International Journal of Population Geography*, 4: 113–33.

Weber, M. ([1919] 1978) *Economy and Society*, trans. and edited by G. Roth and C. Wittich. Berkeley, CA: University of California Press.

Weiner, M. (1995) *The Global Migration Crisis*. New York: HarperCollins.

Wenger, C. (1984) *The Supportive Network: Coping with Old Age*. London: Allen & Unwin.

Williams, A. M., King, R. and Warnes, A. (1997) A place in the sun: international retirement migration from northern to southern Europe, *European Urban and Regional Studies*, 4(2): 115–34.

Williams, R. (1990) *A Protestant Legacy: Attitudes to Death and Illness among Older Aberdonians*. Oxford: Clarendon Press.

Willis, P. (1977) *Learning to Labour*. London: Saxon House.

Willis, P. (1990) *Common Culture: Symbolic Work at Play in the Everyday Cultures of the Young*. Buckingham: Open University Press.

World Bank (1994) *Averting the Old Age Crisis*. Oxford: Oxford University Press.

Index

THE MATURE IMAGINATION
DYNAMICS OF IDENTITY IN MIDLIFE AND BEYOND

Simon Biggs

- What does it mean to possess a mature imagination under contemporary social conditions?
- Is it possible to choose not to grow old?
- How are the core questions for adult identity to be addressed in midlife and beyond?

This innovative and wide-ranging book critically assesses notions of adult ageing as they affect people's lifestyles and their sense of personal and social identity. Drawing on an extraordinary range of theory, original research and empirical sources, Simon Biggs examines the interpretation of these changes within social theory and their implications for practice in therapy and in health and welfare settings.

Biggs' argument develops a number of key concepts, and begins by assessing notions of change arising from psychodynamic and postmodern perspectives on ageing. Whilst these ideas shape our understanding, the study of ageing itself challenges easy theoretical assumptions about adult identity. The author critically assesses the contribution of these key perspectives and develops a model for combining the inner world of the mature imagination with the possibilities and uncertainties inherent in contemporary social life. Central to this analysis are tensions between authenticity and masquerade, personal coherence and continuity, and the role of facilitative and restrictive social space. The reader is invited to transgress traditional subject boudaries and draw on insights from sociology, psychotherapy and social gerontology in new and creative ways. The issues that emerge are of both theoretical and practical importance and are presented clearly and concisely.

The Mature Imagination should be of interest to a broad range of students and practitioners in the areas of counselling, health and welfare as well as readers interested in following debates in contemporary social theory.

Contents

c.224pp   0 335 20102 4 (Paperback)   0 335 20103 2 (Hardback)

CRITICAL APPROACHES TO AGEING AND LATER LIFE

Anne Jamieson, Sarah Harper and Christina Victor

- How are individuals and society ageing towards the end of the twentieth century?
- How can different disciplines help us to understand the ageing process?
- What are the key developments in postmodern thought and critical studies in relation to ageing and later life?

In answer to these questions, the editors of this volume have brought together some of the leading figures in the field. Gathered together for the first time in a single volume, the authors discuss the latest theoretical developments in the international field of ageing. Drawing on research from the USA and UK, the book is strongly multi-disciplinary in content with chapters from both social sciences and humanities. The book provides a critical approach to our understanding of the experience of ageing and later life. It has been written for advanced students of gerontology and those with an interest in ageing and later life, but it is also relevant to policy makers and practitioners in the field.

Key features:
- first time work from the USA and UK has been available in one volume
- wide coverage of the latest trends and theoretical approaches in gerontology
- issues addressed from a range of disciplines – unusual combination of humanities and social science in one volume
- written by leading experts in the field.

Contents
Introduction – Part I: Reflections on gerontology – Talking about age: the theoretical basis of social gerontology – Critical gerontology – From minorities to majorities: perspectives on culture, ethnicity and ageing in British gerontology – The uses of literature in the study of older people – Historical research into ageing, old age and older people – Recalling life: analytical issues in the use of 'memories' – Part II: Conceptualizing age relations and later life – Inter-generational relationships: an autobiographical perspective – Spatiality and age relations – Representations of old age in painting and photography – Citizenship theory and old age: from social rights to surveillance – Illustrating care: images of care relationships with older people – Figuring identities: older people, medicine and time – Constructing later life/constructing the body: some thoughts from feminist theory – Part III: Concluding analysis – Theory and concepts in social gerontology – Index.

208pp   0 335 19725 6 (Paperback)   0 335 19726 4 (Hardback)

ON BEREAVEMENT
THE CULTURE OF GRIEF

Tony Walter

Insightful and refreshing.
Professor Dennis Klass, Webster University, St Louis, USA

A tour de force.
Dr Colin Murray Parkes, OBE, MD, FRCPsych, President of CRUSE

Some societies and some individuals find a place for their dead, others leave them behind. In recent years, researchers, professionals and bereaved people themselves have struggled with this. Should the bond with the dead be continued or broken? What is clear is that the grieving individual is not left in a social vacuum but has to struggle with expectations from self, family, friends, professionals and academic theorists.

This ground-breaking book looks at the social position of the bereaved. They find themselves caught between the living and the dead, sometimes searching for guidelines in a de-ritualized society that has few to offer, sometimes finding their grief inappropriately pathologized and policed. At its best, bereavement care offers reassurance, validation and freedom to talk where the client has previously encountered judgmentalism.

In this unique book, Tony Walter applies sociological insights to one of the most personal of human situations. *On Bereavement* is aimed at students on medical, nursing, counselling and social work courses that include bereavement as a topic. It will also appeal to sociology students with an interest in death, dying and mortality.

Contents
Introduction – Part I: Living with the dead – Other places, other times – War, peace and the dead: twentieth-century popular culture – Private bonds – Public bonds: the dead in everyday conversation – The last chapter – Theories – Part II: Policing grief – Guidelines for grief: historical background – Popular guidelines: the English case – Expert guidelines: clinical lore – Vive la difference? The politics of gender – Bereavement care – Conclusion: integration, regulation and postmodernism – References – Index.

256pp   0 335 20080 X (Paperback)   0 335 20081 8 (Hardback)